MW00782446

Public Record Office MS SP 12 / 289, 40-Verso—containing verse and prose passages from Book III of Elizabeth I's translation: the end of Meter 6, all of Prose 7; all of Meter 7; the beginning of Prose 8, in the hand of Queen Elizabeth I and the hand of the principal amanuensis, with corrections entered in the queen's hand—also indicating the fragile condition of the leaves in the manuscript.

The Consolation of Queen Elizabeth I

The Queen's Translation of Boethius's *De Consolatione Philosophiae*

Medieval and Renaissance Texts and Studies

Volume 366

The Consolation of Queen Elizabeth I

The Queen's Translation of Boethius's *De Consolatione Philosophiae*

Public Record Office

Manuscript SP 12 / 289

Introduction by
Quan Manh Ha

Edition by
Noel Harold Kaylor, Jr.,
and Philip Edward Phillips

ACMRS
(Arizona Center for Medieval and Renaissance Studies)
Tempe, Arizona
2009

Library of Congress Cataloging-in-Publication Data

Boethius, d. 524.
[De consolatione philosophiae. English]
The Consolation of Queen Elizabeth I : the queen's translation of Boethius's De consolatione philosophiae : Public Record Office, Manuscript SP 12/289 / introduction by Quan Manh Ha ; edition by Noel Harold Kaylor, Jr., and Philip Edward Phillips.
p. cm. -- (Medieval and Renaissance texts and studies ; v. 366)
Includes bibliographical references and index.
ISBN 978-0-86698-414-0 (alk. paper)
1. Philosophy and religion. 2. Happiness. 3. Latin literature--Translations into English. 4. Elizabeth I, Queen of England, 1533-1603. I. Elizabeth I, Queen of England, 1533-1603. II. Kaylor, Noel Harold, 1946- III. Phillips, Philip Edward. IV. Great Britain. Public Record Office. Manuscript. SP 12/289. V. Title.
B659.D472E5 2009
100--dc22

2009019817

∞
This book is made to last.
It is set in Adobe Caslon Pro,
smyth-sewn and printed on acid-free paper
to library specifications.
Printed in the United States of America

for

Jo, Deno,

and especially Elena,

who were there when the project began

Table of Contents

Acknowledgments *xi*

Introduction

I. Elizabeth I and her Translation of Boethius's *De Consolatione Philosophiae* 1

II. William Camden on Elizabeth I's Translation of the *Consolatio* 16

III. The Early Tradition of Translations of the *Consolatio* 23

IV. The State of the Manuscript 26

V. Editorial Practice and Notation 32

VI. Works Cited 36

VII. The Printed Editions of Elizabeth I's Writings 38

The Consolation of Queen Elizabeth I 39

The Computation of Days and Hours 41

The Queen's Translation of Boethius's *De Consolatione Philosophiae*

Book I 43

Book II 61

Book III 79

Book IV 105

Book V 131

Appendix I: Two Variant Copies of the Computation of Days 149

Appendix II: A Fragmentary Second Draft of Book I 155

Appendix III: A Fragmentary Second Draft of Book IV 163

Appendix IV: A Third Draft of Book IV, Meter 2 177

Textual and Explanatory Notes 181

Glossary 225

Acknowledgments

The preparation of an edition from a manuscript is exacting and demanding work that requires the cooperation both of institutions and of individuals. The editors owe a debt of gratitude to those who have lent their gracious assistance in various ways during the process of editing Elizabeth I's translation of Boethius's *De Consolatione Philosophiae*.

The editors appreciate the cooperation of the administrators and staff of the Public Record Office at London first and foremost, as well as the cooperation of the administrators and staff of the British Library. Without their generous help and professional support, no edition of Elizabeth I's translation of the *Consolatio* could have been attempted.

They also appreciate the assistance of the librarians at the University of Munich and the University of Regensburg in Bavaria, Germany, who managed to locate materials that otherwise would have been inaccessible. The administrators and staff of the Jean and Alexander Heard Library of Vanderbilt University have been helpful, and their work in locating sources is greatly appreciated.

Quan Manh Ha, Noel Harold Kaylor, Jr., and Philip Edward Phillips are grateful to Robert E. Bjork, Director of the Arizona Center for Medieval and Renaissance Studies, for his support of this project. They are indebted to Roy Rukkila and Todd Halvorsen for their careful supervision of all aspects of the publishing process. It has been a privilege to work with them in the production of this edition of Queen Elizabeth I's translation.

The work of transcribing the manuscript of Elizabeth I's translation has been accomplished at various times with the help of colleagues and students. Jesse Swan, University of Northern Iowa, offered his valuable assistance in the initial stages of transcription. John Jackson, an undergraduate student assistant at Troy University, devoted much time and effort to transcription of the manuscript, as did Quan Manh Ha and Priya Menon, graduate assistants at Troy University.

Quan Manh Ha, who wrote the Introduction to this edition and whose insights into the life and mind of Elizabeth I have added both conceptually and substantially to the realization of the entire project, expresses gratitude to Marion Hollings of Middle Tennessee State University for her advice and encouragement.

Noel Harold Kaylor, Jr. appreciates the major funding for this project that was provided through research grants by Troy University's Faculty Development Committee. It was Troy's generous support that funded some of his numerous trips to

Europe to work with the manuscript of Elizabeth's translation and to obtain access to rare sources on Queen Elizabeth I and her work as a translator. Troy University also provided financial remuneration for the students who assisted in the transcription of the manuscript. He is grateful particularly to Jack Hawkins, Chancellor of Troy University, for his administrative support in funding the research and for his personal encouragement in the realization of this project.

Philip Edward Phillips is grateful to Middle Tennessee State University for generously funding his research through a Faculty Development Grant to travel to Poland to deliver a Faculty Seminar on "Queen Elizabeth I's Translation of Boethius's *Consolatio*" at the Institute of English Philology at the Jagiellonian University, Kraków, in May 2001 and through two Faculty Research & Creative Activity Summer Salary Grants in support of research on the vernacular translations of the *Consolatio*, including Elizabeth I's, in 2002 and 2004. He appreciates the encouragement and support of Professors Bill Connelly and Tom Strawman in this project. He thanks, especially, Sharmila Patel and Edward Phillips for their love and steadfast support during the preparation of this edition.

Quan Manh Ha, Noel Harold Kaylor, Jr., and Philip Edward Phillips express their sincerest gratitude to the reviewers who spent much time noting problems in early drafts of this edition. Jean R. Brink, Karl Heinz Göller, Paul Szarmach, and Leslie MacCoull each diligently read the entire manuscript, commented upon it, noted problems that needed to be addressed, and in some cases supervised the process of making those corrections. They brought the finest potential of the vetting and copyediting processes used by publishers of academic texts in the United States to bear upon the production of this edition. We deeply appreciate their willingness to do work that too often goes unacknowledged in efforts to bring books into print, and we appreciate their willingness to enter actively into the work of creating this text. Without their proactive involvement, errors might not have been noted and corrected.

Unqualified gratitude must be expressed to Dr. and Mrs. Constantine Curris and to their daughter Elena for their enthusiastic encouragement at the very moment when this project was conceived, in London, on the occasion of Elena's high school graduation. Mrs. Alliegordon Kaylor and Mrs. Pauline Hern were present on that evening in London, and their spirit also is reflected in this volume, an edition of the work of an earlier dynamic woman whose legacy, like theirs, is not to be forgotten.

Introduction

I

Elizabeth I and her Translation of Boethius's *De Consolatione Philosophiae*

The life of Elizabeth I has been chronicled many times since her death in 1603; thus it will not be necessary here to rehearse the events that define her seventy years. The article on the life and deeds of Elizabeth I by Patrick Collinson in the 2005 *Oxford Dictionary of National Biography* (18:95–130) presents comprehensive information on the activities of the monarch and the importance of her reign. The following paragraphs will present only a few notes and facts that relate specifically to Elizabeth's intellectual interests and to her educational preparation for translating the *Consolatio.*

Elizabeth's Fluency in Latin

In 1597, André Hurault, sieur de Maisse, arrived at Elizabeth's court as ambassador, sent by Henry IV, the recently converted Catholic king of France. In conversation with Elizabeth, the ambassador noted that it is a "great virtue in a princess" to be a master of languages. "'It is no marvel to teach a woman to talk,' the queen shot back wryly. 'It were far harder to teach her to hold her tongue'."[1] In making this reply, Elizabeth demonstrates, as she often does, her ready wit. Of the six languages alluded to in the report submitted later by this French ambassador, the queen seems to have used Latin, Italian, and French quite frequently, and with above-average fluency. Some Greek, Spanish, and German are also attested. In recent biographies, there is confusion as to whether Elizabeth used Spanish or Italian when she received Spanish ambassadors, but Carolly Erickson affirms that she used Spanish with Count Feria during a famous interview at Brocket Hall just prior to her accession to the throne in 1558 (*First Elizabeth*, 161). Her use of German seems to have been in the occasional introduction of appropriate words or phrases rather than in any display of true agility with the language.

[1] C. Erickson, *The First Elizabeth* (New York: St. Martin's Griffin, 1983), 390.

In regard to Elizabeth's actual intellectual or academic accomplishments in the use of her languages, a question remains largely unanswered in the biographies: did they arise out of an inherent interest and aptitude that perhaps waited in the wings of her court life to be called to center stage when needed, or were they but further decorative elements of courtly stagecraft, worked in from time to time to amplify the mystique of the principal performer in the Elizabethan drama? The most famous, or infamous, evidence of the queen's facility in using Latin *ex tempore* involves the arrival at her court at Greenwich in 1597 of a new Polish ambassador, perhaps the prototype of Shakespeare's Polonius. This famous scene is either mentioned or expounded upon in most biographies, and it is worth examining at some length. In an article on this event, Janet M. Green points out: "Elizabeth's talent at self-dramatization, especially ceremonial self-dramatization, was partly responsible for her success as queen."[2] The following account emphasizes the essentially dramatic nature of the incident that is suggested in all reports of the occasion:

> This [audience with the Polish ambassador] had begun as a routine piece of diplomatic business, but as the Queen preserved pleasant memories of the King of Poland's father, who had visited her once long ago in her giddy courting days [. . .], she decided to honour him with a public reception in the Presence Chamber [. . .].
>
> The ambassador was duly brought in, attired in a long robe of black velvet "well jeweled and buttoned," [. . .] while the Queen, standing under the canopy of estate, waited to listen kindly to the usual complimentary Latin address. But it was not a complimentary address. On the contrary, the Polish ambassador was uttering threats. His master, he said, complained that, despite repeated protests, the Queen was allowing his ships and merchants to be spoiled in the pursuance of her quarrel with Spain, thus violating the laws of nature and of nations [. . .].
>
> But if the King of Poland had expected to flummox the Queen of England, he was about to be disappointed. Her majesty took up the challenge without hesitation, and there and then in fluent and flawless off-the-cuff Latin, proceeded to wipe the floor with his unhappy spokesman.[3]

Alison Plowden narrates this account of the incident, affirming, with some slight reservation, the spontaneity generally accredited to her majesty on this occasion. In Plowden's version, the high drama and stage-business of the moment is placed in the foreground. After carefully painting in the scene presented here, Plowden adds another fact, which generally is contained in the reports: "Justly pleased

---

[2] J.M. Green, "Queen Elizabeth I's Latin Reply to the Polish Ambassador," *Sixteenth Century Journal* 31 (2000):987–1008, here 1000.

[3] A. Plowden, *Elizabeth Regina* (London: Macmillan, 1980; repr. Phoenix Mill: Sutton, 2000), 111–12.

with her *performance* [emphasis added], Elizabeth is said to have turned to the awed and admiring bystanders, exclaiming 'God's death, my lords! I have been enforced this day to scour up my old Latin that hath lain long rusting'" (*Elizabeth Regina*, 112). By introducing this final bit of information, almost as an afterthought, Plowden underlines the wit of Elizabeth, even as the queen applauds herself for her own good performance at court.

Elizabeth well may have been surprised by the tenor and substance of the comments made by the Polish ambassador on this occasion, but she was never one to be taken totally off guard. She had her spies about, and they knew how to gather information: Sir Francis Walsingham had begun constructing an intelligence network when he became Elizabeth's principal secretary in 1573. He would have known in advance of the event at Greenwich that this same Polish ambassador had "delivered a similar tactless message"[4] in Holland some time before he had journeyed to England. If either Walsingham or Essex, who had his own spy network in place, had been alerted prior to the audience at Greenwich, then Elizabeth would have been informed of any negative attitude the Polish ambassador might have borne at the time, and she would have been on her guard, and at least partially prepared with facts, to counter it. In this particular dramatic action, the Polish ambassador unawares may have played his role as Polonius, but Elizabeth consciously may have stepped to center stage as Prospero. In all accounts, the scene has the elements of a staged piece, complete with special sets, costumes, and dramatic lines. We even have an "official" transcription of the incident because Elizabeth suggested that it be recorded by Robert Cecil, so that the Earl of Essex, being absent at the time, might enjoy the details. Cecil's report well might have served also as Elizabeth's note of thanks to Essex for information he might have supplied prior to the event. We will never know what script had been written or at least sketched out prior to the enactment of this famous scene. It was either described or transcribed by various other witnesses, and it is the sum of these reports that gives us our window today on a major event that involved a very new, somewhat naïve, and significantly minor actor on the Elizabethan scene.

The Quality of Elizabeth's Translation of the *Consolatio*

Four years earlier, an unstaged event had occurred in the fall of 1593 at Windsor that gives less mediated, and possibly more insightful, evidence of the queen's true intellect and of her command of Latin. By the reckoning of the Keeper of the Records at Windsor, Mr. Bowyer, Elizabeth translated Boethius's *De Consolatione Philosophiae* from Latin into English during the period of a month, in odd moments that totaled about twenty-four hours. The time affirmed by the Keeper

[4] Green, "Latin Reply," 991.

of the Records might be exaggerated, but the task of rendering so extensive and difficult a text as the *Consolatio* into English in even a month or longer of concentrated effort still would be an academic tour de force.[5]

In her youth, Elizabeth had been instructed by Roger Ascham in his dual-translation method. Ascham's method fostered a literalness in understanding a Latin text, a predilection for approximating its Latin style in English, and a preference for choosing Latin cognates over Anglo-Saxon alternatives in translation. Elizabeth's rendering of Boethius into English manifests all of these characteristics, and it attests to the effectiveness of Ascham's instruction of half a century earlier. A reader sees all of these features very clearly even in the queen's translation of the opening verses of I Meter 1.

The structure of Boethius's *Consolatio* moves from an emotional self-indulgence expressed by Boethius the Prisoner in I Meter 1, toward a rational understanding of the laws of the cosmos expressed ultimately by Lady Philosophy in V Prose 6. It also moves from potential tragedy, which results from emotional railing against the seeming injustices of fate, toward probable consolation, which results from rational acceptance of necessity.

Caroline Pemberton compared the queen's renderings with those of Geoffrey Chaucer throughout her 1899 edition of Elizabeth's translation of the *Consolatio*, even though there is no evidence of influence from the earlier to the later work. It is instructive, however, to compare the reception of these two translations, the earlier by Chaucer and the later by Elizabeth. A pioneer critic of Chaucer's translation of the *Consolatio* (of c.1380), Hugh Fraser Stewart, concluded:

> [. . .] while no one can deny that [Chaucer's] translation abounds with slipshod renderings, with awkward phrases and downright glaring mistakes of a kind to make a modern examiner's hair stand on end, yet its inaccuracy and infelicity is not that of an inexperienced Latin scholar, but rather of one who was no Latin scholar at all.[6]

Some recent reevaluations of Chaucer's translation are more generous. Chaucer's work is fairly accurate, but, more importantly, he has left us his own reading of the *Consolatio* as a philosophical and scientific work, as shown in part by the types of glosses he interpolates into his primarily utilitarian, all-prose translation. The degree of his intellectual comprehension and assimilation of the work and many of its implications is further manifested by the uses to which he puts Boethian concepts in his poetry. The structure of Boethius's *Consolatio* also moves from Boethius the Prisoner's sensing his political misfortunes as arbi-

---

[5] Cf. C. Pemberton, ed., *Queen Elizabeth's Englishings*, EETS o.s. 113 (London: Kegan Paul, Trench, Trűbner, 1899; repr. New York: Kraus Reprints, 1975, 1981), viii-x.

[6] H.F. Stewart, *Boethius: An Essay* (Edinburgh: Blackwood, 1891; repr. New York: Burt Franklin, 1974), 226.

trary wrongs inflicted upon him by fate toward understanding those changes as elements of an ultimate universal good. The epistemology that Boethius and his reader Chaucer employ rises through the successive stages of sensing, imagining, reasoning, and finally understanding (see Book V). Evidently, Chaucer read the Latin work as a philosophical and scientific work, and it is upon these registers that he draws substantially as he creates his subsequent poetic works.

Thematic evidence indicates that Elizabeth, however, read the *Consolatio* as a literary and political work, with special attention to the Latin verses and to the logical arguments on foreknowledge and free will, as shown by her rendering of the Latin meters into English verse and by her attention to meaning in particular philosophical passages in the text. As in the case of Chaucer, early assessment of Elizabeth's translation generally has been negative, but Maria Perry's more recent revisionist assessment of Elizabeth's work on the translation is accurate when she says:

> Derided by some [earlier] critics as her least impressive "Englishing," it has not been generally realized that she was experimenting with the "antique style" favored at the time for translating classical authors [. . .].
>
> When she came to a passage that interested her, Elizabeth forgot about the antique style and went straight for the sense [. . .].[7]

Parry then notes specific lines from Elizabeth's translation of V Prose 6 to illustrate her point:

> Wh^{r}fore
> if thou woldest way [God's] foreknoledge by wch he all und^{r}=
> standith, thou woltst Iudge that he hath not afore=
> knowledge of thingz to co^{m}, alone, but rightlyer
> a science of nev^{r} worn co^{n}tynua^{n}ce. Wh^{r}fore we must not call it
> foresight, but p^{ro}vidence wch being set ov^{r} all thingz, yet in the
> meanest, vewes the^{m} all as out of the very top & spring of all.
> (see edition below, V Prose 6, 55–61, 144)

Parry also points out that "[p]assages of Boethius are echoed in her last two parliamentary speeches, and that in berating Essex, she occasionally parodies the philosopher's method of reasoning" (*Word of a Prince*, 221). Just as we gain a view of "Chaucer the reader of Boethius" in his all-prose *Boece* and the glosses that he interpolates into the text, we possibly gain a view, by way of "Elizabeth the translator of Boethius," of "Elizabeth the reader of Boethius" in her use of both verse and prose in the translation, in passages in which she goes "straight to the sense" of the argument, and in passages that she later alludes to or makes use of in her public life.

---

[7] M. Perry, *The Word of a Prince* (Woodbridge: Boydell Press, 1999), 221.

There was considerable interest in the *Consolatio* during the late Tudor and early Jacobean periods, and, interestingly, particularly among people connected with the court. George Colville published a translation of the *Consolatio* in 1556, which he dedicated to Elizabeth's sister, Queen Mary; Thomas Challoner, who later became for a while Elizabeth's ambassador to Spain, translated the Meters in 1563;[8] and Elizabeth translated the entire Latin text in 1593. Then around 1602, John Bracegirdle, newly appointed vicar of Rye, dedicated a manuscript-translation to his patron, Thomas Sackville, first earl of Dorset,[9] and after Sackville's death in 1608, another translator, designated simply as I.T., dedicated a highly successful translation to Sackville's widow in 1609.[10] The late Tudor and early Jacobean period was one in which "stoic submission to destiny" versus "action through free will" would have been matters of existential consideration, and Boethius was still the recognized authority on those issues. In her translation, Elizabeth probably leaves us an index of her rational interest in Boethian ideas and concepts rather than a record of her emotional need for Boethian *consolation*. Some readers see the fulfillment of an emotional need in Elizabeth's work of translation, as implied in a reference in William Camden's history of Elizabeth's reign,[11] but emotional consolation would not have required the focused attention to the formal and substantial subtleties of the Latin text that Elizabeth demonstrates in her translation.

Elizabeth's concentrated work of translating Boethius at Windsor in October and November of 1593 produced a completed, relatively unpolished first-draft translation, but the draft is amazingly accurate. The queen seems to have "sight-read" the Latin, much as a pianist might "sight-read" a musical score, revealing in the process some probable earlier familiarity with the work. In her draft, the queen generally writes the verse translations of the Boethian meters herself, but apparently she dictates most of the prose passages to her amanuenses. One of these amanuenses has been identified by R.E.G. Kirk as "Thomas Windebank, Clerk of the Signet in 1568, and Clerk of the Privy Seal in 1598 " (Pemberton, *Englishings*, xi). The queen does, somewhat significantly, also write a few whole prose passages, and at least the introductory portions of other prose passages, in her own hand. The prose passages inscribed by amanuenses show many corrections entered upon the dictated passages in the hand of Elizabeth I. Thus, solid evidence indicates that the queen was actively

---

[8] In *Englishings*, ed. Pemberton, 150–60.

[9] N.H. Kaylor and J.E. Streed, eds., *John Bracegirdle's Psychopharmacon*, MRTS 200 (Tempe: ACMRS, 1999).

[10] I.T., tr., *Five Bookes of Philosophical Comfort, Full of Christian Consolation, Written a 1000 yeeres since* (London: John Windet, 1609; repr. in H.F. Stewart and E.K. Rand, eds. and trans., Boethius: *The Theological Tractates and the Consolation of Philosophy*, Loeb Classical Library ([Cambridge, MA: Harvard University Press, 1918; repr. 1962]), 129–411.

[11] See below, "William Camden on Elizabeth I's Translation of the *Consolatio*," 16–23.

involved in the production of the entire first-draft version of the English text, and the complete first-draft translation seems to have been produced by Elizabeth through a personal engagement with the Latin text, and with no broad audience intended. As noted above, she seems to have been interested especially in the meters and in some particular aspects of the content of the prose passages in the Boethian work.

As Maria Perry observes, "*The Consolation of Philosophy* suited Elizabeth's frame of mind that autumn [of 1593], dealing as it does with questions of great magnitude, suitable to be understood by Princes" (*Word of a Prince*, 221). This suitability of Boethius's text to Elizabeth's particular circumstances at the time will be explored in greater detail in the section that follows, and in a later section treating the reference made by William Camden to the queen's translation.

Thematic Links Between Elizabeth's Life and Boethius's *Consolation*

The translation of the *Consolatio* is scarcely indexed or mentioned in biographies of the queen. Her rendering was made, evidently, in one of those rare, relatively quiet and private periods in her life, when there was no staging for the event and apparently no audience other than the queen's personal household and circle of close associates to observe. It definitely was not part of the courtly spectacle and the political dramas that preoccupy the attention of most of her biographers, and that is possibly why her translation too often is trivialized as a bagatelle, or as a diversion contrived to fill some idle hours spent at Windsor.

Elizabeth was a practical thinker whose genius was for politics. Attention must be paid, therefore, to political aspects of the *Consolatio* that too often are overlooked even by specialists on the work, but that Elizabeth might have discerned clearly. Edward Gibbon was aware of this political dimension of the work when he wrote in his *The Decline and Fall of the Roman Empire*:

> While Boethius, oppressed with fetters, expected each moment the sentence or the stroke of death, he composed in the tower of Pavia the *Consolation of Philosophy*: a golden volume not unworthy of the leisure of Plato or Tully, but which claims incomparable merit from the barbarism of the times and the situation of the author. (215)

Behind Gibbon's typically well-crafted words, the *Consolatio* is understood to be a political as well as a philosophical work.

Some of the early prose passages recount the story of Boethius's imprisonment, without benefit of trial, on charges of treason against Theodoric, the Ostrogothic monarch in Italy at the time.[12] In 1554, following the Wyatt rebellion, Elizabeth

---

[12] See H. Chadwick, *Boethius: The Consolations of Music, Logic, Theology, and Philosophy* (Oxford: Clarendon Press, 1981; repr. 1990), 1–68; J. Matthews, "Anicius Manlius

had suffered a similar fate at the age of twenty-one under the reign of her sister, Mary. Unlike Boethius, however, Elizabeth was spared eventual execution for her allegedly offensive, but apparently less precisely documented, political opinions. Later, Elizabeth's own reign was characterized by treasonous opposition and sometimes open rebellion that forced her to imprison and even execute some subjects who too overtly resisted the order imposed by her reign. We can single out here particularly the imprisonment and execution of her cousin Mary, Queen of Scots, in 1587, about six years prior to the October and November that Elizabeth spent at Windsor with her Boethius.

Having been imprisoned herself, but clever enough not to write down any truly incriminating statement, Elizabeth could have found much more than mere consolation in her reading of Boethius; she well may have seen in Boethius a kindred spirit, possibly first encountered during her early schooling under Roger Ascham, a spirit whom she later would decide to revisit, more or less privately, in 1593.

It is often reiterated among the biographers that Elizabeth, although outspoken, still held a carefully guarded tongue. She famously refused to open windows upon the souls of her subjects, and she refused to open windows upon her own. During Elizabeth's reign, one's unexpressed thoughts were not punishable by law, but one's enacted behavior was: this was a lesson that Elizabeth had learned during various storms that she had weathered in her early years—early on as a consequence of the Thomas Seymour affair and later as a consequence of the Thomas Wyatt revolt. Elizabeth maintained the interior and exterior spheres as separate, both in the lives of her subjects and in her own life, which was a key to their survival as well as to her own.

The *Consolatio* is not a work one seeks out to fill idle moments, but it is a work that demands the luxury of time devoted to sustained, concentrated study. Boethius's ideas and his arguments are too densely presented for relaxed reading. Gibbon, in the passage quoted above, must have intended such a period of sustained engagement with the text when he chose the word "leisure" in his often-quoted compliment to Boethius's final statement to the world. Gibbon was aware of some of the translations of the *Consolatio* that had been made into English, first by "the most glorious of the English kings" (*Decline and Fall*, 216), Alfred the Great, c.899, and then later by the Father of English poetry, Geoffrey Chaucer, c.1380. They had turned their devoted attention to the work in quieter moments during the Danish invasions or during the Hundred Years' War, respectively. Gibbon indicates no knowledge of Elizabeth's translation, which was produced about five years after the Armada year of 1588 and at the end of the thirty-fifth year of her eventful reign. As will be pointed out, Elizabeth's

---

Severinus Boethius," in *Boethius: His Life, Thought, and Influence*, ed. M. Gibson (Oxford: Blackwell, 1981), 15–43.

translation was produced during such an interval of leisure as Gibbon recommends, and the text remained unpublished until 1899.

The title of Boethius's volume, the *Consolation of Philosophy*, is deceptive to one who has only casual knowledge of it, because the words *consolation* and *philosophy* require more specific definition than their common usage admits. Gibbon proves himself a good reader of Boethius when he makes a summary statement on the content of the work: "The celestial guide [Philosophy], whom he [Boethius] had so long invoked at Rome and Athens, now condescended to illumine his dungeon, to revive his courage, and to pour into his wounds her salutary balm" (*Decline and Fall*, 215). As Gibbon points out here, and as is stated clearly in the work, Boethius intends "medical attention and healing" as the referent of *consolation*, rather than "commiseration," which has sometimes been inferred. As nurse, Lady Philosophy first applies her milder and then her more stringent remedies to heal her ailing patient (I Prose 6.55–60). Commiseration had been offered by the poetic muses, before Philosophy evicted them in the opening prose passage of Book I (*scenicas meretriculas*: I Prose 1.29). As Gibbon also well understood, the word *philosophy* has as its most direct referent the splendid early education that Boethius, later stripped of all external gifts, kept during his imprisonment as his internal treasure (*mentis sedem*: I Prose 5.23), until the executioner's rope squeezed it from his mind, along with his life. Apart from parallel political incidents, Elizabeth also shared with Boethius the most thorough tuition that an age could provide. For each, early instruction remained a resource to be drawn upon throughout life, and exhausted only with death. The title of Boethius's personal and literary statement to the world does not define the depth of the work, and it should not define or limit Elizabeth I's interest in the profounder dimensions that are both explicit and implicit in the text.

Elizabeth's Education

The excellent humanist education that Elizabeth had enjoyed early on as daughter of Henry VIII benefitted her later as monarch of England. Her intellectual virtuosity revealed itself early in her childhood, as attested in her well-written letters and remarkable childhood translations. The skills that she had acquired as a young student in composing letters and poems, delivering speeches, and translating classical works are the basis of the formal beauty, rhetorical finesse, regal confidence, and occasional aesthetic inspiration that manifest later in her public and even private expression.[13]

Recognition has to be given to Desiderius Erasmus, a Dutch cleric as well as personal friend, frequent correspondent, and occasional guest of the English intellectual and statesman Thomas More, for the significant role he played in

[13] L.S. Marcus et al. eds., *Elizabeth I: Collected Works* (Chicago: University of Chicago Press, 2000), xi-xxiv, here xi.

introducing Renaissance humanism into England and in establishing humanism at Cambridge University. Humanism prevailed among English intellectuals in the latter half of the reign of Henry VIII, fostering the future development of Elizabethan literature and culture. In Tudor England, humanism became tremendously attractive, especially for ecclesiastics and aristocrats, and in the 1500s, education, history, literature, rhetoric, moral philosophy, and the arts all eventually came under its influence. Nicholas Mann defines Renaissance humanism in this way:

> Humanism is that concern with the legacy of antiquity—and in particular, but not exclusively, with its literary legacy—which characterizes the work of scholars from at least the ninth century onwards. It involves above all the rediscovery and study of Greek and Roman texts, the restoration and interpretation of them, and the assimilation of the ideas and values that they contain. It ranges from an archaeological interest in the remains of the past to a highly focused philological attention to the details of all manner of written records—from inscriptions to epic poems—but comes to pervade [. . .] almost all areas of post-medieval culture, including theology, philosophy, political thought, jurisprudence, medicine, mathematics and the creative arts.[14]

The sixteenth century in England also witnessed the humanist reform of Latin instruction and Latin usage as the language of the intellectual and ruling classes, and Latin became a prerequisite to entering into the significant vocations of the time. A humanist education served two primary needs of Tudor government: it provided an elite linguistic medium "for propaganda to legitimize a rather tenuous claim to the throne, and for educated personnel to staff the centralized bureaucracy forged to strengthen its position in relation to the feudal aristocracy."[15] For these reasons, among others, humanist educators laid great emphasis upon a broad humanistic curriculum in literature and rhetoric rather than upon the abstract and complicated systems of philosophy, theology, and logic that had been emphasized by the scholastic educators before them.

The humanistic agendum for education in young Elizabeth's early sixteenth-century England was hierarchical in its vision, and it emphasized education for the aristocrats, especially for the leadership roles to be awarded to the highest-achieving among them in Tudor society. Humanism in the Tudor period "effectively shaped practices of reading, writing and thought as well as the ways subjects imagined themselves and their social and political roles" (Crane, "Early

[14] N. Mann, "The Origins of Humanism," in *The Cambridge Companion to Renaissance Humanism*, ed. J. Kraye (Cambridge: Cambridge University Press, 1998), 1–19, here 2.

[15] M.T. Crane, "Early Tudor Humanism," in *A Companion to English Renaissance Literature and Culture*, ed. M. Hattaway (Oxford: Blackwell, 2000), 13–26, here 18.

Tudor Humanism," 14). Generally, the early humanists in England were teachers rather than writers; their writing was primarily academic and instructive rather than literary. They affirmed in these writings that learning would prompt leaders to rule more justly and generously, thanks to an understanding gleaned from the ideal of public service demonstrated in classical texts. In this way, the educational agendum of humanism fostered not only the skills necessary for effective expression in classical languages but also an appreciation for the values thought to have prevailed in classical civilization.

Elizabeth had been instructed well in Latin during childhood. Any discussion of her early education would contain an egregious lacuna if Katherine Champernowne, Elizabeth's Kate, were not duly acknowledged. Kate was Elizabeth's first governess, and she arrived on the job infused with a knowledge of Tudor family history and of the basics in classical scholarship.[16] She deserves praise for introducing the young princess not only to the canons of courtesy and respectful compliance to her elders that defined decent children of the day but also to the importance of learning Latin. Under Kate's tutelage, Elizabeth learned to read and write in Latin, and at an early age, she proved herself to be an excellent and eager student.[17] Impressed by Elizabeth's high command of the language, Sir Thomas Wriothesley, after a visit with the six-year-old princess, reported to the court, "If she be no worse educated than she now appeareth to me, she will prove of no less honour to womanhood than shall beseem her father's daughter."[18]

Cambridge humanists, sometimes referred to as "the Athenian tribe," from St. John's College, Cambridge, later took charge of Elizabeth's formal education.[19] These scholars, already known for pioneering educational reform and for training students in classical Latin and especially in Greek learning, affected Elizabeth's subsequent career significantly. Dr. Richard Cox, Edward Tudor's first preceptor, taught her parts of speech and Greek and Latin verb conjugations through exercises based on such military metaphors as linguistic problems likened to "a fortress to be besieged or a bulwark to be defended."[20]

Succeeding Dr. Cox, Sir John Cheke, first Regius Professor of Greek at St. John's College, taught the six-year-old Prince Edward, and sometimes he offered Elizabeth instruction as well. Cheke's virtuosity in languages, especially in Greek and Latin, was exceptional. He showed great interest in the Erasmian

[16] D. Starkey, *Elizabeth: The Struggle for the Throne* (New York: Perennial, 2001), 27.

[17] A. Plowden, *The Young Elizabeth* (London: Macmillan, 1971; repr. Phoenix Mill: Sutton, 1999), 68.

[18] A. Somerset, *Elizabeth I* (New York: St. Martin's Griffin, 1991), 11.

[19] M.A. Overell, " Edwardian Court Humanism and Il Beneficio di Cristo," in *Reassessing Tudor Humanism*, ed. J. Woolfson (London: Palgrave Macmillan, 2002), 151–76, here 159.

[20] Erickson, *The First Elizabeth*, 55.

pronunciation of Greek, in Greek philology, and in Greek grammar. At St. John's College, he was the pioneer in applying the improved teaching methods of the humanists, and Roger Ascham claimed that Cheke laid new foundations for the study. He encouraged his students to answer all questions by appeal to scripture, and he taught the best rhetorical methods. The curriculum that he used in the royal school at Hatfield was based on what he also taught at St. John's; Edward Tudor, and probably Elizabeth also, had to learn by heart Latin passages selected from Erasmus and the Bible and develop Latin writing skills by composing letters to family members and close dignitaries. All of Cheke's students read classical works, starting with Cicero's writings and Justin's abridged Latin version of Greek history.

William Grindall, a Latin scholar, master of many languages, and "the best Grecian" at St. John's, was commissioned in 1544 to be Elizabeth's private tutor. Under Grindall's training, Elizabeth was instructed in an increasingly challenging program of Latin and Greek, and she "was steeped in the particular world view of English Protestant humanism."[21] The instruction that Elizabeth received from Grindall, with its emphasis on Latin and Greek, advanced her to ever higher levels of language fluency and proficiency: "[B]esides being able to read and write [Latin] with ease, she spoke it fluently," and her skills in spoken Greek were at least average. Elizabeth's competence in French and Italian soon became remarkable; they were just "like English" to her.[22] Elizabeth enjoyed the superior education that any prince should envy, and she showed a genuine love, enthusiasm, and aptitude for her studies and for scholarship.

Like Cheke and Ascham, Grindall was a strong believer in reformed religion, and like them, he infused some teachings of the Reformation into his lessons. They all, however, were "to the left-of-centre in religious outlook," and Elizabeth later admitted "that she had never been taught the doctrine of the ancient religion."[23] Elizabeth was always conscious of how her religious perspective had been shaped by her education, and she thanked God in one of her self-composed prayers for having "from my earliest days kept me back from the deep abyss of natural ignorance and from damnable superstition, that I might enjoy the great sun of righteousness which brings with its rays life and salvation" (11).

Some credit for Elizabeth's fine education also must be given to her stepmother, Katharine Parr, a devotee of the reformed faith, for her insistence on making sure that Elizabeth received a humanist education that supported the Protestant faith. Although Elizabeth was familiar with Reformation theology and advocated its cause, she remained apparently indifferent, or unimpassioned about religion, but aware of its divisive function in English politics.

---

[21] Erickson, *The First Elizabeth*, 56.

[22] Somerset, *Elizabeth I*, 11.

[23] Somerset, *Elizabeth I*, 10.

Roger Ascham, Grindall's teacher, was selected by Elizabeth to be her private tutor after Grindall's death, and Ascham played the most significant and influential role of all of her tutors in Elizabeth's education. Ascham himself had been interested in gaining the appointment, and once he had gained it, he quickly realized that Elizabeth was much more intelligent than he had anticipated. Under Ascham's tutoring, Elizabeth studied Greek every morning, starting the day with the Greek Testament, sometimes with Cyprian, and Melanchthon, and then learning classical authors such as Isocrates, Sophocles, and Demosthenes. Her afternoons were devoted to the orations of Cicero; she had read Cicero and almost all of Livy by her sixteenth birthday. Employing Ascham's "double translation" method, described in *The Scholemaster*, Elizabeth read and translated authors' works first into English and then back into the original. First she was asked to master the parts of speech and syntax of Latin and then to make a sentence analysis of a passage from an author such as Cicero. Once a thorough linguistic understanding had been demonstrated, she would translate the passage into English in one copybook and later translate it back into Latin in another, and the retranslated version had to approximate the original Latin version closely. In a third book, she would set up lists of words, phrases, and idioms based on the translation. Ascham's "double-translation" method was adopted from his own Cambridge mentor Sir John Cheke, and it also had been advocated by Erasmus of Rotterdam.[24] In *The Scholemaster*, Ascham used Elizabeth's learning as an example of a student's possible success in employing the method.[25]

Trained by Ascham, Public Orator at Cambridge, Elizabeth developed a Classical Latin so perfect that before her accession to the throne, she could deliver Latin speeches naturally and impromptu. Ascham created a classical and Christian curriculum for Elizabeth designed to prepare her for state leadership. Significantly, Elizabeth continued to show interest in learning and scholarship, and even after her formal education with Ascham was completed, he read Greek to her almost every day during her early reign. Understandably, the death of Ascham left Elizabeth with a feeling of great loss: "I would rather have cast ten thousand pounds into the sea than lost my Ascham."[26]

In the years prior to the accession of Edward Tudor (as King Edward VI), Elizabeth had been educated primarily at the royal residence of Hatfield. The group of students instructed there with Elizabeth included Mary Tudor, Edward Tudor, Robert Dudley, and Jane Grey—all of whom played significant parts

---

[24] J. Loewenstein, "Humanism in Seventeenth-Century English Literature," in *The Cambridge Companion to Renaissance Humanism*, ed. Kraye, 269–93, here 275; J.B. Trapp, "Education in the Renaissance," in idem, *Background to the English Renaissance* (London: Gray-Mills, 1974), 67–89, here 83.

[25] R. Ascham, *The Scholemaster*, ed. L.V. Ryan (Charlottesville: University Press of Virginia, 1967), 35.

[26] D.E. Moss, "Roger Ascham," *History Today* 27 (1977): 651–58, here 651.

in English Renaissance history. All of the queen's tutors (Catherine Champernowne, Dr. Richard Cox, Sir John Cheke, William Grindal, and Roger Ascham) carried out an educational agendum at Hatfield that conformed generally with one that was carried out at Cambridge at the time, and perhaps that agendum sheds light on why Elizabeth, decades later, might have chosen to translate the *Consolatio*, which in its very form stood as a major example of Socratic instruction from late antiquity onward and whose author was one of the major sources of humanistic thought through the Renaissance.

It is perhaps in the person of Queen Elizabeth I herself that the success of the humanist agendum for education in England was most fully realized. She may not have enacted her role as monarch perfectly at all times during her reign, but she was both disposed and prepared to rule, and she survived as few rulers have managed to survive. Throughout her brilliant career, she used and developed the skills that her humanist instructors had provided, and she continued to praise such men as Roger Ascham for their part in her success. Throughout her reign, she epitomized the value and worth of their sincere efforts in instruction. Her success as a monarch reflects in tangible ways the success of moral and civic education in Tudor England that humanism's reforms had initiated. The period of her lengthy reign, the era of the triumph of humanism and of the Renaissance flowering in English culture, rightly carries her name today.

Elizabeth and the Scholarly Ideal

Elizabeth undeniably had been well educated in her youth, but to understand the queen's active and continued intellectual development as an adult, it is necessary to look closely at the more quiet periods in the monarch's life, such as one spent at Windsor in the fall of 1593 in the company of Boethius—those periods that appear so fleetingly in the record of her reign, extraneous to the staged events in the drama of her court, but whose presence offers at least a narrow, if perhaps somewhat opaque, window on her mind. In 1601, another such private moment was recorded by William Lambarde, following a brief audience with Elizabeth in Greenwich, shortly after the Essex Rebellion.

Lambarde had written an inventory of the documents for which he was responsible as Keeper of the Records at the Tower of London. Earlier he had finished and published a work begun by his predecessor and mentor, Laurence Nowell, on Anglo-Saxon laws, the *Archaionomia*. Thereafter he wrote and published the *Perambulation of Kent*, the model for a series of county histories to which many other scholars contributed volumes. Among other endeavors, he also published a four-volume study on the office of Justice of the Peace, the *Eirenarcha*, and a study on the high Courts of Justice, the *Archeion*.[27] The queen insisted that

[27] A.L. Rowse, *The England of Elizabeth* (London: Macmillan, 1950; repr. Bungay, Suffolk: Reprint Society, 1953), 54–55.

Lambarde, a true scholar in his day, present his *Pandecta* to her personally, and he recorded the details of the audience in his memoirs.

> [Lambarde quotes Elizabeth] "'You intended to present this book unto me by the Countess of Warwick. But I will none of that; for if any subject of mine do me a service, I will thankfully accept it at his own hands.' Then opening the book [she] said, 'you shall see that I can read,' and so with an audible voice read over the epistle and title so readily and distinctly pointed that it might perfectly appear that she well understood and conceived the same." She then politely asked the meaning of such terms as *oblata*, *litterae clausae* and *litterae patentes*, giving the old scholar the opportunity to expound what she perhaps understood, [. . .] assuring him that she would be a scholar in her [old] age and thought it no scorn to learn during life [. . .]. "And [. . .] being called away to prayer, she put the book into her bosom, having forbidden me from the first to the last to fall upon my knee before her, concluding: 'Farewell, good and honest Lambarde'." (*England of Elizabeth*, 55–56)

It is A.L. Rowse who narrates and comments upon the event enacted here, and to it he adds the interpretative observation that this is "[a] touching interview [. . .] between an old and famous woman and an ancient faithful scholar [. . .]. A couple of weeks and the old man was dead; two years on and she too was no more" (56).

Biographers sometimes omit this incident, even as they so often fail to mention the queen's translation of Boethius. If note is made of this scene at all, it is usually due only to Elizabeth's identifying herself during her audience with Lambarde as Richard II, a king deposed, as Essex somewhat earlier would have deposed her and usurped her throne. The allusion to Richard II tells us much about the queen's knowledge of the details of the political plot against her, because one of the conspirators had paid to have Shakespeare's *Richard II* performed the night prior to the rebellion, but it tells us less about her mind than does the larger, private moment spent with Lambarde and his cherished book, which forms the context of the allusion. This scene, like the one enacted privately at Windsor in 1593, shows a sympathetically scholarly and human dimension in Elizabeth that is not often emphasized in narrations of events enacted publically by the queen in her role as monarch.

Conclusion

The biographies of Queen Elizabeth I are insightful and genuinely thorough in their presentation of the sequence of events that shaped the Elizabethan drama. Each focuses upon different aspects of Elizabeth's life and times, but the various accounts focus generally on the display of courtly sets, political conflicts, and romantic interludes that were recorded in detail during her reign. The few private moments that have been recorded seem to reveal deeper aspects of the queen's mind that too often fall between the cracks in the boards of the Elizabethan stage. There are dimensions in the personality of Elizabeth I that too often are overlooked in most accounts of her public performance of duty to her office. It seems to have been in such a relatively quiet and private interval that the queen involved herself in an intellectual dialogue with Boethius in 1593. That dialogue, unique as it might be, suggests much that is important in appreciating the significance of Elizabeth I's early education and in understanding the complexity of the mature monarch's mind.

Translation is an effort to understand an essence in a text that can be articulated in a parallel text. The essence that Elizabeth articulated out of the Latin of Boethius and into her own English is of an accusation of treason (with or without foundation), of imprisonment, of a possible sentence of execution, and, eventually, of drawing a degree of personal felicity out of general misfortune. These are themes that certainly preoccupied Elizabeth's mind at sixty, and which would continue to preoccupy her thoughts even to the time of her death ten years later. In her sixtieth year, Elizabeth could relate in tangible ways to many themes in the *Consolatio* that may have come to her mind periodically, but which came to thorough consideration only in that October and November of 1593. It is improbable that Elizabeth would have devoted her concentrated attention to translating the *Consolatio* simply as recreation. The work does not lend itself to that purpose.

II

William Camden on Queen Elizabeth I's Translation of the *Consolatio*

William Camden was Queen Elizabeth's first biographer. One of his works about the queen and her reign is entitled *Annales*, which comprises four books. The first volume appeared in 1625, and the subsequent volumes followed soon thereafter. They were printed together in English in two volumes, but with each of the four books paginated individually. The fourth and final book contains the history of the years 1589 through 1603.

The work is constructed as a chronicle, devoting a whole chapter to each year of Elizabeth's reign, and within each chapter Camden generally enters and narrates events in chronological order. The Chapter for 1 January through 31 December 1593, for example, bears the title "The Sixe and Thirtieth Yeere of Her Reign," and it occupies pages 77–95 of Book IV. On page 89 of this chapter, Camden alludes to Elizabeth's translation of Boethius's *Consolatio* in 1593, and he seems to draw a connection between the translation of Boethius by Queen Elizabeth I and the conversion of King Henry IV of France to Catholicism, suggesting that the queen's interest in Boethius was for "ease and solace" to be derived from the text, to console her distress at Henry's having forsworn Protestantism.

Camden's Report on the Conversion of Henry IV

Concerning Elizabeth's first gaining knowledge of Henry's conversion, Camden writes:

> But whilst the Queen only for Religions Sake, aydes the French King [against Spain], distrusting his owne strength, at so great charges, and so great troubles of mind, as if she esteemed his losse, her owne, behold a most certaine report flies over to England, spreading out, that the French King, either had embrassed, or would shortly embrace the profession of the Romish Religion. (Camden, *Annales*, IV, 85–86)

Camden specifies here that Elizabeth I had been relying upon a foreign policy based on support of the Protestant cause to justify her alliance with Henry IV and France. Henry adopted Catholicism on 25 July 1593 at Saint-Denis, where the sepulchers of the kings of France lay. In late July or very early August, upon receiving intelligence on Henry's conversion, the queen's government dispatched Sir Thomas Wilkes to France to discover details on Henry's public profession of the "Roman Catholic Religion" (Camden, *Annales*, IV, 85–86). Camden supplies some details on the meeting between Henry IV and Wilkes, among which he records one reason given by Henry for his conversion: in 1589, when he acceded to the throne, he had promised the people of France "to learn the Catholic faith," but he had delayed his learning and conversion until 1593, four years thereafter (Camden, *Annales*, IV, 87–88). Thus it was for the sake of ending the religious wars in his realm and bringing peace to the people of France that he had converted; his conversion, then, was not a statement of any shift in his political alliance from England to such European Catholic nations as Spain but a statement of good faith to his subjects.

Camden then, at some length, reports on one tangible result of Wilkes's mission to France:

> In the mean time there is an agreement made between the Queen and him [Henry IV] at *Mellum* in August [1593], under their hands and seals, in good faith, and the word of a Prince, that with ioynt forces they shall warre against the *Spaniard*, both with *offensive* and *defensive* warre, as long as hee shall warre against either of them; and that there shall be no peace between him and them, without their mutuall consent thereunto. (*Annales*, IV, 87; emphases in original)

Henry promised England, furthermore, to "protect and defend" Protestants in France. In this way, a political crisis that arose in late July of 1593 was resolved in August of the same year.

Some Points Underlying Camden's Report

In general, Camden focuses his attention upon matters of state, and he tends to interpret most events he reports in political terms. This fact must be remembered as he associates Elizabeth's interest in Boethius with the political crisis precipitated by Henry IV's conversion. A careful reading of Camden's entries on Elizabeth I's reaction to Henry IV's public departure from Calvinism indicates that the queen probably was very much concerned with how her subjects might view her continued support of Henry IV after news began "spreading out" in England that he had ceased to practice Protestantism. As Camden reports on the matter, the queen's support of Henry IV in his continuous war with Spain, justified by a foreign policy based on England's support for the Protestant cause, seemed suddenly to have been discredited.

Once accords between Elizabeth I and Henry IV had been signed in August 1593, the month following his conversion, Elizabeth could continue her support of Henry IV in his war against Philip II, but based more realistically upon a policy of maintaining a strong alliance with France against Spain, which would represent a shift in the rhetoric, but not in the substance, of her foreign policy. The accord assured the queen and her subjects that Henry IV's conversion did not reflect a change in his own foreign policy and alliances, which permitted Elizabeth I to continue her financial and military support, even of a Catholic monarch. If this interpretation is correct, then Elizabeth as queen was concerned during this conversion crisis less about Henry's religious position than about his political position. Once that political position had been defined, then the queen could celebrate her birthday in September without fear that the balance of power in Europe had shifted against England's security, on the one hand, or that her subjects might construe her commitment to Protestantism to be insincere, on the other.

Peter Ackroyd succinctly pinpoints the source of much of Elizabeth I's political anxiety in this and other crises:

> Her principal concern was always for the stability and solvency of the country (and of her position), so that all the imperiousness and ingenuity of her character were dedicated to the avoidance of civil disturbance and external conflict. She feared disorder more than anything else, and fought only when it became absolutely necessary to do so.[28]

Taking this particular view on the crisis arising from Henry IV's conversion to Catholicism lends support to the idea that the diplomatic work of August had settled the matter to the political satisfaction of the partisans, both foreign and domestic.

[28] P. Ackroyd, *Shakespeare: The Biography* (New York: Doubleday, 2005), 12.

Elizabeth I and Her Translation of the *Consolatio*

During the late summer and early spring of 1593, Elizabeth I was at Windsor, where her court was in residence due to a major outbreak of bubonic plague in London. Camden reports that 1593 was, as 1563 earlier had been, a plague year, and that during 1593, in the city of London and in the suburbs, 17,890 of the queen's subjects died. Preserved among Elizabeth's state papers is a message of July 5 from "Thos. Phelippes to Mr. Sterrell, 1593," that dramatically confirms the removal of the court to Windsor: "The plague is hot in London and other places; cannot come so much at the Court which is in out places, and a great part of the household cut off, and therefore cannot write so often, but will do as the season permits."[29]

It was in late October and early November (apparently between 10 October and 8 November) that Elizabeth I translated the *Consolatio*, allegedly to console herself after Henry IV's abjuration of Protestantism. Thus the queen's period of intensive translation began two and one half months after the conversion crisis had begun and about two months after it had been resolved diplomatically.

It should be noted here that Elizabeth Tudor was born at Greenwich at 3:00 p.m., 7 September 1533, and she celebrated her sixtieth birthday in 1593 while at Windsor, in the month following her signing of the August accord with Henry IV. On 17 November 1593, shortly after completing her translation of the *Consolatio*, Elizabeth then celebrated the thirty-fifth anniversary of her accession to the throne. (The thirty-sixth year of her reign, which gives the title to Camden's chapter for all of 1593, actually begins only with that 17 November anniversary, which had become an annual national holiday by that time.)

Elizabeth seems always to have considered both her longevity and her accession to the throne to have resulted from God's foreordained plan for her life, and she expressed this idea in 1558, at the very moment she was informed of her accession by the lords of the Council who came to kneel before her at Hatfield, where earlier she had received her years of humanist education—in several languages as well as in government and other disciplines. She acknowledged the news brought to her by quoting in Latin Psalm 118:23: "[. . .] a Domino factum est istud / et est mirabile in oculis nostris" ["This is the Lord's doing: it is marvelous in our eyes"]. The Boethian themes of free will and predestination, which fill a large portion of the *Consolatio*, certainly would have been of interest to Elizabeth, particularly during the brief interval of time when she could reflect upon the attainment of a milestone in her longevity and anticipate the arrival of a milestone in her reign. Each of these public and personal rites of passage is more proximate to her actual work of translating the *Consolatio* than is the political crisis of the conversion of Henry IV to Catholicism.

---

[29] R.B. Wernham, ed., *List and Analysis of State Papers, Foreign Series: Elizabeth I*, vol. 5 (*July 1593-December 1599*) (London: HMSO, 1989), s.d.

Her birthday celebrations of 7 September and her Accession Day celebrations of 17 November represent the *terminus a quo* and the *terminus ad quem* that would have propelled the queen's rapidity in making her translation in late October and early November of 1593. When the first-draft translation was completed, she asked the Keeper of the Records at Windsor, Mr. Bowyer, to calculate the days and hours that she had devoted to translating the *Consolatio*;[30] justifiable pride in completing her work in good time and in good form would have been one reason for her desire to preserve this information with the manuscript. The constraint upon Elizabeth and her attendants at Windsor of a forthcoming November 17 celebration might also explain why efforts at making a fair-copy second-draft version of the translation were aborted.

Her calendar for the period mentions neither her translation nor Boethius,[31] so she seems to have devoted focused attention to rendering the Latin *Consolatio* into English during a brief period at Windsor, sandwiched between two of her highly public, but also significantly personal, celebrations of 1593—first of her sixtieth birthday and then of the thirty-fifth anniversary of her accession to the throne. During that interval, she translated only in those private hours, regularly set aside from the scheduled public hours devoted to matters of state, which she used, according to Mr. Bowyer, in three relatively private ways: in Sunday and holiday activities, in riding into the country to take the air, or in translating the *Consolatio*. In his "Computation of Days and Hours," Bowyer lists these three activities under one category of alternating recreational possibilities. Interestingly, Camden mentions neither Elizabeth's sixtieth birthday nor her thirty-fifth Accession Day, probably because these milestones seemed to have had little impact upon political matters, which were his primary interest.

Two Recent Historians on Elizabeth I's Reaction to Henry IV's Conversion

William Camden states rather emphatically that Elizabeth I was able to discuss Boethian thought during her summer and fall at Windsor, and he ties her interest in Boethius to the political crisis effected by the spiritual conversion of the former Calvinist Henry IV to the Catholic faith. Camden writes:

> In this her trouble she found ease and solace from the holy Scriptures, the writings of holy Fathers, often conferences with the Archbishop, and even sometimes out of the Philosophers she drew comfort. For certainly I know,

[30] Perry, *Word of a Prince*, 221; Pemberton, ed., *Englishings*, ix–x; see below, "Computation of Days and Hours," 41.

[31] M.A.E. Green, ed., *Calendar of State Papers, Domestic Series of the Reign of Elizabeth, 1591–1594* (London: Longmans, 1867), s.d.

> that at that time she was very conversant in the Booke of Boëthius and that she then translated it into English. (Annales, IV, 89)

It is this passage that some later commentators have used to equate Elizabeth's supposed need for consolation at the conversion of the French monarch with her need to make a translation of Boethius.

A highly regarded historian, J.E. Neale, reports: "Henry IV, much to Elizabeth's disgust, though not to her surprise, had turned Catholic in 1593 in order to reunite his people. 'Paris,' he is said to have remarked, 'is worth a mass'."[32] Maria Perry translates a message (written originally in French) sent from Elizabeth to Henry on the occasion of his conversion:

> My God! Is it possible [she asks Henry] that worldly considerations can so erase the fear of God which threatens us? Can we in reason expect any good result from an act so impious? He who has supported and preserved you through the years, can you imagine that he will forsake you in time of greatest need? Ah! It is dangerous to do evil, even for a good end. I hope that you will return to your senses.[33]

To her English translation of this message, Perry appends this note: "Despite his defection, Elizabeth remained in firm alliance with Henry IV" (*Word of a Prince*, 220).

Each of these reliable sources indicates that Elizabeth was perhaps more disappointed than devastated by Henry's conversion, but neither suggests any need on the part of Elizabeth for extraordinary personal consolation over his decision and action. Most historians view Elizabeth's reaction to Henry's conversion in this way, as rational rather than emotional.

A Further Caveat on Connecting Elizabeth's Translation with Henry's Conversion

George Colville, who dedicated his translation of the *Consolatio* to Elizabeth's sister, Queen Mary, opens his prefatory summary of the argument in Book I with:

> There was a noble man, a consul of Rome named Boecius, this man was a catholic man and dysputed for the faith in the comon counsayle agaynste the herytykes Nestoryus and Euticen, and confuted them, as it appeareth by a booke that he made, wherein he proveth two natures in Chryste. (n.p.)

[32] J.E. Neale, *Queen Elizabeth I* (Chicago: Academy Chicago Publishers, 2001), 361 (emphasis added).

[33] Perry, *Word of a Prince*, 220.

Colville's statement, published in 1556 and reprinted in 1561, thirty-seven and thirty-two years prior to Elizabeth's work of translating Boethius, respectively, leaves little doubt that the *Consolatio* would be an odd choice for someone seeking personal consolation over the conversion of the Protestant monarch, né Henri de Bourbon-Navarre, to Catholicism. Many authorities have maintained, as Colville seems to affirm here, that Boethius was martyred for his Catholic faith by the Arian king Theodoric. In her reading of Boethius, Elizabeth may have identified herself with Theodoric, but that seems improbable.

Camden notes that Elizabeth I had become conversant on Boethian matters only after he had discussed Henry IV's conversion, but before he discusses the August accords signed between England and France. Camden, who generally enters events in his *Annales* in chronological order, thus mentions the translation of the *Consolatio* out of sequence: Elizabeth made her translation not in early August of 1593, at the time of the conversion crisis, but in October and November, at the time of two celebrations in her life and reign. When Camden writes, "For certainly I know, that at that time [of Henry IV's conversion] she was very conversant in the Booke of *Boëthius* and that she *then* translated it into English" (Annales, IV, 89; emphasis added), his use of the word *then* can be misleading because it does not indicate clearly the actual sequence of events.

Elizabeth's translation of the *Consolatio* is rarely read today or commented upon in the biographies. Her translation seems to have been made in one of those rare intervals in her life, during the quiet moments between two major public and personal celebrations. Apparently she had no audience in mind for her translation other than her small circle of associates at Windsor, and the fact that no fair-copy inscription ever was completed indicates that Elizabeth had gained from the text, through study and translation, whatever she might have sought. She may have taken a printed copy of the *Consolatio* from her shelf to read and to discuss at the time of Henry IV's conversion, but the motivation to devote her concentrated attention to translating the entire Latin work into English verse and prose probably did not result from any need for self-consolation over the conversion of her continental ally. The equation of "conversion / translation" that seems to be suggested in Camden's report contradicts both thematic and sequential evidence.

Conclusion

At the end of the thirty-fifth year of her reign, Elizabeth well could have remembered the day at Hatfield when she was informed of her accession to the throne. She well may have remembered also the period of her instruction under Roger Ascham and the formal translations that she prepared under his guidance as gifts at that time. She may have looked back fondly upon her education at Hatfield and decided to prove that she still could do at sixty what she had learned to do, and did, during her first twenty-five years.

As noted earlier in this Introduction, Elizabeth also could have seen in the themes and occurrences that are recorded in the *Consolatio* a mirror of many of her own political and personal experiences. She would have found little consolation, however, for the conversion of a Protestant monarch to Catholicism in its major themes and narrated events.

It is impossible to conclude exactly why Elizabeth might have been inspired to spend a period of intense study and work with the *Consolatio*. Her interest well may have originated in a need for consolation, but the effort she brought to bear on translating the entire Latin work indicates intellectual more than emotional needs, which could have been aesthetic, biographical, political, or some combination of these factors. In fairness to the intellect of the mature monarch, the translation should not be trivialized. It merits greater attention by scholars and historians who want to understand Elizabeth as an intelligent human being as well as the monarch of England.

III

The Early Tradition of Translations of the *Consolatio*

The English tradition of translations of the *Consolatio*, and indeed the entire European tradition,[34] begins with King Alfred the Great, about 899. The translation and adaptation of Boethius's Latin text made either by or under Alfred is the earliest vernacularization recorded. The work was rendered into Old English prose, and most of the meters were subsequently rendered into Old English alliterative verse. Traditionally, these translations are assigned to Alfred the Great. About the year 1000, Notker Labeo translated Boethius's final work into Old High German, as a macaronic text in which the German translation is interlinear with the Latin. This effort in Germany was followed most immediately by efforts in France that produced a series of translations into Old French, appearing at various times and in various places during the Middle Ages.[35]

Nicholas Trevet produced an important Latin commentary on the *Consolatio* in England shortly before 1307. It survives in over a hundred manuscripts, and it was used by Chaucer as he produced his prose translation of Boethius's text. Independently of King Alfred's work, Geoffrey Chaucer translated the *Consolatio* into his own Middle English. Chaucer's *Boece* survives in eleven manuscripts and in an incunabulum published by Caxton about 1478. His is the most well-known

[34] See Pierre Courcelle, *La Consolation de Philosophie dans la tradition littéraire: Antécédents et postérité de Boèce* (Paris: Études augustiniennes, 1967).

[35] See N.H. Kaylor, *The Medieval Consolation of Philosophy: An Annotated Bibliography* (New York: Garland, 1992).

English rendering, and it is a very careful and literal translation of the original. Chaucer produced an all-prose translation that begins:

> Allas! I wepyng, am constreyned to bygynnen vers of sorwful matere that whilom in floryschyng studie made delitable ditees. For lo, rendynge muses of poetes enditen to me thynges to be writen, and drery vers of wretchidnesse weten my face with verray teers. (397)

In the early fifteenth century, an adaptation with commentary of Chaucer's translation of Book I of the *Consolatio* was produced by an Oxford Anonymous (Oxford MS. Auct. F.3.5 [fols. 198r through 220v]), but it remained as a unique manuscript at Oxford, in the Bodleian Library, until it was first edited and published in 1993 and reedited and published in 2007.[36]

John Walton (Johannes Capellanus), under the patronage of Elizabeth Berkeley, versified Chaucer's prose translation in 1410, rendering the *Consolatio*'s earlier books into seven-verse stanzas and the later books into eight-verse stanzas. In an edition prepared by Mark Science, Walton's opening stanza reads:

> Allas I wrrecche that whilom was in welthe
> And lusty songes used for to write
> Now am set in sorowes and unselthe.
> With mournyng now my merthe I most respite;
> Lo re[n]dyng muses techith me to endite,
> Of wo with wepyng weteth thay my face.
> Thus hath disease distroyed al my delyte
> And brought my blisse and my bone cheefe all bace. (13)

The translation survives in nineteen manuscripts; it was printed in 1525, and of this printing, three copies survive. Elizabeth I may have known about the edition of Chaucer's *Boece* produced by Caxton a century earlier, and possibly about the printing of Walton's versification of Chaucer, but her translation shows no influence of either.

In 1556, George Colville (sometimes spelled Clovile or Coldewel) translated the *Consolatio* under an oddly ungrammatical title, *Boethius: De Consolationae Philosophiae*. The problem in the grammar here may result from "back spelling" by the translator, due to the scribal practice of writing a final "e" so that it might have been interpreted as an "ae." He renders Boethius's opening meter into the following English prose lines:

---

[36] N.H. Kaylor et al., "*The Boke of Coumfort of Bois*," *Carmina Philosophiae* 2 (1993): 55–104; N.H. Kaylor and P.E. Phillips, "[Re-edition of] *The Boke of Coumfort of Bois*," in *New Directions in Boethian Studies*, ed. eidem (Kalamazoo: Medieval Institute Publications, 2007), 223–79.

> I that in tyme of prosperite, & floryshing study, made pleasaunte and deletable ditties, or verses: alas now beyng heauy and sad ouerthrowen in aduersitie, am compelled to fele and tast heuines and grief. Beholde the muses Poeticall, that is to saye: the pleasure that is in poetes verses, do appoynt me and compel me to writ these verses in meter, and ye sorrowfull verses do wet my wretched face with very waterye teares [. . .]. (n.p.)

He dedicated this translation to "the hygh, and myghty pryncesse, our Soueréigne Ladye, and Queen, Marye by the grace of God, Queen of England, Spayne, Fraunce, both Cicilles, Jerusalem, & Ireland [. . .]." A comparison of Colville's style with that of Elizabeth I indicates that there is no connection between the renderings of the two translators. Elizabeth I seems to have worked independently of any preceding English translations as she prepared her own English rendering of the Latin text. Elizabeth I's translation mirrors the Latin more exactly, probably for reasons discussed above, than do the translations prepared by her antecedents:

> Righmes that my growing studie ons p^{er}formed
> In teares alas cumpeld woful staves begin[.]
> My muses torne behold what write I shold indite
> wher tru woful verse my face w^{t} dole bedews
> Thes at Lest no terror aught Co^{n}strain
> that felowes to our mone our way they shuld refrain[.]
> (See edition below, I Meter 1, 1–6, 43)

She captures in these opening verses both the sense and syntax of the Latin lines in ways that the earlier translators had not attempted to coordinate. She is also one of the few translators of the *Consolatio* to maintain Boethius's opening word, *carmina*, as the opening word in the vernacular rendering of the Latin work.

Since 1593, over thirty full translations of the *Consolatio* have been made into English, with a recent translation appearing as late as 2001.[37] In addition, such luminaries as Henry Vaughan (1651), Alexander Pope (1717), and Samuel Johnson (1750) rendered some of the meters of the *Consolatio* into the English of their day. Elizabeth I became part of an illustrious group when she turned her attention to translating Boethius's Latin work in October and November of 1593, and her efforts prove that she holds a well-deserved place within it.

[37] J.C. Relihan, trans., *Boethius: Consolation of Philosophy* (Indianapolis: Hackett Publishing Company, 2001).

IV

The State of the Manuscript

Queen Elizabeth I's translation of Boethius's *De Consolatione Philosophiae* is preserved in MS SP 12 / 289 in the Public Record Office at London. In many ways, the volume actually resembles a scrapbook more than a manuscript, and the folios and leaves upon which the translation is inscribed vary in size and state of preservation. Some short, neatly rewritten fragments of the translation also are preserved in the manuscript, inscribed on folios that show minimal damage or wear, but Elizabeth I's translation was completed only in its first-draft inscription: its final appearance as a manuscript seems not to have been so important to her as accuracy and completeness in the translation itself. It is the completed, first-draft inscription that has been incorporated into the body of this edition, because all evidence indicates that the first-draft version is the only one in the production of which the queen actively involved herself. Readers will not come to this edition for Boethius's *Consolatio*; they will consult this volume either for Elizabeth's translation or for her reading of Boethius. Therefore, the body of this edition contains the finished draft that reveals evidence of Elizabeth's actual attention to its production. The fragmentary drafts that do not show evidence of Elizabeth's actual involvement are found in the Appendices.

Some of the folios and sheets are badly worn at the margins and damaged by repeated folding, widthwise, into thirds, or into halves and then into quarters, and some pages also have been damaged by ink spots and by accidental perforation. Some of the folio entries might, in fact, represent the later joining of sheets that had been torn apart for convenience of size during the work of inscription. Many folios and sheets that have been badly frayed around the edges have been repaired by affixing paper strips to create even edges all around, and especially at the binding edge (see frontispiece above for an example of this practice). It seems that the leaves that eventually were collated into the manuscript were not stored together at all times and did not necessarily share the same history of preservation. In spite of this fact, the first-draft translation is complete, with all prose passages rendered into English prose and all metrical passages into English verse.

The Textual Units in MS SP 12/289

As noted above, the volume into which the queen's translation is bound contains pages of varying size, so a detailed outline, presented section-by-section and page-by-page, seems necessary for accurate description.

External Elements
Black Archive Box [Heavy Card Stock]
Inscription on the Box Cover:

Queen Elizabeth's Translations, A.D. 1593
Inscription on the Box Spine:
Queen Elizabeth's Translations

Manuscript Binder [Red Leather over Heavy Card Stock] [28cm × 33 cm]
Inscription on the Binder Cover [gold lettering on red leather]:
Queen Elizabeth's Translations A.D. 1593

Internal Elements
Running End Sheet [marbled (red, blue, yellow) on recto; off-white on verso]
Inscription in pencil on upper-verso:
Rebound April 1888

First Textual Unit
Unnumbered Manilla Sheet [26½ cm × 32½ cm] [not card stock] [blank]
Unnumbered Manilla Sheet [26½ cm × 32½ cm] [card stock] [blank]
Unnumbered Manilla Sheet [26½ cm × 32½ cm] [card stock] [blank]

1-recto–2-verso [11 cm × 17½ cm] [folio]
[a partial list of English translations of the *Consolatio*, added later]
3-recto–6-verso [19 cm × 30 cm] [a *vita* of Boethius, added later]
3-recto–4-verso [folio]
5-recto–6-verso [folio]

Second Textual Unit
Unnumbered Manilla Sheet [26½ cm × 32½ cm] [card stock] [blank]

7-recto–8-verso [21 cm × 30½ cm] [Computation I] [folio]
[inscribed sheets affixed to folio backing paper]
9-recto/verso [21½ cm × 24½ cm] [Computation II] [single sheet]
10-recto–11-verso [20½ cm × 30 cm] [Computation III] [folio]

Third Textual Unit
Numbered Manilla Sheet [11-A] [26½ cm × 32½ cm] [card stock]
[blank]

12-recto–15-verso [19 cm × 27½ cm] [Book I begins 13-recto, top]
12-recto–13-verso [folio]
14-recto–15-verso [folio]
16-recto–19-verso [20½ cm × 30½ cm]
16-recto–17-verso [folio]
18-recto–19-verso [folio]
20-recto-23-verso [15½ cm × 20½ cm]

20-recto–21-verso [folio]
22-recto–23-verso [folio]

Fourth Textual Unit
Numbered Manilla Sheet [23-A] [26½ cm × 32½ cm] [card stock] [blank]

24-recto/verso [21 cm × 30½ cm] [single sheet] [blank] [water mark]
25-recto–30-verso [18½ cm × 26 cm]
25-recto–26-verso [folio] [watermark] [Book II begins 26-recto, top]
27-recto–28-verso [folio]
29-recto–30-verso [folio]
31-recto–35-verso [21½ cm × 30½ cm]
31-recto/verso [single sheet]
32-recto–33-verso [folio]
34-recto–35-verso [folio]

Fifth Textual Unit
Numbered Manilla Sheet [35-A] [26½ cm × 32½ cm] [card stock] [blank]

36-recto–47-verso [19½ cm × 30½ cm]
36-recto–37-verso [folio] [Book III begins 36-recto, top]
38-recto–39-verso [folio] [hole–possibly an ash burn]
40-recto–41-verso [folio]
42-recto–43-verso [folio]
44-recto–45-verso [folio]
46-recto–47-verso [folio]
48-recto–49-verso [21½ cm × 30½ cm] [folio] [Book IV begins 49-recto, mid-page]
50-recto/verso [20 cm × 30½] [single sheet]
51-recto-52-verso [20 cm × 30½] [folio]
53-recto–56-verso [18 cm × 27½ cm]
53-recto–54-verso [folio]
55-recto–56-verso [folio]
57-recto/verso [21½ cm × 30½ cm] [single sheet]
[contains the queen's inscription of IV Meter 2]
[Inserted Textual Sub-Unit (fragmentary rewrite of Book IV)
58-recto–63-verso (20½ cm × 30½)
58-recto–59-verso (folio)
60-recto–61-verso (folio)

62-recto–63-verso (folio)]
64-recto–65-verso [20 cm × 31½] [folio]
[first-draft inscription recommences with IV Meter 4
64-recto, top]
[contains IV Meter 5, the only meter having no
corresponding version in the Queen's hand,
64-verso]
66-recto–69-verso [18 cm × 28 cm]
66-recto–67-verso [folio]
68-recto–69-verso [folio]
[contains IV Meter 6, the only meter having a
mixture of the queen's hand with that of an
amanuensis, 68-verso]
70-recto–71-verso [15½ cm × 28] [folio] [70-recto blank]
[misplaced inscription of IV Meter 7, on three separate
¼ sheet fragments, affixed to top ¼ of three separate
mounting sheets: 70-verso, 71-recto, 71-verso]
72-recto–73-verso [18 cm × 27½] [folio]
[contains the final, misplaced, lines of IV Prose 7, 72-recto]

Sixth Textual Unit
Numbered Manilla Sheet [73-A] [26½ cm × 32½ cm] [card stock]
[blank]

74-recto–81-verso [20½ cm × 30½ cm]
74-recto–75-verso [folio] [Book V begins 74-recto, top]
76-recto-77-verso [folio]
78-recto–79-verso [folio]
80-recto-81-verso [folio]
82-recto–83-verso [17½ cm × 27½] [folio]
[contains the end of Book V, first-draft inscription, 83-verso]

Seventh Textual Unit
Numbered Manilla Sheet [83-A] [26½ cm × 32½ cm] [card stock]
[83-A-recto inscription in pencil:
De Arte Poetica] [fragmentary translation]

[Inserted Textual Sub-Unit (fragmentary *De Arte Poetica*)
84-recto–89-verso inserted as "booklet"
84-recto/verso & 89-recto/verso (18½ cm × 28 cm)
(folio) ("booklet cover")
85-recto/verso (18½ cm × 28 cm)
(inserted single sheet)

86-recto–87-verso (18½ cm × 28 cm)
(inserted folio)
88-recto/verso (18½ cm × 25½ cm)
(inserted single sheet)]
89-recto/verso (see above)

Eighth Textual Unit
Numbered Manilla Sheet [89-A] [26½ cm × 32½ cm] [card stock]
[89-A-recto inscription in pencil:
De Curiositate] [complete translation]

90-recto–91-verso [18½ cm × 26½] [folio]
92-recto–93-verso [18½ cm × 25½] [folio]
94-recto–95-verso [19½ cm × 27½] [folio]
96-recto–97-verso [18½ cm × 26½] [folio]
98-recto–99-verso [18 cm × 26] [folio]

Ninth Textual Unit
Numbered Manilla Sheet [99-A] [26½ cm × 32½ cm] [card stock][blank]
[99-A-recto inscription in pencil:
Fair Copy]

100-recto–105-verso [three folios folded together as booklet,
sewn down spine]
[containing the fragmentary rewrite of Book I;
inscribed in the finest penmanship in the
entire manuscript]
100-recto/verso & 105-recto/verso ["booklet cover"] [folio]
101-recto/verso & 104-recto/verso [inserted] [folio]
102-recto/verso & 103-recto/verso [inserted] [folio]
[inscriptions of fragmentary rewrite on:
100-recto/verso; 101-recto/verso;
102-recto (bottom half); 102-verso (top half)]
[105-recto inscription:
END]
[105-verso numbered:
105-D]
[contains a receipt for the purchase
of wool, dated January 18, 1607]

Unnumbered Manilla Sheet [26½ cm × 32½ cm] [card stock][blank]
Unnumbered Manilla Sheet [26½ cm × 32½ cm] [card stock][blank]
Running End Sheet [white on recto; marbled (red, blue, yellow) on verso]

Some Fragmentary Rewrites

A fragmentary second-draft inscription of Book I is bound into the manuscript many pages after the completed first-draft inscription of the translation of the *Consolatio* ends. The fragment contains I Meter 1 through the opening portion of Prose 3 (100-Recto-102-Verso), which terminates after the ninth line; that ninth line is found earlier, in the primary inscription, in Elizabeth I's italic hand, as the fifteenth and bottom line on 15-Verso. In the fragment, the passage terminates abruptly at mid-page, on 102-Verso; in the primary, first-draft inscription, the passage continues in the queen's hand on the following page, 16-Recto.

A fragmentary second-draft inscription of Book IV (Prose 1 through Prose 4) is bound into the completed, primary or first-draft inscription of Book IV, between Prose 4 and Meter 4, on pages numbered there sequentially as 58-Recto-63-Verso. This second-draft inscription is preceded immediately in the manuscript by a page-fragment, affixed to an otherwise blank sheet, containing a copy of IV Meter 2, inscribed in Elizabeth I's italic hand (57-Recto); that same meter appears earlier in the manuscript, in its proper place among the primary, first-draft inscriptions, but in an amanuensis's italic hand. It is probable that the queen's own inscription of Meter 2 and the fragmentary second-draft inscription of Book IV were inserted as extraneous units–between the two sections of the primary, first-draft inscription of Book IV–at some time during the process of collation, perhaps to be reviewed later for placement elsewhere.

The primary inscription of Elizabeth I's translation of the *Consolatio* ends, complete, with the final prose passage of Book V, on 83-Verso. The fragmentary second-draft inscription of Book I is bound into the manuscript at 100-Recto-102-Verso. The second-draft inscription of Book I comprises the final unit in the manuscript. Thus, the unique manuscript preserves portions of Books I and IV as revised or fair-copy inscriptions, but, as noted earlier, any further attempt to produce a complete revision of the whole translation seems to have been abandoned. The fair-copy fragments show no evidence of the queen's involvement in their production. Perhaps complete fair-copy inscriptions of all five books of Elizabeth's translation of the *Consolatio* will one day be discovered, but the unfinished state of the two fragments bound into the manuscript make this possibility seem dubious.

Some confusion occurs in the manuscript's pagination, but it entered at the later collation and binding stages of manuscript production. This confusion is further evidence that all of the folios and sheets of the translation probably were not stored together at all times. Indeed, some seem to have been recovered piecemeal, inserted during the process of collation, perhaps in anticipation of a later consideration of their final disposition, but then subsequently bound in where they had been inserted.

The bound volume is entitled *Queen Elizabeth's Translations, A.D. 1593*. It contains not only the queen's translation of Boethius's *De Consolatione Philosophiae* but some other translations as well (84-Recto-99-B-Verso). The manuscript, comprising Elizabeth I's translation of the *Consolatio* and the other, shorter renderings bound up with it, ends at 105-Verso, after a few blank pages that follow the fragmentary second-draft inscription of Book I.

As noted in Pemberton's 1899 edition, the other translations bound up with the translation of the *Consolatio*, Plutarch's *De Curiositate* (complete) and Horace's *De Arte Poetica* (fragment), date from 1598. Appearing five years after Elizabeth had produced her full translation of the *Consolatio*, they are from another time, and from a state of mind conditioned by other political and biographical circumstances. They appear at the end of Pemberton's volume, but because they have little if any affinity with the *Consolatio*, they have not been included in this edition. This edition is of Elizabeth's translation of the *Consolatio* of 1593 and not of any or the queen's prior or subsequent renderings into English.

V

Editorial Practice and Notation

For the diplomatic edition presented here, the transcription of Elizabeth I's translation of Boethius's *De Consolatione Philosophiae* was prepared using a "blind reading" of the manuscript, without any reference to the edition of 1899, made by Caroline Pemberton and published by the Early English Text Society, which was not prepared as a diplomatic edition. Pemberton makes no distinction for differences in orthography and reading between the first-draft inscription of the text and the later fair-copy inscription. It was only after a complete transcription had been made and rechecked many times that a comparison with the earlier transcription was undertaken. The comparison revealed that Pemberton was creating a text in which some orthographic normalization is imposed and in which no attention is given to the nature and structure of the manuscript; Pemberton's edition provides a smooth and continuous reading of the translation, for its content. Her work has served scholarly needs for over one hundred years, which is positive testimony to the value of her contribution to Elizabeth I scholarship.

For this edition, another approach has been taken. An attempt has been made here to produce consistency by placing only "first-draft" inscriptions of all prose and meter passages into the body of the edition, while all "second drafts" or "third drafts" have been removed to appendices. Thus, an attempt has been made to place the actual work of Elizabeth I in the foreground, and to separate it from the copying and polishing that was accomplished by her amanuenses—apparently independently of the queen, because the fragments show no evidence of the queen's attention to them or interest in them. The present edition has incorporated as many of the orthographic peculiarities found in the manuscript, or close typographic analogies of those peculiarities, as possible. Maria Perry justly remarks: "Elizabeth's spelling is a law unto itself."[38] The queen's own spelling idiosyncracies have been maintained in this edition.

In this edition, where problems occur in the sequence of prose and metrical passages in the unique manuscript, elements have been moved to create a continuous reading of the first-draft inscription consistent with the order of a Latin text of the *Consolatio*. All such reorganization has been noted in the edition and described in the Textual and Explanatory Notes.

An effort also has been made to account for all numbered pages in the collated manuscript so that a reader may follow the process of editorial rearrangement among the various elements. As stated, the goal here has been to produce a smooth textual surface, presenting the first-draft inscription of the text for readers interested either in Elizabeth I as translator or in the vernacularizations of the *Consolatio* in general, but also to provide clear notations that should answer questions that specialists might have concerning the nature and structure of the manuscript. In this diplomatic edition, an asterisk [*] refers the reader to the Textual and Explanatory Notes and a "dagger" symbol [†] refers the reader to the Glossary at the back of this volume.

As often as possible, scribal features of the manuscript have been maintained and noted throughout the edition, in order to convey a sense of the original scribal work. For example, the line numbering added in the edition corresponds to the occurrence of the lines in the manuscript. Length of lines vary because of the many markings out within the lines and because of the often multi-layered, caret-inserted additions of words or phrases above the lines in the first-draft inscription. Lines of exceptional length in the manuscript have been divided and appear on two lines in the edition, with an indentation at the start of the unnumbered second line. Where hyphenation of words at the ends of lines occurs in the manuscript, indicated in Elizabeth's translation by an "equal sign" [=], it has been retained in the edition. If words or phrases have been clearly marked out and replaced by corrections in the manuscript, then the items marked out have been disregarded and the corrections presented in the edition. Underlinings of words have been maintained because, it appears, an underlining in the manuscript indicates that the translation of a particular word or phrase was designated to be revisited and perhaps corrected later. Such underlinings, therefore, might be of interest to scholars who compare Elizabeth I's translation with the Latin original.

As a young student, Elizabeth I was taught to write in "secretarial italic," and her penmanship was regarded at that time as quite elegant. In later years, her script became less deliberate, and some readers refer to its appearance as "spidery." This is a good adjective to describe her script in the translation of the

---

[38] Perry, *Word of a Prince*, 221.

Consolatio. In this edition, all entries inscribed by Elizabeth I in the manuscript are presented in italic type, which includes almost all of the meters and some of the prose passages. Occasionally, an amanuensis enters italicized words or phrases into otherwise non-italic passages; these also appear in italic type, but they are marked and described in the Textual and Explanatory Notes, as are corrections entered in Elizabeth I's hand upon the passages that were otherwise inscribed by an amanuensis. All corrections made in Elizabeth's hand appear in italic in this edition, although she did inscribe some words in a non-italic hand. Corrections entered by Elizabeth I are valuable indications of her active and continued involvement with the entire first-draft inscription of the manuscript. There is no evidence of any such personal involvement with the production of the fragmentary fair-copy inscriptions of Book I and Book IV.

Abbreviations in the manuscript are indicated in the edition. The standard Elizabethan abbreviation for both "m"s and "n"s in the manuscript appears in the edition as the superscripted letters, respectively. In the case of abbreviations for "ar"s, "er"s "ir"s, "or"s, "ur"s, or the reversals of such combinations, following "p"s, the abbreviation appears in the edition as a fully expanded superscription, to facilitate reading. Elizabethan ampersands in the manuscript appear as modern ampersands in the edition. Other unique abbreviations were occasionally entered by amanuenses, and these have been reproduced (as technology permits), noted, and described in the Textual and Explanatory Notes.

Spellings of words vary throughout the manuscript, even between their appearance in catchwords and their repetitions as the initial words on the following page, whatever the actual order of their inscription might have been. All such orthographic peculiarities that appear in the manuscript are maintained in the edition; for example, both in the manuscript and in the edition, "the" can be interpreted as "the," "thee," or "they"; "to" can be interpreted either as "to" or "too"; and "of" can be interpreted as either "of" or "off." Perry notes that "[i]t is not uncommon to find three different renderings of the same word in one manuscript, but in the draft of Boethius, [Elizabeth] has occasionally crossed out Windebank's version of a word, deliberately replacing it with a more archaic form."[39]

Elizabeth also seems generally to have paid little attention to punctuation, and the distinction between commas and periods in the manuscript often is amorphic. Bracketed periods and commas have been entered in the edition only when reading can be facilitated or when clarification is needed. Elizabeth, and also her amanuenses, used capitalization in idiosyncratic ways. In the edition, upper-case letters are maintained as they appear in the manuscript at the beginning of words, but the upper-case letters that occasionally appear in the middle of words, particularly with the upper-case "L" in Elizabeth's italic script, have been

[39] Perry, *Word of a Prince*, 221.

ignored in the edition. Such internal occurrences of upper-case letters seem to indicate only a personal predilection, as in Elizabeth's preference for the flourish of her upper-case "L," but little else. The letters "u" and "v" are used in idiosyncratic ways, and at times apparently interchangeably. We have normalized these letters in the edition to facilitate reading.

Page numbers were stamped into the manuscript at some late date, after the individual folios and sheets were collated. This numbering has been maintained in the edition, and explanations are given in the Textual and Explanatory Notes when redundancies or other problems occur. Some rubrics were penciled in at a later date, as were some marginal notes, and these have been maintained in the edition, noted, and registered in the Textual and Explanatory Notes. Catchwords are reproduced as they appear in the manuscript. Probably they once proved useful in collation of the pages prior to numbering them, and now they prove useful in identifying some of the problems in pagination that entered at the time of collation.

Elizabeth I's completed translation remains a first-draft inscription, in which the dramatic nature of the dialogue between the prisoner Boethius and the personification Philosophy was totally disregarded (in capitalization, in punctuation, and often in grammar) as the queen translated, and even as an amanuensis later polished and recopied portions of the translation. In order to facilitate both the reading of the text and a comparison with a Latin original, the alternating interlocutors have been indicated in the edition with bracketed letters: either as [B] or as [P]. Boethius has two distinct voices in the *Consolatio*: one as interlocutor and another as narrator. Only passages in which he acts as interlocutor have been indicated with the addition of a [B]. This sort of clarification for a reader of the edition seems not to conflict with the primary objective in preparing this edition: to produce an accurate representation of Elizabeth I's engaged work as translator of Boethius's *Consolatio.* As noted above, to do justice to the work of Elizabeth I herself, the first-draft inscriptions (those showing evidence of Elizabeth's personal supervision in production) appear in the body of the edition, and minimal emendations have been imposed. Readers should find evidence in this edition of the queen's linguistic and intellectual accomplishments, on the one hand, and a record of how she read Boethius's final statement to the world, on the other.

As a first-draft inscription, Elizabeth I's translation is impressive. It stands on its own merit, as the queen's own reading of the work. This fact has guided the editors as they prepared this diplomatic edition of Elizabeth's translation of Boethius's *Consolatio.*

VI

Works Cited

Ackroyd, Peter. *Shakespeare: The Biography.* New York: Nan A. Talese-Doubleday, 2005.

Ascham, Roger. *The Scholemaster.* London: Iohn Daye, 1570; Ed L.V. Ryan. Charlottesville: University of Virginia Press, 1967.

Camden, William. *Annales: The True and Royall History of the Famous Empresse Elizabeth*, etc. 2 vols. London: Beniamin Fisher, 1625.

Challoner, Sir Thomas. "Sir Thomas Challoner's Translation of Some of the Meters of Boethius, from a MS. in the Public Record Office [State Papers, Domestic, Elizabeth, Addenda, Vol. 11, No. 121]." In *Queen Elizabeth's Englishings*, ed. Caroline Pemberton, 150–60. EETS o.s. 113. London: Kegan Paul, Trench, Trübner & Co., 1899.

Chaucer, Geoffrey. *Boece.* In *The Riverside Chaucer.* 3rd ed. Ed. Larry D. Benson et al. Boston: Houghton Mifflin Company, 1987.

Collinson, Patrick. "Elizabeth I." In *Oxford Dictionary of National Biography*, ed. H.C.G. Matthew and Brian Harrison, 18: 95–130. 60 vols. New York: Oxford University Press, 2005.

Colville, George. *Boethius: De Consolationae* [sic] *Philosophiae.* London: Iohn Cawoode, 1556.

Crane, Mary T. "Early Tudor Humanism." In *A Companion to English Renaissance Literature and Culture*, ed. Michael Hattaway, 13–26. Oxford: Blackwell, 2000.

Elizabeth I, trans. *The Consolation of Philosophy.* MS SP12/289. Public Record Office. London.

Erickson, Carolly. *The First Elizabeth.* New York: St. Martin's Griffin, 1983.

Gibbon, Edward. *The History of the Decline and Fall of the Roman Empire.* Vol. 4: 987–1008. New York: AMS Press, 1974.

Green, Janet M. "Queen Elizabeth I's Latin Reply to the Polish Ambassador." *Sixteenth Century Journal* 31 (2000): 987–1108.

Green, Mary Anne Everett, ed. *Calendar of State Papers, Domestic Series of the Reign of Elizabeth, 1591–1594.* London: Longmans, Green, Reader, and Dyer, 1867.

I.T. *Five Bookes of Philosophical Comfort, Full of Christian Consolation, Written a 1000 yeeres since.* London: John Windet, 1609. Reprinted in H.F. Stewart and E.K. Rand, eds. and trans., *Boethius: The Theological Tractates and the Consolation of Philosophy*, 129–411, Loeb Classical Library. Cambridge, MA: Harvard University Press, 1918, repr. 1962.

Kaylor, Noel Harold (Jr.). *The Medieval Consolation of Philosophy: An Annotated Bibliography.* Garland Medieval Bibliographies 7. New York: Garland Publishing, Inc., 1992.

———, and Jason Edward Streed. *John Bracegirdle's* Psychopharmacon*: A Translation of Boethius'* De Consolatione Philosophiae (MS BL Additional 11401). MRTS 200. Tempe: Arizona Center for Medieval and Renaissance Studies, 1999.

———, Jason Edward Streed, and William Watts, eds. "*The Boke of Coumfort of Bois.*" *Carmina Philosophiae* 2 (1993): 55–104.

———, and Philip Edward Phillips, eds. "[Re-edition of] *The Boke of Coumfort of Bois.*" In *New Directions in Boethian Studies*, ed. eidem, 223–79. Kalamazoo: Medieval Institute Publications, 2007.

Loewenstein, Joseph. "Humanism in Seventeenth-Century English Literature." In *The Cambridge Companion to Renaissance Humanism*, ed. Jill Kraye, 269–93. Cambridge: Cambridge University Press, 1998.

Mann, Nicholas. "The Origins of Humanism." In *The Cambridge Companion to Renaissance Humanism*, ed. Jill Kraye, 1–19. Cambridge: Cambridge University Press, 1998.

Marcus, Leah S., Janel Mueller, and Mary Beth Rose, eds. *Elizabeth I: Collected Works*. Chicago: University of Chicago Press, 2000.

Moss, D. E. "Roger Ascham." *History Today* 27 (1977): 651–58.

Neale, J.E. *Queen Elizabeth I.* Chicago: Academy Chicago Publishers, 2001.

Overell, M.A. "Edwardian Court Humanism and *Il Benificio di Cristo.*" *Reassessing Tudor Humanism*, ed. Jonathan Woolfson, 151–76. London: Palgrave Macmillan, 2002.

Pemberton, Caroline, ed. *Queen Elizabeth's Englishings*. EETS o.s. 113. London: Kegan Paul, Trench, Trübner & Co., 1899; repr. Millwood, NY: Kraus Reprints, 1975, 1981.

Perry, Maria. *The Word of a Prince: A Life of Elizabeth I from Contemporary Documents*. Woodbridge: Boydell Press, 1999.

Plowden, Alison. *The Young Elizabeth*. London: Macmillan, 1971; repr. Phoenix Mill: Sutton Publishing, 1999.

———. *Danger to Elizabeth*. London: Macmillan, 1973; repr. Phoenix Mill: Sutton Publishing, 1999.

———. *Marriage With My Kingdom*. London: Macmillan, 1977; repr. Phoenix Mill: Sutton Publishing, 1999.

———. *Elizabeth Regina*. London: Macmillan, 1980; repr. Phoenix Mill: Sutton Publishing, 2000.

Relihan, Joel C. *Boethius: Consolation of Philosophy*. Indianapolis: Hackett Publishing Company, 2001.

Rowse, A.L. *The England of Elizabeth*. London: Macmillan,1950; repr. Bungay, Suffolk: Reprint Society, 1953.

Somerset, Anne. *Elizabeth I.* New York: St. Martin's Griffin, 1991.

Starkey, David. *Elizabeth: The Struggle for the Throne*. New York: Perennial, 2001.

Stewart, Hugh Fraser. *Boethius: An Essay*. Edinburgh: Blackwood, 1891; repr. New York: Burt Franklin, 1974.

Trapp, J.B. "Education in the Renaissance." In idem, *Background to the English Renaissance*, 67–89. London: Gray-Mills, 1974.

Walton, John, trans. *Boethius: De Consolatione Philosophiae*. Ed. Mark Science. EETS o.s. 170. London: Oxford University Press, 1927.

Wernham, Richard Bruce, ed. *List and Analysis of State Papers, Foreign Series, Elizabeth I*. Vol. 5 (*July 1593-December 1594*). London: Her Majesty's Stationery Office, 1989.

VII

The Printed Editions of Elizabeth I's Writings

Please note that among the editions of writings by Elizabeth I listed below, only Pemberton, *Queen Elizabeth's Englishings*, contains the translation of the *Consolatio*.

Bradner, Leicester. *The Poems of Queen Elizabeth I*. Providence, RI: Brown University Press, 1964.

Bruce, John, ed. *Letters of Queen Elizabeth I and James VI*. Camden Society Publications 46. London: n.p., 1849.

Elizabeth I. *Queen Elizabeth's Englishings of Boethius, Plutarch and Horace*. Ed. Caroline Pemberton. EETS 113. London: Kegan Paul, Trench, Trübner, 1899; repr. Woodbridge: Boydell and Brewer, 1997.

Harrison, G.B., ed. *The Letters of Queen Elizabeth, 1533–1603*. Westport, CT: Greenwood Press, 1981.

Marcus, Leah S., Janel Mueller, and Mary Beth Rose, eds. *Elizabeth I: Collected Works*. Chicago: University of Chicago Press, 2000.

———. *Elizabeth I: Autograph Compositions and Foreign Language Originals*. Chicago: University of Chicago Press, 2003.

May, Steven W., ed. *Queen Elizabeth I: Selected Works*. The Folger Shakespeare Library Series. New York: Washington Square Press, 2004.

Mueller, Janel, and Joshua Scodel, eds. *Elizabeth I: Translations, 1544–1589*. Chicago: University of Chicago Press, 2009.

Shell, Mark. *Elizabeth's Glass*. Lincoln, NE: University of Nebraska Press, 1993.

The Consolation of Queen Elizabeth I

*1-Recto-1-Verso

2-Recto-2-Verso

[Blank]

*3-Recto-5-Recto

5-Verso-6-Verso

[Blank]

*7-Recto-8-Verso

[The Computation of Days and Hours]

*9-Recto
*The Queenes Matie, being at Windsor in the xxxvth yeere of her Raigne,
began her translation of Boethius,
upon the xth of October, a^{o}. 1593, and ended it
upon the eighte of November then next following, wch were
xxx days.
*Of wch tyme there are to be aco^{m}pted xiij dayes
in Sondayes and holly dayes, and parte in *[w^{ch}] her Ma[^{tie} rode]
abrode & taking her ayre, upon wch her Matie did
forbeare to translate.
*So that xiij dayes being deducted from xxx, Remaynth
*17 dayes xvij dayes, In wch her Matie finished her transla^{ti}on.
*And in those xvij dayes, her Matie did
nev^{r} exceed one hour & a half at a tyme in following her transla^{ti}on.
Wherby it appeerith that in xxvj or xxvij houres
*[2]6 houres her Matie p^{er}fo^{r}med the wholle translation.
*The number of leaves in my book are 88, so that it must be that her
Matie did translate v. leaves at ech tyme, and
iij leaves over and above in the wholle tyme.

*9-Verso

*10-Recto

10-Verso-11-Recto

[Blank]

*11-Verso

11A-Recto-12-Verso

[Blank]

[The Queen's Translation of Boethius's *De Consolatione Philosophiae*]

13-Recto

*[Book One]

**1. Myter.*
**Righmes that my groing studie ons p^{er}formed*
In teares alas cumpeld woful staves begin[.]
My muses torne behold what write I shold indites
Wher tru woful verse my face w^{t} dole bedews
Thes †at Lest no terror aught Co^{n}strain
that felowes to our †mone our way they shuld refrain
The glory ons, of happy †griny Youthe
Now, fates of grunting Age, my Co^{m}fort all
Unlookt for Age hied by mishaps is Come
And Sorow bidz his time to add w^{t}al
Unseasond hore heares upon my hed ar †powrd
And Loosed skin in feable body shakes
blessed dethe that in switest yeres refraines
but oft Calld Co^{m}es to the woful wights
O w^{t} how defe eare she fro^{m} †wretched †wries
And wailing yies Cruel to shut denies
While Gileful fortune w^{t} †vading goodz did †chine
My life †welny the doleful houre bereved
Wha^{n} her fals Looke a Cloude hathe cha^{n}ged
My wretched Life tha^{n}kles abode protractz[.]
Why me so oft my frendz have you happy cald[?]
Who fauleth downe in stedy step yet never stode[.]

While of all

13- Verso

[Blank]

14-Recto

[Prose 1]

**While of al this alone in silence I bethoght me and*
tearesful Complaint[,] †*in stiles office ment*[,]
over my hed to stand a Woman did apeare
of stately face with flaming yies of insight
above the Comun worth of men of fresche coulor
and unwon strengh thogh yet so old she wer
that of Our age she seamed not be One
her stature suche as skarse Could be desernd
for sume while she †*skanted her to the Comen*
stature of men strait she semed w^{t} Crowne
of hed the heavens to strike, and lifting
up the same †*hiar the heavens them selves*
she enterd begiling the sight of Lookars o^{n}
her †*wedes the wer of smalist thrides*
p^{er}faict for fine workma^{n}ship and Lasting substa^{n}ce
as after by her selfe I knewe was by
her ha^{n}des al wroght Whose forme as
to smoky Images is wo^{n}t a certain dimnis
of despisid antiquitie overwhelmed[.] *Of thes* †*wides*
in the Lowest skirtz Π in the upper side
a Θ was reade al woven and betwine
bothe lettars Ladar wise certain steps wer
marked by wiche fro^{m} Lowest to hiest
Element ascent ther was. Yet that selfe
garment the handz of violent men had
torne and pices suche as get the Could
away the stole[.] *Her right hand held*
a booke the Left a sceptar who whan
she spied poetz musis standing by my bed
and to my teares inditing wordes
some what moved inflamed w^{t} Gloting yies[:]
[P] *Who sufferd q^{t} she thes stagis harlotz*
aproche this sik man wiche not only

wold not ease

14- Verso

Wold not ease his sorow w^t no remedies, but
w^t swit veno^m nourris the^m, thes the be
that w^t baren affectio^{n}s thornes destroies
the ful †Eares of reasons fruitt, and mens
*mynds with disease in *†vres not fries,*
but if of vane ma^n, as vulgar wontz,
your alurements had deprived me
w^t Les griefe had I borne hit for by
suche, Our worke had got no harme
but this man have you touched who^m
Stoike and Academiq^{ue} study broght
out. Get you away Sirenes swite
til ende be seene to my musis Leve
him for Cure and helthe. to this the
Checked rabel w^t Looke downe Cast w^t wo
w^t blusche Co^{n}fessing shame doleful out
of doores the went, but I whose †sisght
drowned in teares was dimed, Could
not knowe what she was of so empirius
rule, and setteling my yies on ground,
what she wold more do[,] *in Silence*
I attended. Than she drawing nar
on my †bedsfete sat downe and vewing
my Looke of hevy woe and w^t my
dole to the erthe throwne downe, in
versis thes of my mynds †pane
Co^{m}plaineth thus[:]

*2. *Myter.*

[P] *Ô in how hed Long depth the drowned mind is dark*
and Losing Light her owne to others darkenis drawn
as oft as driven w^t erthely flawes the har^{m}ful care upward grows[.]
†wons this man fre in open feld used skies to vew
of †Rose son the Light beheld

of frosy moone

15-Recto

of frosy mone the planetz saw
And what star elz runs her wo^{n}ted cours
bending by many Circles this man had won

by numbar to knowe them all
Yea Causis eache †whe^{n}s roring windz the seas p^{er}turbz
acquainted w^{t} the spirit that rolles the stedy world
And whi the star that falz to the Hisperas waters
fro^{m} his reddy roote dothe raise herself
Who that gives the spri^{n}ges mild houres ther te^{m}p^{er}
that w^{t} rosy floures the erthe be deckt
Who made the fertile Autume at fullist of the yere
Abound w^{t} Grape al †Solne w^{t} ripest fruits[.]
he wo^{n}ted to serche and find sondry causes of hide^{n} nature
downe lies w^{t} mindz Light bereved
W^{t} brused Nek by overhevy Chaines
A bowed Lowe Looke by waight bearing
driven alas the †Sely erthe behold.

pr. [2]
[P] **but fittar time q^{t} she for medecin tha^{n} Co^{m}plant*
than fixing on me her stedy yies art thou
the same q^{t} she who ons nourriched with my milke
fed w^{t} our foode art growe^{n} to stre^{n}gh
of manly mynd? On who^{m} we bestowed suche
weapons as if thou hadst not Cast away, had
saved the w^{t} invi^{n}cible strength, dost thou
me knowe? Whi art thou †doum? is hit shame
or wo^{n}dar makes the Silent? but wha^{n} she
spied me not only stil but woordles and dum,
on my brest gently Layd her hand, Said[:]
ther is no danger, he is enterd in a Letharge
a Co^{m}men †diseace of mynd, distract
he hath a litel forgotten himself easily his
memory wyl retourne wha^{n} first he hathe reme^{m}bard me

And that he

15-Verso
And that he may[,] *a litel Let us wipe his*
yies overdimd w^{t} Cloude of erthely things
thus speaking my yies flowing w^{t} teares
Folding her garment she dried[.]

*3. *Myt.*
than Night overblowen the darkenis Left me

and formar strengh unto my yies retornd
As wha^{n} the heavens astound w^{t} hedlo^{n}g wind
and †Pole amidst the Cloudy mistes
the Son is hid and in the heavens no stars aperes
fro^{m} hy the night on erthe is spred
The same if boreas sent fro^{m} his †tracien den
dothe strike and Opens the hiden day
Shines out and w^{t} his Soudan †Ligh Φebus shake^{n}
Withe his beames strikes al Lokars On[.]

[prose 3]
**No*[*w*] *otherwise mistz of my wo dissolved*
to heaven I reached and raised my mynd
to knowe my †Curars face than whan
on her I rolled my yies and Loke I fixed[.]
my nurs I saw in whose retired †Romes
in my Youthe I dwelt. [B] *And how q^{t} I*
art thou Come to the Solitarenis of our
exile, O, pedague of al Vertus, fallen fro^{m}
the hiest step shalt thou w^{t} me be torme^{n}ted
to w^{t} falz Crimes[?] [P] *Shal I q^{t} she O skoler*
myne, the Leve and not to ease thy
burdane wiche for my sake thou berest
in easing thy Labor w^{t} felowing of the paine
hit il becumes Φilosoφie to Leve alone
an innocentz way. Shal I dread †my none blame

And as

16-Recto
and as if any nouvelty had hapt shal I feare? Ar you
now to knowe how amonge wicked folkes wisedo^{m}
is assailed w^{t} many dangers? *Have we not wrestled
with follies rashnes among the elder sorte afore our Platoes age
and made therewith great battaile? yea he alive his master Socrates
uniustely claymed the victory of deathe when I was by! whose
inheritance when after the vulgar Epicurian and Stoick and all
the rest each man for his part ment to bereave
me, sundred, as in parte of their pray my garment though
I resisted and exclaymed: For being the workmanship of myne
own hande, they plucking some ragges from it, supposing they
had all, departed from me. Among which for that some trims

of my garment appeared, folly supposing they were my familiars abused some of them with error of the vayne multitude. Though thou haste not knowen Anaxagoras flight nor Socrates Venim nor Zenos torment because they are strange, yet *Cauni[,] Senecæ, Sorani thou maist knowe for they are not *[. . .] nor of unhonored memory, whom nothing else to their bane brought but that instructed with our conditions, they seamed unlike the wickeds endevors. Thou oughtest not therefore to wonder if in the sea of lyffe we be tossed with many a tem=pest rising, whose purpose is this chiefest to dislike the wickedest. Whose army though it be great, ought be *despi[sed] as whom no Guide rules, but hurled rashely with a dimme error, which if once setting battayle against us should fortune prevayle[.] Our guide will drawe our troupes to castle while they be busy to †ravyce Unproffitable baggage, and we from hye shall skorne them while they spoile that is vyle, sure from the furious tumulte and saffe in such a trenche whether those foolish raveners may never attayne[.]

who so

16-Verso

*4. Myter.

[P] *Who so quiet in setled Life*
proude fate kepes underfote
And stable defending eache fortune
His chire †unwonne preserves
him shal no rage nor Seas threates
fro^{m} depthe that hurles her fome
Nor wood Vesevus with holy pittz
that burstz out his smoky fires
Nor way of flaming Sulφar wont to strike
the towers †hie can move
Whi so muche Can wretched men
at †fiers tirants wo^{n}dar forsles furious
Hope thou naugh ne feare
disarmst thou may the powreles Ire
but who so quaking feares or wische
Not being stable and in his strengh[,]
downe falz his shild and changing place
Linkes the chaine by wiche he is drawen.

4. prose.

[P] **Knowest thou al this and yet hast forgotte the? art thou the Ass to the Lute? heare and reme^{m}bar, If thou Looke for thy Curars ande discover thy wound.* [B] *Than I gathering my mynd to his ful strengh, have I yet nide of warning, hathe not the †sowernis of Cruel fortune Overtopt me by herself alone doth not the vew of this place the move*[.] *Is not this the †shop wiche surist seat in all my inward romes for the I chose me *w^{ch}* by me oft sytting, of science divine & humain matters thou disputest? was this thy habite? was this thy Looke? when w^{t} the I serched natures secretes? when to me w^{t} Ruler thou discribedst the starres wayes & framedst o^{r} woorkes & wholle trade of lyfe after the trade of celestiall order shall we receave such rewardes for obeying the? when thou thy self this sentence †paste of Platos mouth, that happy were those co^{m}mon welthes if eyther wisdom studiers Ruld them, or their Rulers wisdom imbraced. Thou by the self same mans mouth didst teache that this was the necessariest cause, for wyse

17-Recto

for wyse men to rule the co^{m}mon wellth, leste that the raynes th^{r}of left to the wicked & harmfull citizens might breede the plague & harme to good. This autoritie I following, wch in thy secret leysure thou taughtest me, made me wish to tourne for action of co^{m}mon Rule. God & thy self doo witnes beare, wch he inspirede to wyse mens myndes, that no care brought me to magistrate Rule, but co^{m}mon care for all good men whence greate & unappeased discorde w^{t} wicked folkes I had. And that freedom that co^{n}science libertie gave me for to save right, I preserved, dispising the mighties offence. How oft have I crossed Conigastus, using violence to eche mans weke fortune? How many tymes have I ov^{r}throwne Triguyl[e] In court cheefe officer, from his begon & almost ended iniurye? How oft have I protected poore men, who^{m} unpunished avarice of so Barberous w^{t} infinite slanders vexed, throwing my autoritie against their perills. Nev^{r} could any man, drawe me fro^{m} Law to Iniury. I sorowed for the provinces misfortunes, wrackt by private †ravins and publick taxes, no lesse than they that suffered the^{m}. whan Campania province seemed afflicted through want in tyme of greatest famyne & such as could not

be exprest, when buying & selling was forbyd, I began a quarrell against the
pretorian Ruler for cause of co^{m}mon good. I strave w^{t} him the king knowing it, &
won it that no sale were made. Paulin the consul whose goodes the
palatine doges w^{t} hope & ambitio^{n} had devoured, from the gapers Iawes I
drew. I opposde myself to the hate of Ciprian the bakbyter that the payne of the †preiudical
accusation might not fall to the share of Albinus the co^{n}sul. Have not I, suppose you,
sha^{r}pned quarrels against me ynough, and ought to have ben defended among the
rest, evin them that for love of Iustice among the Courtiers might have
saved me, by wch I should be safer; by what accusers am I now stricken
of who^{m} Basilius fallen fro^{m} princes service is driven to slaunder of o^{r} name, for
dettes sake. when by kinges Iudgem^{t} a censure was given for banishment for
Opilion & Gaudensius for their Iniuries & many wronges, And when they denyeng
to obeye, saved them selves w^{t} defence of holy Sanctuary, & that the King
knowing, proclaymde that w^{t}out they dep^{ar}trd fro^{m} Ravenna towne at the
p^{re}scribed daye, they should be driven out w^{t} their †forheades markes. What might

be

17-Verso

be thought to crosse such severitie? but yet in that daye, themsellves deferring
the slaunder touched me. what tho? Hath o^{r} science deservid this, or their foreru^{n}ning
condemna^{ti}on, made their aucusers Iust? So fortune was nothing ashamde if not
[of] th[']accused innocency, yet of th[']accusers *[basenis] Wickednes: but what is o^{r} faulte? will ye
seeke the p^{ri}ncipall? we are sayde to wish the Senates surety: The waye you desire.
A sclaunderer, lest he might delay his Lessons by wch he might make me
guilty of treason, we are accused to have †letted him. What then think you, ô
pedagogue myne? shall we deny the facte that shame the we might not[?]
but I wolde, & nev^{r} to will, willes leave. shall we co^{n}fesse it[,] but they shall
the worke of hinderi^{n}g the sclaunderer ceasse[?] shall I call it a faulte, to
wish the surety of that state? he himself by his own decrees against me, hath
made this unlawful: but folie that lyes ever against her self, the worth
of thinges can nev^{r} change. neth^{r} Lawfull is it for me by Socrates Rule, to

hyde trouth or grau^{n}te a lye, but this[,] what it is[,] to yours & wyse folkes iudgem^{t} I leave the censure, whose manner of matter & trouth that posterite may knowe to my silent memory, have co^{m}mitted, for as for false supposed *tres in wch I am accusde to hope for Romayne libertie, what bootes it speak? whose fraude had lyen all open, if I might have usde my accusers co^{n}fessio^{n}, wch in all matters beares greatest swaye, for what left liberty may be hoped for? that wold god there were any. I had aunswered then as **Canius* did, who accused by **Caius Cesar Germanicus* sonne, to be guilty of the coniuration against him. **Yf I had knowen, thou hadste not knowen.* In wch matter, sorow hath not so duld my senses to *co^{m}play[n] of wicked men for dooing mischefe against vertue, but rath^{r} much wonder how they could hope p^{er}forme it. For to will the worst, p^{er}chaunce might be o^{r} faulte, but to have powre against Innocency, for ech wretch to doo what he conceaves, god being Looker on, seemes monstrous. Whence ther is a question not w^{t} out cause, of thy familar: **Yf ther be a god, q^{t} he, whence coms the evill? The good fro^{m} whence, yf he be not?* but it may be lawfull

ynough

18-Recto

ynough for wicked men that thursted the blud of all the senate & all good men, to seek o^{r} †wrak, who^{m} they have seene defend the good & save the Senate, but did we deserve the lyke of the fathers or no? Yo^{u} reme^{m}ber I suppose, for what I sayde or did present you directed me. You call to mynde quoth I, At Verona when the king greedy of †co^{m}mon fall did stryve to bring the treason layde to Albinus, to the Senates order, how I defended then the innocency of all of the Senat w^{t} most assurance of my owne danger.

You know all this that true it is I tell & that no boste I make of any my prayse. for th[']assurance of a grau^{n}ting co^{n}science diminishith it self in a sorte as oft as bosting receavith rewarde of fame. But you see what end my Innocency hath. for true virtues rewarde, we suffer false factes payne. For whose manifest co^{n}fessio^{n} of wicked facte, ev^{r} made all Iudges so agree in severitie that eyth^{r} the faulte of humaine witt, or th[']incertayne state of fortune, may not leave out somwhat? Yf we had been sayd to have burned the sacred houses, to have slayne the preestes w^{t} wicked sworde, & bred de-structio^{n} *[of] all good men, the sentence had punished present co^{n}fessing & convicted, now allmost fyve hundred thousand paces †of, though farre of & †unwearyed, we are condemmde to death & exile, for o^{r} ready indevors for the Senates good. O woorthy men, For such a faulte, none of the^{m} shall be co^{n}vinced, the value of whose guiltynes, they themselves have seene that brought it, wch to dym w^{t} mixture of som wickednes, they have false belyed me to have stayned my co^{n}scie^{n}ce w^{t} sacrilege for Ambitio^{n} sake. And thou thy self grafted in me, all desyre of mortall thinges from seate of my mynde hast pluckt, for under thy sight *[. . .] was no place for sacrilege faulte, to my eares thou didst instill, & to my thoughtes this Pythagorian worde, **Obey thy God*, neyth^{r} did it becom me to seeke the help of vilest spirites, who^{m} thou hadst framed to such an excellency, that lyke to god thou madest the^{m}. Agayne, the Innocent closet of my house, resorte of honest frendes my holy lawes fath^{r} **Symmacus*, And for his deedes reverenced, defendes us from all suspicion of this cryme, but Ô mishap! They beleeved all this cryme, & for this synne we were co^{n}fyned, for that

18-Verso

for that we were indewed w^{t} thy lesson, & framed of thy conditio^{n}. So bootes it not ynough, that thy revere^{n}ce should p^{ro}tecte me, but that w^{t}all thou shouldest be vexed w^{t} my offense. but this is greatest heape to o^{r} mishap, that the valuing of most[,] regardes more fortunes event, than causes merit, And Iudgith that best p^{ro}vided, that felicitie reco^{m}mendith. W^{ch} makes that true waight first leaveth the unhappy man. What now the rumors be, how variable, & increasing their Iudgem^{tes}, to remember, it greeves me. This only can I saye, that the last burden of fortune is, that †whilest faultes be layd to the wretchedest charge, they are beleeved to deserve that is layde to their charge, And my self bereved of all my goodes, spoyld of my dignities, spotted in my fame, for benefitt, receave punishm^{t}, Me thinkes I see the wicked †shops of vilest men flowing w^{t} Ioye & mirth, And every wickedst man, overlayeng me w^{t} new fraudes of accusation. I see the good lye downe p^{ro}strate for feare of my fall. Ech wicked man be bolde unpunishd to faulte. To doo the wch thorow rewardes be styrred, but Innocent folk not only of surety, but of defense deprived. wherfore thus may I exclame:

**5. Myter.*

[B] *Ô framar of starry Circle*
who lening to the lasting †grounsto^{n}e

Withe whorling blast heve^{n}s turnest
and Law Co^{m}pelst the skies:
Now that w^{t} ful horne
meting all her brothers flames,
the Lessar stars the mone dimmes
Now darke and pale her horne
†*Nar to Son Loseth her Light*
And she that at beginning of night
Hesperus frosen rising makes
And Luciφar palled by Φebus uprise
Againe her wo^{n}ted raines excha^{n}geth
thou by the Cold of †*Lefe falne shade*
straightist thy Light w^{t} shortar abode
Than wha^{n} the fervent so^{m}mar Comes
Easy nights houres devidest
Thy power tempers the changing year
that what †*Leves boreas blastz bereves*
Gentel †*Seφirus brings as fast*
Sedes that the Northe star doth behold
at hiest blade the †*dokstar burnith up*

*[no catchword]

19-Recto

Naught †*loused fro^{m} au^{n}cient Law*
Leves the worke of her owne place
Al giding w^{t} assured end
Mans workes alone thou dost †*dispice*
O gidar by right desart fro^{m} meane to †*kipe*
for why so many slipar fortune
turnes doth make oppressing †*fautles*
dew paine for wicked mete
but in hy Seatz the wicked factz abide
And wicked stamps o^{n} holy necks
With uniust turne
And Cleare vertu dimmed
With thick blackenis Lurketh
And iust ma^{n} the wickeds Crime doth beare
fals †*othe in fraude doth the^{m} annoy*
Who whan the Can use ther forse
Who^{m} many vulgar feare
the mightiest kings them can subdue

**O now behold of wretched erthe*
thou who so ties the bondz of all
Us men regard of thy great worke not vilest part
how †tost we be with fortunes waves
O weldar †apeace the Roring floudes
And w^{t} what bondz the great heave^{n} thou gidest
**the stable erthe do stedy.*

This

19-Verso

*The First Booke

20-Recto

5. prose

This when w^{t} contynuall *wo[es] I had burst out, seeing her w^{t} mylde cou^{n}tena^{n}ce nothing mooved w^{t} my mones, [P] when the quoth she, sad & wayling I sawe, straight a wretch & exile I knew the, but how farre of thy bannishm^{t} was, but that thou toldste, I knew not, but thou how farre fro^{m} cou^{n}trey art not expulst, but strayed, yet thou hadst it rath^{r} be thought expulst, thou thy self haste throwne it. For that for oth^{r} was nev^{r} lawfull than the to doo. For if thou remember from what cou^{n}trey thou ca^{m}mest, not guyded as Athens was, by rule of multitude, but one ys King & Ruler, that Ioyeth more in subiectes number than their expulse, w^{t} whose raynes to be guyded & Iustice obeyde, is greatest libertie. Art thou ignorant of the auncientest law of thy Citie, wch co^{m}mandes that no man may be banisht fro^{m} it, who choosith there to build a seate[?] For who so in her trench & suerty is co^{n}teynde, no feare shall have, nor exil deserve to be, but who so leaves to will her habitation, †wantes allso deservith. Wh^{r}fore thy Looke, not this place so much moovith me, nor doo I desyre my †shops walles adornid w^{t} yvory or glasse, rath^{r} than the seate of thy mynde, In wch I placed not bookes, but that that gives the^{m} price, sentences of myne owne woorkes. Thou haste rehersed truth of thy

20-Verso

of thy desert for co^{m}mon good, but little hast thou told of nombers greate thou hast receaved. Thou hast remembered thinges, knowen to all, obiected against the eyth^{r} for good or falshode. Of mischefz or fraudes of thy slaunderers rightly thou haste straightly touched that they might the better & farder be knowen w^{t} prayse of vulgare folk. Vehemently hast thou invayde against the Senates Iniustice, of o^{r} co^{m}playnt haste moned, & bewaylde the wrack of estima^{ti}ons Loste. The last thy wo agaynst fortune invayed, complayning that she equalled not desertes rewarde. In end of thy raging muse, requirst a grau^{n}te that the same peace wch ruleth the heaven might so rule th[']earth. But for that a greate heape of affections ov^{r}whelme the, & sorow, ire, wo, diversly distractes the, such as thy mynde is now, as yet thy remedies be no greater, wh^{r}fore easyer lett us use a while, that such as by growing paynes in swelling hath bene hardenid, that they may beare more sharp †receites, w^{t} a soft touch be doulced.

**6.M.*

[P] *Whan hevy Cancer* *[*sm^{e}*]
by Φebus beames inflames
than he that Lent Plentyes sead
to †*forowes that denied them*
bigiled by Ceres faithe
Let hi^{m} seake the Acorne tre

The decked

21-Recto [top half]

the decked wodz seak not
Wha^{n} thou violetz gather
Wha^{n} w^{t} the Northy blastz
Ther roring fildz affrightz
Nor Seake not thou w^{t} gredy ha^{n}d
The springing Palmes to weld

Grapes if thou wische inioy
In Autume bacchus rather
hys giftes bestowes
Times God assigneth fit
for eche mans office best
Nor the tournes that he apoints
Suffers to be mixte
So what so Leves by rachelous way
the Certain rule[,]
Ioyful ende shal never hit *seest *suffer*[.]

*21-Recto [bottom half]–22-Verso [top quarter]

22-Verso [bottom three quarters]

*6.pr.

[P] First then suffre me w^{t} questions few thy myndes state to touche, & it to proove that better may I know of thy cure the way. [B] Ask me q^{t} I, according to thy will, what thou woldest my au^{n}sweres be. [P] Then she, thinkes thou that this world is wheeled by rash & happing chaunce? or dost suppose that Reasons rule is in it? [B] I can no way think, q^{t} I, that w^{t} so rash chaunce, so c^{r}tain thinges are moved; but I know that God ye maker hit guides, nor ev^{r} shall co^{m} day that fro^{m} truth of this opinio^{n} shall draw me. [P] Is it so? q^{t} she. A little afore this thou hast tolde & hast bemonde that men were so furr fro^{m} godes care deprived; For w^{t} the rest thou art nothing moved, but that w^{t} reason they were led. Good Lord I wonder much why placed in so right a mynd thou canst be sick? But let us s^{er}ch a little hyar. I wote not what, somwhat lackes I trowe. But tell me, For that thou †doutst not the world by god be rulde, seest thou by what raynes it is guided. [B] Scarce doo I know, said I, the meaning of the questio^{n}, ne yet can I au^{n}swer thy dema^{n}des. [P] was I ignorant that somwhat lackt? by wch like cliff of Ramp^{ar}[t] shrinking the woes desease into the mynde is crepte. but tell me dost thou

reme^{m}ber

23-Recto

remember what is the end of all? And whith^{r} tended the intent of all nature[?] [B] I have hard it au^{n}swerd, but my memory dampt sorow hath made. [P] but whom dost thou know whence all p^{ro}ceedes? [B] I know q^{t} I. And God is he I au^{n}swere. [P] How can it be then, that begynning knowen, the end therof thou knowest not[?] but this is the fasho^{n} of troubles, & such is theyre wont, that moove they *may a man fro^{m} his place, but ov^{r}throw or wholly pluck up they can not. But this wold I have the au^{n}swer. Re=membrest thou thy self a man? [B] What else q^{t} I[,] should I not reme^{m}ber that? [P] Canst thou tell me what man is then? [B] Dost thou ask me this, whith^{r} that I know that I am a reasonable creature & mortall? I know it, & that to be I must co^{n}fesse. [P] Then she, knowest thou not thyself ought els? [B] nothing. [P] but I know q^{t} she, that the greatest cause of thy disease, is to have left to know what thou art. wh^{r}fore eyth^{r} fully have I founde the reason of thy sicknes, or a waye to reco^{n}cile the home agayne. For being co^{n}founded through thy oblivio^{n}, thou hast bewaylde thy self an exile & spoyled of thine owne goodes, for being ignorant of thy end, thou haste supposde mighty & happy the wicked folkes & lewde, & forgetting by what brydle the world

is guided

[*23-Verso]

*

is guided the *[. . .] of fortune thou supposest w^{t}out a guide to run. Greate causes not only to disease but to ruine to. But thanked be *†<u>thy hoste</u>, that nature hath not yet wholly destroyde the. We have the *great[est] foode for thy helth[:] thy true opinio^{n} of the worldes Rule, who^{m} thou beleevest not subiect to chaunce, but Ruled by divine Reason. Feare nought th^{r}fore, Allready from this little sparke thy vitall heate is sprong, but because the tyme is not yet for stro^{n}ger remedyes, & that the nature of the myndes is such, that when they have cast away the true, & are *[. . .] w^{t} false opinio^{n} by wch a springing darknes of woe co^{n}foundes that true sight, I will assay a while th^{r}fore w^{t} †lenitives & meane †fomentations to †skant them, that darknes of deceaving affectio^{n} remoovid the shyne of true light mayst obtayne.

*————————————————————————

*————————————————————————

*Dym cloudes

*The fyrst booke

*————————————————————————

*21-Recto [bottom half]

*7.m.

[P] *Dim Cloudes*
Skie Close
Light none
Can afourd
If Roling Seas
boustius Sowth
Mixe his fome
Griny †*ous*
Like the Clirristz
days the water
straight †*moude*
sturd up al foule
the Sight gainsais
Running Streame
that poures
fro^{m} hiest hilz
Oft is staid
by Slaked
stone of Rock
thou if thou wilt
in Clerest Light
the trothe behold
by striaght lin
hit in the pathe

Chace Ioyes

21-Verso-22-Recto

[Blank]

*22-Verso [top quarter]

Chase Ioyes
repulse feare
thrust out hope
Wo not retaine
Cloudy is the mind
With †*snafle bound*
Wher they raigne[.]

*here endith ye first

booke /

*——————————————————————————

*22-Verso [bottom three-quarters]-*23-Verso

23-A-Recto-23-A-Verso

[Blank]

*24-Recto

*24-Verso

*25-Recto

25-Verso

[Blank]

26-Recto

The second Booke / .

1 Pro.

After this, a while she pawsde, & when my heede by my modest silence she markt, thus she began: [P] If alltogith^{r} thy cause of greefe & state I know, thou pynest w^{t} the affectio^{n} & want of form^{r} fortune. She so much changyth the state of thy mynde, as thou ymaginest ov^{r}throwes **hit*. I understand the many **shaped* deceites of her wonder, & so farre exercisith a flattering familia=ritie, w^{t} the^{m} she myndes deceave, till she co^{n}found w^{t} intollerable woe, who^{m} w^{t}out hope she hath left. Whose nature conditions & desert, if thou remember, thou shalt know that thou hast neth^{r} had nor lost by her any thing ought worth, but as I suppose, I shall not neede to labo^{r} much to call these thinges to thy memory. For thou art wont when she was present & flattered the, to invay against her w^{t} manly woordes in chassing her fro^{m} o^{r} doores, w^{t} thy sentence invaydst her. but ev^{r}y souden change nev^{r} hapes w^{t}out a greate streame of the mynde. So doth it **bifal* that thou a while hast parted fro^{m} thy ease. but tyme it is for thee to drawe & taste som sweeter thing and pleasant, wch passing to the inward p^{ar}tes may make a way for behoofuller draughtes. let p^{er}suasion of sweete Rhetorik assist the, wch then goith in rightest path only, when she leaves not o^{r} p^{re}ceptes. And w^{t} this musick the guest of o^{r} home, soundes now easyer now weightyer notes. What is it th^{r}fore O man that **hath* thrown the down to wo & wayle? Thou hast seene I beleve som new unwonted thing. Thou yf thou thinkest that toward the fortune be changed, art deceaved. This was ev^{r} her manner[,] this was her nature. She hath ev^{r} kept toward the, rath^{r} her own co^{n}stancy in her mutabilitie. Such one was she wha^{n} she beguild the, & did deceave w^{t} allurem^{tes} of false felicitie. Thou hast understode now, the doutfull face of the blynde Goddesse, wch though she hyde her self to others, hath made her self to the manifest. Yf thou allow her use her fashon, co^{m}playne not th^{r}of; Yf thou *_hatest_ her treason, skorne her & cast her of, that so falsely beguylde the, for she that now is cause of thy woe the self same ought be of thy quyett. She hath left the, who^{m} no man can be sure that will not leave him. Canst thou beleeve flyeng felicitie precious,

& can

26-Verso

& can thy *†_p^{re}nt_ luck be deere; nev^{r} faythfull in abode, & when she partes bringes naught but woe: And if neth^{r} she can be kepte w^{t} iudgem^{t}, & whan she flyes, makes the^{m} wretched, what ought els meanith her flight than a show of a co^{m}ming calamitie? For alone it suffisith not to beholde, what afore o^{r} eyes is sett, wisdom the end of all measures. For her mutabilitie in bothe neth^{r} makes her fortunes threates feard, nor her beguylinges *_wisched_. Lastly, thou must pacie^{n}tly beare, what so befalles in fortunes Co^{r}te, whan once to her Yoke thy neck thou bowest; but if thou wilt p^{re}scribe her lawe, to byde or parts, who^{m} thou hast freely chosen thy gouvernesse, shoulst thou not be iniurious & sharp thy lucke w^{t} thy impatience, wch change thou canst not? Yf thou woldst throwe the sayles to wynde, not whith^{r} will wolde, but whith^{r} the blast doth dryve so furr thou goest. Yf thou doo lend the furrowes seede, thou must beare w^{t} deere yeeres & barren: Yf to fortunes guide thou hast betaken the, thou must obey thy Dames conditions. woldst thou stryve to staye the co^{r}se of a turning wheele? but thou of all mortall men the foolisht, if hap byde, it leavith to be chaunce.

*_1. Myter_

[P] _This wha^{n} her proud hand cha^{n}geth cours_
And Euripus foming Like is throwne
Whilo^{m} she fierce Kings Cruel destroies
_and Lowe Looke of_*† _won ma^{n}_ _decettful raiseth_
She hereth not the wretche nor hedeth not his teares
Willingly skornes the sighs that spitful she made
Thus playeth she and so her strengh doth trie
A wo^{n}dar great to hers she shewes
If any man you view One houre
both thralz him and
Extolz[.]

2. prose

[P] A few woordes wold I pleade w^{t} the on fortunes syde, mark thou then, whith^{r} she call the not in plea, why me ô man guilty dost thou make of daily quarrells? What wro^{n}g doo I the? What goodes fro^{m} the have I drawne? Pleade thou against me afore any Iudge but for the possessio^{n} of thy goodes & dignities. And if thou showest that any mortall man have

p^{ro}pertie

27-Recto

propertie of any of the^{m}, that thou pretendst thyne owne, that thou aske willingly I will yelde. When Nature brought the out of thy mothers womb, naked of all & needy, I up tooke the and nourisht the w^{t} my substance, & that that breedes now thy rage w^{t} speedy favo^{r} carefully I bred the, And did indue w^{t} plenty & glory of all such thinges as were my owne. Now is it tyme[,] now may I if I list draw back my hand, Yeld thankes for using not thyne owne. Thou haste no lawe for quarrell, as if thy owne lost thou hadst. Why sighest thou than? W^{t} no violence have we used the, goodes[,] hono^{r} & all such lyke, of right myne own, my maydes knowes their Lady, w^{t} me they com, & whan I parte, give place. Boldly I affirme, if thyne they were that lost thou co^{m}playnst, at all thou hast not lost the^{m}. Am I alone forbyd my right to use? To heavens is lawfull to bring the pleasant dayes & dark the same w^{t} misty nightes. To yeare is lawfull *[to] adorne the earthes face w^{t} floures & frute, Som tyme w^{t} cloudes and coldes co^{n}found. The Sea may w^{t} quyet calme be pleasd, now terrible by waves & tempest, the unsaciable desyre of men, shall it bynd us to co^{n}stancy? furr fro^{m} o^{r} conditio^{n}. This is o^{r} powre, this contynuall plan we make, The wheele by turning Rolle we whirle, and Ioye the lowest change w^{t} hyest, & hyest makes the same to matches. Com up & yo^{u} will, but on that conditio^{n} that ye cou^{n}te it not iniury to descend whan the fashon of my dalyance requires it. Wert thou ignorant of my conditions? Knewest thou not Cresus king of Lydia, a little before fearfull to Cyrus straight way wretched man bequethed to flamy heate, defended fro^{m} heaven by a mist sent downe? Dost thou not reme^{m}ber how *Paul shed many an honest teare for the calamitie of Perseus king, who^{m} he tooke? What does Tragedies clamo^{r} more bewayle, than a man turning happy Raigne by blynde fortunes stroke? Hast thou not learnt that there lay in Iupiters thressholl

*[no catchword]

27-Verso

*thressholl, twoo barrells fyld one w^{t} yll, the oth^{r} of good? what yf thou suckest up more largely of the better part? what yf I left the not all alone? what if this my right mutabilitie have bred the cause to hope for better? but be not thou †amasde, that sett in the co^{m}mon raigne of all oth^{r}, to lyve by thine owne lawe **desirest*.

*2. *Myter.*

[P] *If sandz suche store by raging †flawes*
as Stured Sea turnes up
Or Skies bidect w^{t} mighty stars
the hevens al that Lightz
And suche welthe bestowes
Nor ple^{n}ty w^{t} fullist horne w^{t}drawes her ha^{n}d
Mankind yet Ceaseth not
W^{t} wailing mones bewail him
thogh God his vowes willingly receve
the Liberal dolar of golds ple^{n}ty
And †gridy folke w^{t} honors great indues
Naught to have got they seame
but Raving devouring what they had
stretcheth the †Chawes for more
What raignes Can drawe bak
hedlong desiar to stable end
Wha^{n} thirst of getting inflames
the flowing *[*ove^{r}*] *w^{t} Largist gifts*
No man thinkes him riche
Who quaking mones beleves a beggar[.]

3. prose.

[P] Yf fortune for her self had spoken thus to the, thou hadst no cause to grudge
agaynst her, but if ought there be wherby thy quarrell by law thou canst defend, tell it thou must, place to speak we give. [B] Than fayre thes be in show, q^{t} I,*†*florist* **over* **Retorik* & musik w^{t} the ho^{n}ny of there sweetnes, *th[e]y
only delite whan they be †hard, but deep^{er} sense of yll the wretched hath. wherfore

28-Recto

Wherfore, when these have don, to sounde o^{r} eaeres, ingraffed wo o^{r} mynde

oppressith. [P] And she, So it is, sayd she. * . . . . . .
* ~ / ~ / ~ / ~ / ~ ~ ~ ~ ~ ~ for These be not yet remedyes for thy
disease, but serves for bellowes against the cure of thy resisting sorowe for
when I see thine, I shall apply such remedyes as shall pearce deep^{er}. But
leste thou shouldst suppose thy self a wretch, Hast thou forgotten, the tyme &
meane of thy felicitie? I leave untolde how desolate of parentes, the care of
greatest men fosterd the, & chosen to affinitie of the cities Rulers, And
that kynde
that is of kyndred the neerest, First thou wert deere afore thou were
next. Who wold not have famed the most happy w^{t} so great hono^{r} of
father in lawe, of wyfes modestie, and seasonable obtayning of a man
childe[?] I ov^{r}passe (for so I will co^{m}mon thinges) dignities receavid in yo^{u}th
denyed to elder folkes: it pleasith me, That this is happed to the singuler heape
of thy felicitie. yf any frute of mortall thinges may beare a waight of blessednes,
can the memory of such a daye be scrapte out by any waight of growing
harmes? When thou hast seene twoo Consuls at once, thy children
acco^{m}anyed to w^{t} nomber of the fathers, & peeples Ioye, when they sitting
in the Court as Curules, thou the Orato^{r} of kinges prayse, deservest thou not
glory of wit & eloquence? when amidst the^{m} both thou satisfidest the
expecta^{ti}on
of co^{n}suls w^{t} all the rowte, w^{t} a liberall tryomph? Thou flatterest fortune as
I suppose while she stroked the & cherisht as her darling. Thou tokest away
the rewarde that to p^{ri}vate man she nev^{r} lent afore. will yo^{u} now spurne at her?
hathe she w^{t} a heavy eye now strayned the? Yf thou doo †wayen the no^{m}ber
&
†trade of pleasant & wofull, thou canst not yet deny thy self happy: yf
th^{r}fore thou thinkst not thy self fortunate for seeming Ioyes by past, no
cause why thou thy self a wretch suppose: For passe they doo that
wofull now be thought. Camst thou now first into the stage of lyfe, of
a souden, & stranger? Supposest thou any co^{n}stantcy to be in humayne matters
whan speedy houre a man himself undoes? For tho rare credit of abode owght
happing
chaunce to have, yet the last daye of lyfe may serve for fortune that remaynes.
What meanest thou to speak? wilt thou leave her dyeng, or she the flyeng?
In pole

28-Verso

**3. M.*
[P] *In †poole whan Φebus w^{t} reddy waine*

the light to spred begins
The star dimed w^{t} flames oppressing
Pales her whitty Lookes
Wha^{n} wood w^{t} †seΦirus mildding blast
blusheth w^{t} the springing Roses
And Cloudy Sowthe his blustering blastes
Away from †stauke the beauty goes
Sometime w[^{t}] Calmy fayre the Sea
Void of waves doth run
Oft boistrus tempestz the North
With foming Seas turnes up
If rarely stedy be the Worldz forme
If turnes so many hit makes
belive slippar mens Luckes
trust that sliding be ther goodz
Certane and in Eternal Law is Writ
Sure standeth †naugh is made[.]

4. prose.

[B] Than I, truth hast thou told me, ô of all vertue the nursse, nor can I blame the speedy co^{r}se of my prosperitie, but this is it, that in co^{n}sidering, most vexith me, that in all fortunes adv^{r}sitie I finde this most miserable to have bene happy. [P] That thou q^{t} she, beares payne for false opinion, that Rightly thou oughtest not on matters the^{m}sellves impose. For if the vayne name of chauncing felicitie moove the, Repete w^{t} me w^{t} how many & greate thou aboundest. Yf the preciousest of all thou didst possesse in fortunes Censure, that to thy self unharmd or broken be kepte, canst thou when best thinges be retaynde, co^{m}playne by right, of yll hap? Safe doth remayne Symmachus thy fath^{r} in lawe, of all mankynde most worth. And that w^{t} price of lyfe thou careles should not buy

29-Recto

buye, that man made of wisdom & vertue, sure of his own, mones for thy wronges. Thy wyfe of modest wit, excelling for her shamfastnes & that all her guiftes in short I may include, her fath^{r} lyvith I say, & keepith thy spirit, though hatyng lyfe, from wch dep^{r}vd my self will grau^{n}te †skantey thy felicitie, And for Lack of the, w^{t} teares & woe pynith. What shall I speak of thy children Consuls, in who^{m} fath^{r}s & grandfathers witt appeerith as their yo^{n}g yeeres p^{er}mitt[?] Whan then the cheefest care for mortall men is lyfe to keepe, ô happy thou yf know thou couldst thy good, to who^{m} such thinges do hap, as no man doubtes the deerest *_thinges_ in lyfe. Dry up th^{r}fore thy teares. Fortune hath not yet hated all men, neth^{r} hath †to greevous a tempest ov^{r}whelmed the, for Ankers holde remaynes, wch neth^{r} suffers p^{re}nt co^{m}fort, nor co^{m}ming hope to leave the. [B] And let the^{m} holde q^{t} I, fast still I pray. For they enduring, howsoev^{r} the world goes, out we shall wade. But yo^{u} see q^{t} I, how much hono^{r} we have lost. [P] Then she, we will help the, yf thou be not weary of all thy lott. But I can not abyde such yor delytes, as dep^{ri}ved of som of thy felicitie, wayling & carefull thou co^{m}playnst, for what man is of stayde felicitie, that quarrels not w^{t} som degree of his estate? Carefull is the co^{n}ditio^{n} of mans goodes, wch eyther nev^{r} all happes, or ever bydes. This man hath hono^{r}, but his blotted blud shames him. This man nobilitie makes famous, but inclosed w^{t} neede, rather unknowen he choosith: An oth^{r} man having both, the sole lyfe bewayles: An oth^{r} for mariage happy, childles keeps his goodes for an others heire. Som Ioye w^{t} children, w^{t} teares bemoanes the faultes of sonne or daughter, no man th^{r}fore easely agrees w^{t} his fortunes state, generall to all, that the untryed knowes not, th[']expert abhorrith. Add to w^{t}all that ech man hath a most delicate sense of his own felicitie, and w^{t}out all hap to his beck, throwen down he is, w^{t} any unwontid adv^{r}sitie, though in †leste matters. Such tryfles they be that drawes fro^{m} happyest men the top of bliss. How many be there supposest thou that wold think the^{m} neerest heaven, if skraps of thy fortune hap to *_ther_ share? This place which thou

29-Verso

wch thou thy bannishm^{t} callst is the inhabitantes cou^{n}trey. So nothing is wretched but when it is thought so, & blessed is all luck that hapes w^{t} sufferers ease. What man is so happy that hath given hand to impatie^{n}ce, that wisshith not his fortune changed? The sweetnes of mans lyfe, w^{t} how many bytternesses is it mixt, wch if they seemid to the enioyer delitefull when he wolde, it is gon, therfore he may not keepe it. The blessednes of mortall goodes, plainly is miserable, that neth^{r} p^{er}petually duryth w^{t} the co^{n}tented, nor wholly delites the afflicted. why doo ye mortall men seeke outwardly yor felicitie w^{t}in yo^{u}? Error & blyndness co^{n}founds yo^{u}. I will shew the shortly the thressholl of thy felicitie. Is there to the ought more precious than thy self? [B] Nothing, q^{t} I. [P] Then if thou be wise thou shalt possesse that neth^{r} thou canst lose, nor fortune take away.

And that thou mayste knowe felicitie not to stand in happing chau^{n}ces, consider it this. Yf happynes be the greatest good of nature lyving by Reason, nor **hit* the greatest good that may be taken away, the cause **hit* doth exceede that may not so. It is manifest that fortunes change can not attayn to the **getting* of bliss. Besydes, who^{m} falling felicitie caryes, eyth^{r} knowith **her*, or seeth her mutabilitie. Yf he be ignorant, what happy luck can blynde felicitie have? Yf he know it, he must needes feare to lose that he is sure can not be kepte, His co^{n}tynuall feare then, dep^{ri}vith his happynes. or if he have lost, will he not care for it? for **hit* should be a slender good, that a man **wold* easily lose. And because thou art the same that art p^{er}suaded & holdes it sure by many demonstra^{ti}ons, mens myndes not to be mortall, And when it is playne, that chauncing felicitie, **w^{t}* bodies death is finished no man can doubte, Can this bring felicitie, but rath^{r} all mortall folkes in misery **by* deathes end is brought. Yf many we knowe to have sought the frute of blessednes, not only by death, but by woes & tormentes, for that how can the p^{re}nt lyfe make the^{m} happy, who^{m} miserable the passed could not?

who

30-Recto

**4 Myter*
[P] *Who Lasting wyl*
Wary settel seat,
And stable not of Roring
Eurus blastz ben won
And Careth skorne
the waves of thretning Sea
Shuns Soking Sandes
and top of hiest mount
One the froward Southe
With all his affrightz
The other Loused refuse
A hanging Waigh to beare
†*fleing perillous Lot*
Of pleasantz Seat
On Lowe stone reme^{m}ber
thy house sure to place,
Thogh wynde blowe,
Myxing Waters to boto^{m}

Thou happy †*plast in stre*^{n}*gh*
Of quietz Rampar[*t*]
happy shalt Live
And smile at Skies
Wrathe[.]

5. prose

[P] But because the fomentations of my reason have entred in the, I suppose I must use som stronger remedies. Go to, yf now the giftes of fortune be not fleeting & changeable, what is ther that eyth^{r} thou canst make thyne, or if thou seest & p^{er}cevist, wilt not dispise? Are riches eyth^{r} thyne or by their nature pretious? what is the gold th^{r}of? but heape of gathered pence?

30-Verso

pence? and such as shynes more w^{t} their spending than w^{t} their heapes. Hatefull men doth Avarice mocke, but bou^{n}tie noble. And if it can not byde by a man that is given to an oth^{r}, Than mo^{n}ey is most p^{re}tious when turnd to others by liberall use, hath lost the possession. The same, if but w^{t} one abyde from how many it be pluckt, the rest it leaves full needy. The fame th^{r}of fills many mens eares, but Riches not distributed may not passe to many: wch when it is don, they must make poore who^{m} they leave. Ô skant & needy riches, wch all to have is not lawfull for many & com not to any one w^{t}out they begger of the rest. Doo Iewels luster drawe thyne eyes? Yf any beauty they have, it is the †stones light not mens; W^{ch} I muse why men so admire. For what is there that wontes a spirit & lymmes †partage, that Iustly may seeme fayre to the myndes and Reasons nature? wch tho as Creators goodes & his divisions, may draw som later beauty, placed under yor worth, no way deserve yor wonder. Doo sick mens palenes please you? What eles: for it is a fayre portio^{n} of a goodly woork. So somtymes we delite in face of smothest sea. So doo we vew the heaven, the starres, sonne & moone. Doo any of these touch the? Darest thou boste at any of their lusteres? o^{r} Shalt thou be paynted out for the florishing springes sake, or shall thy plenty increase to so^{m}mer frutes? Why art thou drawne w^{t} vayne Ioyes? Why dost thou cherish others goodes for thyne? Fortune shall nev^{r} make those thyne, that nature hath made oth^{r}

folkes. The earthes frutes doutles be due to best nourishment, Yf thou wilt fill the neede that nature Requires, thou needest not seeke fortunes plenty, for w^{t} few or little nature is co^{n}tented. Whose

ynough

31-Recto

ynough if thou wilt make to much, that noyfull & unpleasant to taste will make. But now, Thou thinkest it beautifull to shyne w^{t} divers garmentes, whose show yf it please the eye, eyth^{r} they will wo^{n}der at nature of the substance, or the witt of the Craftes man. But shall the long trayne of many servantes happyn the, who if they are of vile co^{n}dition, it is an yll burden for the house, & most foe to his Lord: but if goode they be, how canst thou sett oth^{r} mens vertue amo^{n}g thy goodes? By wch all, It is playne seene, that those thou reckenst for thy goodes, are none of thyne: In wch if ther be no beauty got, what is it that thou waylest for losse, or Ioyest to have? If by nature they be fayre, what carest thou? for such thinges of themselves separated fro^{m} thy substa^{n}ce should have pleased, for precious they be not to have co^{m} amo^{n}g thy ryches, but because they were p^{re}cious, thou chosedst rath^{r} place the^{m} among the^{m}. Why, lack you fortunes *exclama[^{ti}]on? I beleeve you seeke to beate away beggery w^{t} plenty: but this happes awry. For ye had neede of many helps to p^{re}serve the variety of deere goodes. And this is true, that they neede many, that possesse much. And agayne they lack †leste, that mesure their own abunda^{n}ce by natures necessitie, not Ambitions greedynes. But is it so? Is ther *[no] proper good ingraft in yo^{u} of yor own, that yo^{u} should seeke it in *outwar[d] & meane matters? Ys the world so changed that the divine Creature for Reasons sake should no otherwise florish, but that it neede possession of Co^{m}on ware, And all oth^{r} thinges co^{n}tented be w^{t} their owne, but we lyke god of mynde, shall we take the ornamentes of excellent nature fro^{m} basse thinges? nor shall not understand how much therby we Iniure o^{r} Creat^{r}? He wold have us exceede all earthly thinges, but yo^{u} throwe yor worth among basest stuff. For if every mans possessio^{n} seemes more dere that it is his owne, when the meanest thinges your own you Iudge[,] to them yo^{u} yeld *[yo(u)] w^{t} yor prising: wch not w^{t}out desert happs, for this is the state of *humayn[e] nature, that then it exceedes all oth^{r}, whan it self it knowes, but is made baser than very beastes, if to know it self, it leave for naturall it is for oth^{r} beastes, not know the^{m}selves. In man it is a vice. How farre stretchith yor erro^{r} wch doo suppose to be deckt w^{t} oth^{r} mens ornamentes.

For yf

31-Verso

for yf of outward thinges, any lyke be had, those be praysde fro^{m} whence they cam: but if ought ther be hid or unknowen, bydes in his own spot: but I deny that is good, that harmes the haver. Doo I saye untruth? No, wilt thou saye, And riches oft have harmed their owners whan ech wicked man, (and th^{r}fore greedier of others goodes), hath thought him only woorthyest, that hath obtayned golde or Iewells. Thou that the speare & sword carefully hast feared if wandering †empty man, of lyfe the path hadst enterd, afore a theefe woldest sing, o beautifull hap of mortall goodes, wch when thou hast taken, sure hath left the.

*5. *M.*

[P] *happy to muche the formar Age*
With faithful fild co^{n}tent
Nor Lost by sluggy Lust
that wontz the Long fastz
to Louse by son got Acorne
that knew not baccus giftz
With molten hony mixed
*Nor *serche Shining †flise*
With tirius †venom die
Sound slipes Gave the grasse
ther drink the running streme
Shades gave the hiest pine
The depth of sea they fadomd not
Nor wares chosen fro^{m} fur
Made Stranger find new shores,
Tha^{n} wer Navics Styl
Nor bloudshed by Cruel hate
Had fearful weapo^{n}s staned
What first fury to foes shuld
any armes Rayse
Wha^{n} Cruel woundz he Saw
and no reward for bloude,
Wold God agane Our formar time

to wo^{n}ted maners fel
But Gredy getting Love burnes
†Sorar than Etna w^{t} her flames
**O who the first ma^{n} was*
of hide^{n} Gold the waight
Or Ge^{m}mes that willing Lurkt
The deare da^{n}ger digd.

what

32-Recto

6. pr.

[P] **What shal I dispute of Dignities and rule wiche you ignora^{n}t of true worthe and power withe the skies domaine, wiche happening to any wicked man what Etnas fire w^{t} brusting flames or what deluge suche ruine makes Surely as I thinke you reme^{m}ber how Co^{n}sulz rule beginar of liberty for ther pride our fathers soght to put downe, who for like faulte out of the citie the name of kings Abolisshed, but if sometime as seldo^{m} haps, honors On Good men be bestowed, what els in the^{m} doth please the usars goodnis? So haps* *that hono^{r} is not given to v^{r}tue or her worth, but v^{r}tue esteemd by dignitie, but what is this, yor craved & beautifull force? Do yo^{u} not see how earthly be the †bestes that yo^{u} Rule, for evin among the †myse, yf ye see any one chalinging rule or gouernment above the rest, what a laughter doo ye moove? but what if ye have respect to the body? what can be weaker than man, who^{m} somtyme the byt of a flye & somtyme the passage into any secret p^{ar}te may destroye[?] How farre ought the Rule of any man stretche but on the body alone & his circu^{m}stanes, I mean fortune her self? will you ev^{r} guide ought w^{t} free mynde, & will ye remoove the same sticking to her self by good reason, fro^{m} the state of her own quiet? Whan a tyrant thought to afflicte a poore man w^{t} his tormentes to confesse the knowers of a co^{n}spiracy against him, his tongue he byt & threw away, throwing it to the face of the wicked tyrant. So the torture that he supposde to make stuff for his cruelty, a wise man made for his v^{r}tue. For what is it that any man can doo to any oth^{r}, that to be don to himself can he beare? *Bucidides we heare was wont his guestes to kyll, slayne himself by Hercules his host. Regulus cast many p^{ri}soners into yrons in the Punik warr, but straight himself sett handes on †victorerers chaynes. Dost thou think his powre ought, what himself may, can not lett that an oth^{r} should doo him? Besides, if evin in Souveray^{n}ties & powres, there should be any naturall & prop^{er} good, nev^{r} should they hap to wicked, for co^{n}trarieties seld consorte, Nature denyes that **disagreing* be Ioyned[.]

Wh^{r}fore when playn it is that many men beare greate office, this is sure that of their nature, they be not **good*, **wiche* stick to wickedst folke. The greatest

worth

32-Verso

worth that fortunes guiftes worthyest can give, be such as in abondant sorte to wicked folkes do hap who so quicknes hath, hit swift a ma^{n} doth make. So musick the musicall, phisick the phisician, Retorik Rhetorician maketh, for the nature of ech thing doth his prop^{er}tie, nor is myxt w^{t} effect of co^{n}trarietie. And freely expells that is against it: neth^{r} can riches unsaciable avarice refrayne, nor makes not free his own, who^{m} †vitious lust w^{t} unbroke chaynes, holdes bound. And dignitie on wicked bestowde, not only makes the^{m} not worthy, but betrayes & discovers their indignitie. Why doth it hap so? You Ioye somtyme to falsifie w^{t} oth^{r} name, whose effect shames themselves. Wh^{r}fore neth^{r} those riches, nor same powre nor lyke dignitie, can by right be called.

Lastly, the same we may co^{n}clude of all fortune, that hath nothing in her as it is playne to be desyrde, not of naturall goodnes: *who^{m} eyth^{r} nev^{r} acco^{m}panyes the good, nor makes the^{m} good who^{m} she is neerest[.]

**6. M.*

[P] *We knowe how many ruines made*
Whan flamed Citie and fathers slain
that tirant who ons brother kild
Imbrued w^{t} mothers bloude
With Looke overvewed her body Cold
No teares bedewes his face, but was
A †domar of †dedded beautye
the same yet w^{t} Sceptar peple Ruled
Evin suche As Son espies at furdest west
fro^{m} the Orison Come

Who^{m} frosty seven stars Overlookes
Who^{m} wrothful North with drie heat
†*Affraies in sithing of the burning sandz*
Could al his Lofty power at Lenghe
Turne the rage of frantiq^{ue} Nero?
O grevous hap wha^{n} wicked Sword
To Cruel Veno^{m} Ioingnes[.]

7. pro.

[B] Then I, Thou thy self knowest that no a^{m}bitio^{n} of mortall thinges did Rule us we were not guided by the **pride* of any mortall glory, but wish

a ground

33-Recto

a ground in o^{r} †affayres, by w^{ch}, silent v^{r}tue should not growe olde. [P] Then she, This is that that noble myndes by nature but not yet brought by p^{er}fectio^{n} to the uttmost top of vertue, might intice, I meane Gloryes desyre & fame of best actes for co^{m}mon welth: wch how small it is & empty of all waight, co^{n}sider this, As Astrologers demo^{n}stra^{ti}ons have told yo^{u}, all the Earthes circle, is playne, gettes som meane to know these partes of the heavens face, that if it be matched w^{t} the greatnes of the celestiall globe, It is supposde to have no space, and is of this little regio^{n} of the world, almost but the forth portio^{n}, As thou hast learnd by ptolomes grau^{n}te, wch is inhabited by us **Creatures* **knowe* Fro^{m} this fourth if in thy mynd thou draw away, as much as Sea & marish covers, & so much as wasted ground by *drynes hath **distended*, the straytest roome is left for mans habitation. If in this so small a point of title, we be hedged in & inclosed, what think we so much of enlarging fame & name p^{ro}moting? For what large & magnifick thing hath glory bounde in so straight & small lymites? Ad to this that it self though but small, is environd w^{t} habitatio^{n} of many nations, to^{n}gues and conditions that in all trade of lyfe differs, To wch not only no report of ech man, but not of Cities can com through hardnes of way & differe^{n}ce of speeche, and divers traffik. In Marcus Tull. tyme as he himself in place hath sayde, the fame of Romayn Empire nev^{r} past Caucasus mounte, & yet it was florishing & fearfull to the Parthians & to all peeple inhabiting such places. Dost thou not see then, how narrow &

neere presst glory is wch to stretch out spred thou labourst? shall the glory of a Romayn go so furr, as where nev^{r} Romayn name hath past? What for that the divers natures of peeple & their orders disagree? so that what amo^{n}g so^{m} is prayse, among the rest sett for cryme. So haps that if any mans prayse delyte, to him the same doth nev^{r} p^{ro}ffit to many peeple sent. Is any man co^{n}tent that amo^{n}g his own, his glory byde, & Immortalities fame be tyed in boundes of his own soyle? but how many noble men in their tymes fayling oblivio^{n} of writers **have* dasht? but what proffites writinges? Whe^{n} w^{t} their

office

33-Verso

office, a long & dark age suppressith, but doo yo^{u} think to get immortality w^{t} thought of co^{m}ing tyme? Yf thou Ioyne it w^{t} the infinit spaciousnes of eternitie, what hath thou to Ioye of thy lasting name? For if the abode of one moment, if w^{t} ten thousand yeeres be co^{m}pared, for that both space is ending, It shall have, tho a little, som portio^{n}, but this number of yeeres, How oft so ev^{r} multiplyed, may not co^{m}pare w^{t} the unending lasting: Somtyme som **outward* thinges ther be co^{m}pard amo^{n}g themselves, have end **twixt* **infinitie* **and* **ending* no co^{m}parison may beare. So is it that the lasting of any longest tyme, if it be matcht w[^{t}] unbounde eternitie, not small but none shall seeme. For w^{t}out yo^{u} be ignorant how rightly to please popular eares & vayne rumors, & leaving care of co^{n}science & vertue, ask rewarde of oth^{r} mens frute, see how in the myldnes of such an arroga^{n}cy, How pleasantly a man may be begylde. for when one once had skornde a man that clothed him not w^{t} Philosophy for true v^{r}tues use, but for proude gloryes sake, & saide he wold try him whith^{r} he were a Philosopher that easely could beare in patie^{n}ce iniuryes, he took upo^{n} him to be suffring, & taking the skorne as a ragi^{n}g man. Dost thou, at length, understand me a Philosoph^{r}? Then nippingly he said, I should have understode it, if thou hadst bene silent. What meanes it? that cheefest men (for of the^{m} I speake) that seeke through v^{r}tue glory, what hath death to doo w^{t} the^{m}, after the body is dissolved, as their end? for be it that o^{r} Reason it self denyes us to beleeve that all men dye, then ther is no glory, when he is not of who^{m} she speakes, but if the mynde it self w^{t} co^{n}science good dissolved fro^{m} earthly *†*gial* all freed seekes heaven, wold she not all earthly thinges despise, who heaven enioyeng, Ioyes earthly thinges to want.

who so

34-Recto

*7. *Myter*

[P] *Who so w^{t} hedlong mynd glory*
alone belives as Greatest thing
And quarters of Largist hevens behold
With straightid seat of erthe
Wyl blushe that hit not filz
The Short Co^{m}pas of †*Gridy desire*
Why proude men do you Crave,
Your necks fro^{m} mortal yoke retire
Thogh fame by people strange
flying spred the tonges Open
And noble house by Great titelz shine
dethe hates the hiest glory
Intangels Low and hauty hed
And equalz †*Lest to most*[.]
Wher now lies faithful †*fabritius bones?*
Wher brutus or Currish Cato
Smal Lasting fame Signes
A vaine name w^{t} fewest lettars
But why do we knowe noble names
Do we not See the^{m} to co^{n}sumed[?]
Ly you shal unknowe at all
Nor fame shal uttar Who
If you Suppose that Life be Lo^{n}gar draw^{n}e
For brethe of mortal fame
Tha^{n} the Second dethe Expect[.]

8. pro.

[P] **but Lest you shuld suppose against fortune*
I make an Endles war, Ther is a time whan
she the begiling one, somewhat wel of men desarves
Eve^{n} tha^{n} wha^{n} discoverd, herself she shewes and
maners hers detectz, p^{er}chanche yet tho^{u} wotz
not what I say, wo^{n}dar hit is that I mynd tel
and mening skars w^{t} wordes can Expres
For men I suppose more get by adverse
than Lucky fortune for she ever w^{t} shewe
of blis, w^{t} seming al false deceves and ever
true she is *in change when unstable she seemes. The one beguyles, the oth^{r}
instructes. This tyes the enioyeres myndes w^{t} show of lyeng

good

34-Verso

good, the oth^{r} loosith the^{m} w^{t} knowledge of frayle felicitie. This know th^{r}fore for wyndy, fleeting, & ignorant of her self. The oth^{r} sober, ready & wise by adv^{r}sitie exercise. At last happy he that drawes the strayeng w^{t} deceite fro^{m} greatest good, but adv^{r}sitie oft tymes retourning the^{m} to surest haps as by a hook doth drawe. Thinkst thou this for †lest good, that this Currish & fearfull Fortune hath discovered the mynde of thy faythfull frendes? The oth^{r} hath shewed the *fellow sure lookes & doubtfull, in dep^{ar}ting hath taken hers, & thyne hath left the. W^{t} how much woldest thou in p^{ro}sperous state have bought this when thou thoughtest it most? Leave to seeke lost goodes. The preciousest kynde of ryches, frendes thou hast founde.

**8. Myter*

[P] *That world w^{t} stable trust*
the changing seaso^{n}s turnes
And divers sedes stil holdes League
That Φebus the ruddy daye
With Golde^{n} Car bringes furthe
that the †Mone may rule the night
Wiche hesperus broght
The gridy Sea her Streame
in Certain limites †kipt
That Lawful be not to wide world
to bancke her spatius boundz
Al this †hole molde ties
in Ruling erthe and Sea
Love Ruling heavens
Who if the raines he slake
What so now by love is linked
Straict maketh war
And seakes to wracke that worke
Whiche Linked faithe
hit quiet motions moved
He in holy peace doth hold
the bounded peoples pact
And Linkes Sacred wedlok
With Chast Goodwyl
Who Lawes his owne
to true Associates gives
**O happy humain kind*
If love your mindz

The same that heven doth rule
Mygh gide[.]

*Here endes y^{e}
second booke

35-Recto

[Blank]

35-Verso

*The second Booke

35-A-Recto-35-A-Verso

[Blank]

36-Recto

The *thrid book .

[1] pro.

Thus ended she her song, when greedy me & astond w^{t} lyfted eares, the doulcenes of her verse, perced. [B] wh^{r}fore a little after, o cheefest co^{m}fort q^{t} I, of wearyed myndes, how much hast thou revived me, w^{t} waight of sentence, or pleasa^{n}tnes of song, so as heerafter I shall think me not inferio^{r} to fortunes strokes, and so the remedyes that a little before thou saidst †to sharp not only doo I not feare, but ernest to heare of I greedely beseech. [P] Then she, I p^{er}ceavid q^{t} she, when silently o^{r} wordes w^{t} attentyve eare thou †cacht, that this state of thy mynde eyth^{r} I lookt for or that is truer, my self have made. The rest that doth remayne, be such that tasted, smartes, but inwardly †rxd. sweetens, but for that thou namest thy self ernest to heare w^{t} what desyres shouldest thou be inflamed, yf thou couldst know whith^{r} we meane to bring the. [B] Whith^{r} q^{t} I. [P] to true felicitie, wch thy mynde dreames of, whose eyes being used to pictures, it self can not beholde. [B] Than I, doo I *bese[c]h the, & w^{t}out delay shew what is the true one. [P] willingly shall I doo it q^{t} she for thy sake, but cause that thou doost better know, the same in woordes I shall describe and seke to inform the that she knowen when eyes thou turnst to co^{n}trary p^{ar}te the show of truest good, thou mayst knowe.

*1. *Mytre*

[P] *Who frutfulst fild wyl sowe*
first †fried of fruit must make his †Leas
With †Sithe must fern and busches Cut
that Ceres may swel with new sede
The flies Labor swetar is
If strongar tast be first eate

As LuciΦar dothe the darkenis chase
  A fayre day spurs the ruddy †*hors*
Thou Looking So on falsed Good
  begin thy neck fro^{m} *yoke to pluck*
Therby the mind may true obtaine[.]

2. prose

Than, fixing her looke awhile, and as taken w^{t} straight co^{n}ceite of mynde, thus begyns: [P] All mortall care wch labo^{r} of many studyes usith, goes on in divers pathes, & yet stryves to com to one end of bliss: but that is right good wch a man obtayning no farder may desyre, wch is of all the greatest good, & in it self

36-Verso

*in it self co^{n}taynes them all, of wch if any want, it can not be the moste[,] For outwardly were left somthing to be wisht. Playne then it is, that state of all good thinges p^{er}fect in his gathering, is onely blisse. This as we sayde by divers path all mortall men indevors gett. For nature hath ingraft in mens mynd desyre of truest good, but strayeng erro^{r} to falshode doth seduce us among who^{m} som beleeving hit greatest good nothing to want, stryve to be rych.

som supposing hono^{r} best, when gotten they have, seeke of their Citizens hono^{r}.

others ther be that settels greatest good in hyest powre. such will or raigne themselves, or stryve to cleave to such as doo, but they that suppose hono^{r} greatest good, they eyth^{r} w^{t} warre or peaces worth hast to inlarge a glorious name, but many good men measure the frute of good w^{t} ioy & mirth, and they think it happyest to wallow in delytes. Ther be to, that enterchange ech end & care w^{t} oth^{r}, as they that Riches & delyte for powres sake desyre, the oth^{r} powre for mo^{n}nyes sake or glory doo desyre. In these & such lyke humayne actes or desyres, intent abydes, as nobilitie & popular fame they seeme to get som show, wyfe & children for plesure sake desyre, but partaking of *of frendes (that holyest is) not recken by fortune nor force. The rest eyth^{r} *fo[r] powres sake or delyte be taken. It is playne that bodyes good to hyer thinges be referd, whose strength & bygnes it is that makes their woork co^{m}mended beauty & agilitie their fame, hath their delyte to who^{m} only bliss they ad, for that that ech man thinkes above the rest exceede, that greatest good he thinkes. And greatest we suppose bliss to be, wch makes men think blessedst thing, that ech man above the rest covetes before thyn eyes thou hast the forme sett out of mans felicitie, Riches,

honor, powre, glory & delyte, wch last only, the Epicure considering hit followes that the greatest good he thought, for that delyte bringes all delytefull thing to mynde. but let me retourn to mans study, whose mynde albeit wt blynded memory, yet seekes the greatest good, but as drunken man knowes not the path to bring him home. Doo they seme to err that nothing to neede desyres? For that naught can so well obtayne happynes
as flowing

37-Recto

as flowing state of all good thinges, not needing others, contented wt it self, be they deceavd that hit supposith best that worthyest is of Reverente respecte[?] *no sure. nethr is that vyle to be despised that the care of ech mans labor **covetz*. Is not force to be nombred among good thinges. what then, is that weake & to be estemid feeble that of all othr thinges exceedes? Is not honor to be regarded? It can not be denyed, but that that is most worth, ought be most honord. For carefull & sorowfull, blisse we can not call, nor subiecte to care & woe we may not saye, when in †lest thinges that is desyrd, that most delytes have & enioye. And these be those wch men wold obtayne, & for their cause desyre ryches, dignitie, †Raygnes, glory & delytes, for that by these they beleeve they may gett ynough honor, powre, glory & Ioye. Good it is thrfore that men by so many ways doo seeke, In wch, what force of nature there is, is showed, that tho dyvers & sondry opinyons, yet in looving goodnes end, they all consent.

**2. Myter.*

[P] *how many raines of Causes gideth*
nature powreful by wiche the great
World wt Lawes provident kepes
and †tijnge Strains wt unlousing
Knot eche thing wel pleased wt shirllest
note expres wt drawing strings
Thogh †Afriche Lionnes faire
gives beare and takes given food wt paw
And Cruel kipar feares the wonted stripes that bare
If bloud have ons dyed ther Looke
Ther courage retournes to formar state
and wt rorings Lowde them selves remembring
Slacks from tied knotz ther necks
**and furius first wt Cruel tothe*
On kipar raging wrath bestowes

The Chatting bird that sings o^{n} hiest bow
In holow den Shut is she
to this thogh Cups w^{t} hony Lined
And Largest food w^{t} tendar Love
begiling Care of man bestowes

yf yet

37-Verso

If yet skipping on the Eves
Spies pleasing shady wood
With †fote she treds her skatterd meat
in †Soroing seakes the woodz alone
And w^{t} swit vois the trees †Resontz.
the twig drawen ons w^{t} mighty fors
bowing plies her top
the same if bending ha^{n}d do slack
The top upright doth turne
The Son to Hesperius waters falz
but by Secret pathe againe
his Cart turnes to Est
Eache thing Sekes owt his propre Cours
and do reiois at retourne ther owen
Nor ordar given to any remains
onles he Ioining to end his first
And So stedyes his holie round[.]

*3. pr.

[P] You allso o erthly wightes, though by single figure doo dreame of *yo[ur] own begynning & that true end of blissednes p^{er}ceave, tho w^{t} no †playne yet w^{t} som thought, understand. And thith^{r} bringes you a naturall insti^{n}ct to true goodnes, & increasing erro^{r} leades yo^{u} fro^{m} the same. Consider th^{r}fore whith^{r} men can obtayne their end desyred, by those meanes that men suppose gettes happynes, for if eyth^{r} mon^{n}y, honors or such lyke can bring such thinges to who^{m} nothing is lacking of, best, let us then co^{n}fesse that som men may be happy by their obteyning. For if neyth^{r} they can do that they p^{ro}mise & wantes greatest good, Is it not evident that they have but a false show of blissidnes? first th^{r}fore let me ask the that a little afore aboundest in ryches. Among thy flowing heapes, did not co^{n}ceyte of co^{n}ceavid iniury †amase thy mynde? [B] I can not reme^{m}ber q^{t} I that ev^{r} my mynde was so free but somwhat greevid it[.]

was it

38-Recto

[P] Was it not because that was a waye that thou woldest not forgo, or was w^{t} the that thou caredst not for? [B] I answerd, so it is. [P] Then thou desyredst the ones p^{re}sence, & the oth^{r}s want. [B] I co^{n}fesse. [P] Does *[any] man neede than, q^{t} she, that every man wantes & needes? He that lackes, is not wholly co^{n}tent? [B] no sure. [P] When thou hadst welth ynough, hadst thou not this want? [B] What els, said I. [P] Then Riches can not make a man lack nothing, nor yet co^{n}tent himself. And this is that promise they seemed. This I suppose ought most be co^{n}sidered, that mo^{n}ny of his own nature hath nothing *[ ] he ca^{n} not be spoyled of that possesses it. [B] I co^{n}fesse it. [P] Why shouldst thou not co^{n}fesse yt, whan a mightyer takes it away fro^{m} the unwilling[?] Whe^{n}ce *coms these Courtes co^{m}playntes? but that coyne is taken away fro^{m} the losers by force or guyle? He shall have neede th^{r}fore of outward help by wch his mo^{n}ny he may keepe. [B] Who can this deny? [P] He should not neede such help that possest of mo^{n}ny lose he wold not. [B] This is doutles. [P] The matter is fallen oth^{r}wise now. For such riches as were thought sufficient of the^{m}selves, are needy of others ayde, but what is the way to dryve away lack fro^{m} ryches? for rych men can they not ho^{n}ger, can they not thirst, *[nor] can not sometyme the cold wynter hurt the ly^{m}mes of the rich man? But yo^{u} will say they have ynough thurst & colde to dryve away, but by this meanes yo^{u} may saye the lack of rich men may be co^{m}forted, nev^{r} taken away. For if she ev^{r} gapes & serch for som thing els, tho fild w^{t} ryches ynough, it must be that there something remayns that it should be filld w^{t}all. I neede not tell you that nature w^{t} †lest, & Avarice w^{t} nothing is co^{n}tented. Wh^{r}fore if neth^{r} Riches can take away their lack, & they make their own neede, why should we think the^{m} sufficient?

Though

38-Verso

**3. M.*

[P] *Thogh riche man with flowing golde^{n} †golfe*
Covetous hepes not richis that Suffice
his neck adornes w^{t} geme of Reddis Sea
W^{t} hundred oxe the fruitful fildz doth til
Yet Eating Care leves not him quicke
Nor ded the fliting good acco^{m}pagnies[.]

4.pr.

[P] But thou wilt say dignities makes honorable, rev^{r}enced to who^{m} they hap. Have *the[n] dignities this force? that they can ingraff in users myndes v^{r}tue, & expulse vice. nay they are wont, not to chace iniqutie but to adorn it, so as we disdayne somtyme that they should hap to wickedst men: wh^{r}fore Catullus tho nonnius sate as Curule, calld him Lump of flesh. Dost thou see how great a shame somtyme dignity recevith, wch indignitie should not be so evident if hono^{r} should not show it. You allso, could you have been brought by so many perils to acco^{m}pany Decoratus in office when in him you sawe a mynde of a wicked Ruffin, & slanderer tongue? For we can not for honors sake iudge the^{m} worthy Reverence who^{m} we suppose unworthy of their dignites, but if thou sawest a wyse man, couldst thou not think him wo^{r}thy of rev^{r}ence evin for that wisdom he enioyes[?] [B] Yes surely. [P] for ther is a peculier dignitie for v^{r}tue, wch alltogith^{r} is bestowde on the^{m} to who^{m} she haps, wch because they cannot ev^{r} have popular honores, they may not enioy the beauty of their worth, whe^{r}in this is to be noted, that if it be the lesse worth that it is dispised of many, when they can not make them reverenced thorow the co^{n}tempt that many makes it. Then hono^{r} makes many wicked, but yet not w^{t}out punishm^{t}. For wicked men gives this good turn to dignitie, that they spot the^{m} w^{t} their own infectio^{n}. And that thou, mayst know that true hono^{r} can not hap by these shaded dignities, gath^{r} it this. Yf a man have oft tymes bene Co^{n}sul, & fortune to com to

barbarous

39-Recto

barbarous nations, shall there hono^{res} make him be esteemd, Yf this be a naturall gyft to all dignities, whith^{r} ev^{r} they go they should use the self office, As the fyre in ech Cou^{n}try nev^{er} leaves to burne but because not their own force but false humayne opinio^{n} hath bred it, straight they vanish when to the^{m} they co^{m} that esteemes not such dignities, but thus much for †foren nations. Amo^{n}g them that made the^{m}, doo they ev^{r} last? The Prefectures office was once a greate powre, now a vayne name, & a co^{m}bersom waight of Senators Censure. He was wont be greate that cared for the peeples p^{ro}vi^{ti}ons. *N[ow] what baser than that office. For as a little afore I said, That it had nothing in it self of his own prop^{er} valor, that takes or loses luster by the users opinion. Yf then honors can not make men rev^{r}enced wch are despisd by wicked mens infectio^{n}, if by change of tyme they leave to be famous, yf by vulgar opinio^{n} despysd, what beauty have they in the^{m}selves or can give others?

*4. Myter.

[P] *Thogh the proude man w^{t} Tirius Shelles*
be dekt and shining stone
hated yet of all Lived Nero
for Cruel Lust
but ons Thogh wicked he gave
Unmete Curules to revere^{n}t fathers
Who yet happy thoght them
Who^{m} wickedz Sort estemed[.]

*5. Prose.

[P] But kingdomes & kinges familiaritis, can they not make a man happy, what els? yf their felicytie ev^{r} last. but full be old examples & of p^{re}nt age that kinges have changed w^{t} misery their lott. O noble powres, wch is not able to kepe the^{m}selves. Yf this Raigne of kinges be †auto^{r} of felicitie, shall it not bring misery in part that lackes, and so diminish Luck? For tho mens Dominions stretch furr, yet more peeple ther must needes be, nev^{r}
unacquay^{n}ted w^{t} kinges Raigne. for wher the making felicitie
endith

39-Verso

endith, there †skanted is the force, & so wretched makes. Thus must it needes follow that greatest portio^{n} of mysery of kinges have. The tyrant that proved the danger of his Lot, dissembled his Raignees
feare by sword hanging on his head. What then is powre? that can not chace bittes of Care nor then the stinges of feare? will they have to lyve secure, but may not, and yet boast of
their force? Dost thou suppose him mighty, who^{m} thou seest can not what he wold, p^{er}forme: dost thou think him stro^{n}g that fills his sydes w^{t} *garde[s th]at who^{m} he affrightes, himself doth feare? who that he may seeme mighty, throwes himself to the handes of slaves. what shall I speak of †kes favorites, whe^{n} the kingdoms the^{m}sellves I have showde full of such weaknes? Who^{m} oftymes less force hath p^{rr}servid, som tymes opprest. Nero co^{m}peld Seneck his familiar & tuto^{r} to chose his own death. Antony threw to soldie^{r}s †glaives Papinian long in Co^{r}te, of Credit. And both wold willingly give up their autoritie. Seneck offerd nero all his goodes & strove to return to his own ease, but while the waight it self thrust the^{m} down, neth^{r} that he wold obtayned. What is this autoritie then? wch the havers feare such as when thou woldst have, art not safe, & seekest putt of, canst

not shun? o^{r} Shall thy frendes be helpers, who^{m} not v^{r}tue but fortune got the. but who^{m} felicitie made a frend, misery makes an ennemy. What plague is there more of strength to **harme* than a familiar Ennemy?

**5. M.*

[P] *he that Sekes mighty to be*
Cruel myndz must tame
Nor wo^{n} w^{t} lust his neck
filthy raynes subdue
Thogh India Soyle far of
at thy Lawes do shake * A * A *And uttermost Island serve the to*[,]
Yet is hit not thy powre
hiden Cares Expel
Nor wretched mones
Expulse thou Canst not[.]

But glory

40-Recto

*6. prose.

[P] But glory how begyling, how fowle is she?

Wh^{r}fore the Tragik poet wro^{n}gfully exclaymes not, O Glory glory on thousandes of men nought worth, a greate name thou hast bestowed. For many have lost greate renoune through vulgar false opinio^{n}, than wch what can be worsse? For they that falsely *be praised needes must they blush at their own *laude wch if *hit may be got by desart, what may they allow the co^{n}science of a wise man? who mesurith not his good by popular fame, but Co^{n}science trouth. And if to stretch fur mens fame, seeme best, it followes then, to †skant the same is worst, but since as I have afore tolde, it must nedes be that many nations ther ar to who^{m} the fame of one man could nev^{r} com, It followes then that who^{m} yo[u] thought most glorious, in the next climate of the earth, seemes unspoke^{n} of. Among all this I suppose not popular favo^{r} woorthy of memoriall, who^{m} neyth^{r} Iudgem^{t} bred, nor steddy lastes. But now how vayne, how slippery is noble name, who sees it not? wch if to hono^{r} yo^{u} refer, an oth^{r} man make it, for nobilitie seemes to be a prayse p^{re}ceeding of pare^{n}tes desart, And if the speche th^{r}of make it knowen, they must be noble that be spoken of. Wh^{r}fore if thyne own thou have not, an oth^{r} mans lawde shall nev^{r} make the famous. And if ther be any good thing in nobilitie, this I think it only, that it breedes the havers a co^{n}straynte that they may not degenerate fro^{m} their au^{n}cestors v^{r}tue.

*6. *M.*

[P] *Al humain kind on erthe*
fro^{m} like begininge Comes
One father is of all
One Only al doth gide
he gave to †*So^{n} the beames*
and hornes on †*mone bistowed*
he men to erthe did give
and Signes to heaven
he closed in †*Limmes Ons Soules*
fetched fro^{m} hiest Seat
A noble †*Sede therfor broght furth*
all mortal folke

what crakst

40-Verso

What †*Crake you of your stock,*
Or forfathers Old
If your first spring and Author
God you view
No ma^{n} bastard be
Unles w^{t} vice the worst he fede
And Leveth So his birthe[.]

*7. prose.

[P] But what should I speake of the bodyes pleash^{r}, whose greedie desyres be full of wo, and †sacietie of repe^{n}tance, what diseases, how intollerable paynes is wont as frute of wickednes hap to the enioyers body. what pleasure soev^{r} their motions have I know not, but who will reme^{m}ber his own delites, shall und^{r}stand what so wofull end those plesures have. wch if they could yeld men happy ther is no cause why beastes should not be lyke, whose wholle delite hyes to satisfy their lust, most laudable shuld be delite of wyfe & childe but I know not how somtyme against nature it haps that children have tormented them, whose state how wearing it is. I neede not now tell the, but knowst it well ynough, & nedest not now wayle it, W^{ch} makes me allow Euripides opinio^{n}, who said, he was happy in mishap that lackt ofspring.

*7. Myter

[P] *Al* †*deligh hathe this w^{t} hit*
W^{t} †*stinge inioyars hit*
Like to the winged flies
Wha^{n} hony the have made
Away the go and w^{t} stikking
bite the stinged hartes strikes[.]

*8. prose.

[P] Doubte then ther is none but that these to blesse, be crooked steps, we thith^{r} can any man bring *whither they p^{ro}mise leade him. How wrapt they be in evills, shortly I can shew yo^{u} for what wilt thou snatch mo^{n}ney. Thou must take it fro^{m} the haver. Wouldst thou shyne w^{t} dignities? Thou wilt pray the giver

41-Recto

giver, & thou that desyrst to advau^{n}ce others in hono^{r}, w^{t} †lowlynes of request, art dasht. Dost thou desyre powre? to subiectes ambushes thou shalt lye in danger. Dost thou seeke glory? Thou leavest to be sure, that art drawen by so sharp wayes. pleasurable lyfe Dost thou desyre? but who wold not despise or throwe away the bodyes bondage so frayle & vile? but now, such as cares for bodyes stre^{n}gth, on how frayle & meane a possessio^{n} doo they trust. Can yo^{u} in force exceede the Eliphantes waight or bulls strength? Shall yo^{u} forego the Tigres swiftness. Look thou on heavens co^{m}passe, stabilitie, & speede & leave to wonder at that is base. A **marvel* in reason it were that Skye itself were better than he by who^{m} it is guided. Whose form is so much the fayrer as it is caryed w^{t} *†*soudan* & speedy change of springes flowres[,] Yf as Aristotle sayes, men could use †Linxes eyes to pierce throw that they sawe, wold they not whan bowells all were seene, suppose that that fayre body whose covering Alcibiades spoke of, should fowlest seeme? Wherfore not thy nature, but weaknes of Vewars sight makes the seeme fayre: Esteeme how much yo^{u} will of bodyes goodes when this you knowe, what so yo^{u} wonder a †fyre of a †Tercian may dissolve, of wch all, this in some yo^{u} may gath^{r}, that these wch nethy^{r} can p^{er}forme that they p^{ro}mise be good, nor when they are alltogith^{r} can be p^{er}fecte. Such [as] These neth^{r} can add stre^{n}gth to bliss, nor make the^{m} blest that have them.

*8. Myter

[P] *O in how begiling pathe*
men Ignorance Leades
Seake not the Golde in †*griny tre*
nor Lo[o]ke for precious stone on Grape
Hide not on hily tops your baites
Your dische with fische to fil
And gotes if thou wylt take
The †*Tyrrhene Sea not Serche*
for hid in the waves man †*knoes the Waters streame*

*[no catchword]

41-Verso

And what fiersist river have whittest pearle
Or wher the Reddys rubies
And shores also fild most w^{t} smallest fische
Or have most †*porpos skales*
but hiden for they knowe not
The Good the Seake
Blinded Ignorant must the bide
to †*Cerche byonde the Northe^{n} Pole*
drowned in the earthe the rake
What †*hest shal I for dullardz make*
Even this that whan w^{t} †*Carke the falz have got*
Truist than shal Knowe
the best[.]

*9 Prose

[P] **Hitherto hit sufficeth to shewe the forme of gileful*
felicitie wiche if you Clirely beholde the
ordar tha^{n} must be to shewe you the true.
[B] *Yea I* †*se quoth I that ynough suffiseth not riches*
nor Powre Kingdomes nor honor dignities
nor glory the prising nor Ioy the pleasure[.]
[P] *hast thou gathered the cause of this?* [B] *Methinkes I*
see hit as by a †*rife slendarly but do desire plainar*
of the to knowe hit. [P] *Ready is the reason*
whan that whiche unmixt and by natur
unparted is that humain error partz and fro^{m}
the true and right to falz and wanting brings.

*Dost thou suppose that nothing he wantes, that powre needes[?] [B] I think not so. [P] Truly thou
hast sayde. For if ought be that is of weakist worth, must needly neede so^{m} oth^{r} help.
[B] So it is[,] said I. [P] Th^{r}fore the one & self same is nature of sufficiency & powre. [B] So
it seemes. [P] but that ther is such thing, dost thou think it to be despised or wo^{r}thy
all regarde? [B] This is not to be doubted. [P] Let us ad to this sufficiency,
powre, rev^{r}envce that these three we may Iudge one. [B] Let it be, for
trouth we will co^{n}fesse. [P] Dost thou think this any obscure matter
or ignoble, or of more show than any oth^{r} dignitie? but Consider
lest it

42-Recto
leste it be grau^{n}ted that that needes not, is most of powre & wo^{r}thyest most hono^{r}
yit wanti^{n}g estima^{ti}on wch to it self it can not give. And th^{r}fore may seeme in so^{m}
p^{ar}te to be lesse wo^{r}th. [B] We can not but grau^{n}te that this is most reverenced.
[P] Then it followes that we co^{n}fesse a show of glory doth nothing differ fro^{m} the oth^{r}
three. [B] Yt followes q^{t} I, [P] Than that that nedes none oth^{r}, that doth all of his
own strength, that is beautifulst & most reverenced. Is it not playne, that
so is most pleasing to? [B] I can not imagine how to such a man any sorow
can happen wh^{r}fore necessarily it must be co^{n}fest, that he is full of
Ioye, if the forenamed remayne. [P] And by all this, it needfully follows that
th[']effect of sufficiency, powre, hono^{r}, Rev^{r}ence, plesh^{r}, be div^{r}s names[,] in substa^{n}ce
nothing differs. That that is then one & symple by nature, humayn synne
desp^{er}sith. And in seeking to obtayne such thing as wantith partes, myndith the
same to gett, And so neth^{r} gettes that portio^{n} that is none, nor that partie
that desyres *none. [B] How may this be so q^{t} I. [P] He that seekith riches
by shu^{n}ning pe^{n}nury, nothing carith for powre, he chosith rath^{r} to be mean & base,
and w^{t}drawes him fro^{m} many naturall delytes, lest he lose the mo^{n}ny that he
gat, but this waye, he hath not ynough, who leves to have, & greeves in woe
who^{m} neerenes ov^{r}throwes & obscurenes hydes. He that only
desyres to be able, he throwes away riches, despisith pleash^{res}, nought

esteems hono^{r} nor glory that powre wontith, but how many thinges these men lackes, thou seest. Somtyme he lackes that necessary is, so as his want doth byte him, & whan he can not †throwe of this, that that most he sought, hability he wantes. Thus may we reason of hono^{r}, glory & plesh^{r}. For if all these thinges weare ioynd togith^{r}, if any one were had w^{t}out the rest, he can not gett that he requires. [B] What then q^{t} I, yf any man all this can gett, shall he have the greatest felicitie[?] [P] shall he fynd her in these that we have shewed yo^{u}, promise more than they give[?] [B] Not so q^{t} I. [P] In such thinges as ech man desyres to excell in, the true blesse is nev^{r} to be found

42-Verso

be found. [B] I co^{n}fesse it, q^{t} I, Than this nothing can be truer. [P] Thou hast q^{t} she, heere a forme of false felicitie & the cause. Turn thy self now to the co^{n}trary syde of the mynde, for ther sha[l]t thou see strait way the true that I promysd. [B] This evin to a blinde man is playne, q^{t} I, and a little afore thou showedst, In opening the faulse cause. For els I am deceaved, that is the true & parfet felicitie, that makith man co^{n}tent, mighty, rev^{r}nced, honord & pleasant. And that thou mayst know, I have inwardly lookt wch of all these might trulyest all exceede. This I co^{n}fesse to be true bliss that is w^{t}out a doubt. [P] O scholler myne, happy art thou for this opinio^{n}, yf thou wilt ad one thing w^{t}all. [B] Whats that q^{t} I[?] [P] Dost thou think that ought in mortall & fleeting thinges, can make such a state? [B] No q^{t} I. That thou hast showde sufficiently, as nothing more doth neede. [P] For these thinges as pictures of true good, seeme to give som imp^{er}fet good to mortall men, but the true & p^{er}fet bring they can not. Because thou knowest now, what be the true good, & what belyeth the true bliss, now it followith, that thou mayst knowe whence thou mayst ask the true. [B] That is hit q^{t} I, I have long lookt for. [P] but as Plato in his †Timeo wills, that we should ask for divine help in meanest maters what now thinkest thou to be don, wh^{r}by we may merite to fynde the seate of greatest good. [B] We must call q^{t} I, to the fath^{r} of all, who leaving out, no good founda^{ti}on is nev^{r} layde. [P] Rightly[,] said she[,] And thus began to sing:

**9. M.*

[P] *O thou in Lasting sort the world that rulest*
Of erthe and heaven the framar who time fro^{m} first
bidst go and stable stedy al elz dost while
Who^{m} outward Causis forst not to forme
The worke of sliding substance, but shape
of Greatest good that envy wantz thou al
by hiest sample gides the fairest thou
The goodlist world that mindst and of like †mold hit made
bidding the p^{er}faictz the Co^{m}plete partz p^{er}forme
In nu^{m}bar thou Elementz ties as ryming Colde
to melting flames be ioinged Lest purist fire faile
Or waights to drowned Land befall
thou binding the Soules spirite that moves
al that Co^{n}cernes the triple nature
and dost devide them into agrying limmes

who

43-Recto

Who Cut in Circles two the motio^{n} glimmars
And brething to her selfe retournes
The depe mind bisetz and alike heavin rules
Thou w^{t} like Cause the Soules Co^{n}sernes
and Lives that meanar be to swiftist wains
Thou fitting hiest Spirites
In heave^{n} and erthe dost sowe
Who^{m} w^{t} a gentil Law to the retourned
thou makest be broght to fire fro^{m} whe^{n}ce it Came
Graunt that the my^{n}d O father Clime to thy hiest Seat
And On thy vew the clirest Sigh may Set
Away Cast erthely Cloude and Waight of this †mold
do thou with Lustar then them Grace
Thou art the Cleare and quiet rest for best folke
The to admire is first last helpe Gide
pathe and stedy †Last[.]

10. pr.

[P] For that now thou hast seene the forme of imp^{er}fett & true good, now I think to shew
the by what the p^{er}fectio^{n} of this felicitie is made, In wch first this I think to be inquyrd of, whith^{r} any such good ther be, as thou hast defynd a lyttle afore,

among natures workes, leste a vayne imagina^{ti}on of thought deceave us wyde fro^{m} the truthe of that we talke of. And to prove it so, It ca^{n} not be denyed, that this is the fountayne of all good thinges. For all that we call imp^{er}fett, is shewed such by the definitio^{n} of p^{er}fectio^{n}! So haps it, that if in any thing ther be imp^{er}fectio^{n}, In the self same, somthing must needes be that ca^{n} be p^{er}fect. For p^{er}fectio^{n} taken away, we ca^{n} not ymagyne what that is that is imp^{er}fect. For Nature tooke not her begy^{n}ning of thinges diminished & worne, but of hole & absolute, & so cam downe into thes barren & uttmost partes. And if as a little before I told yo^{u}, ther be imp^{er}fect felicitie of a frayle good, It can not be doubted but that ther is a solide & parfet one. [B] This is sure & truly co^{n}cluded; [P] but wher this dwellith q^{t} she, in this wise

co^{n}sider

43-Verso

co^{n}sider. The co^{m}mon co^{n}ceite of mens myndes allowes, that God of all thinges the Ruler, is good hit self. For when nothing can be imagined better than himself, who ca^{n} doute that that is the best, who^{m} nothing can better. For so doth reaso^{n} shew that god is good, that is won to co^{n}fesse he is the p^{er}fect good. For w^{t}out such he were, the **Prince* of all thinges he could not be. For so much the rath^{r} doth he possess p^{er}fectio^{n} that he was the first & above all. for the p^{er}fetest doo show the^{m} sellves first afore the lesser sorte, and lest o^{r} reaso^{n} should nev^{r} have end, we must co^{n}fesse that the greate God is indued w^{t} the wholle & p^{er}fett good. And we doo saye that true blisse co^{n}sistes in p^{er}fectio^{n}, we *[to] must then co^{n}clude, that true felicitie is in the greatest god. [B] I take it so q^{t} I. nether can any thing gayne say it. [P] but I pray the q^{t} she, Look how proovest thou that most holyly & w^{t}out spot, that we say God is the full p^{er}fectio^{n} of greatest good? [B] How shall I proove this said I? [P] P^{re}sume not to think that the fath^{r} of all thing[s] *have taken this great good w^{t} wch he is fulfilld eyth^{r} of outward cause or naturall, in so ymagining a divers substance of him that hath the obtaynid felicitie. For if fro^{m} outward cause thou supposest he has taken, thou mightest than think that better than he that gave. But most worthely we co^{n}fess that he excellith all. Yf nature have don any thing in him, & in a divers sorte, whe^{n} we speak of god the guyder of all thinges, who can imagine to have Ioynd all these div^{r}sities? Last of all, that that differs fro^{m} any thing, that cannot be the same that is not hit, Wh^{r}fore that is co^{n}trary fro^{m} the greatest good that can not be hit selfe wch were sacrilege to think of god, who^{m} nothing can exceede. For nothing in nature ca^{n} be better than her begy^{n}ning. Wh^{r}fore that was the first of all, in his own substa^{n}ce by a right argum^{t} I co^{n}clude the greatest good. [B] Rightly q^{t} I. [P] But it is grau^{n}ted that the greatest good is blesste. [B] So it is. [P] Therfore it needes must be grau^{n}ted that God is blisse it self. [B] neth^{r} can the foresaid

reasons

44-Recto

reasons fayle me, & by the^{m} I finde the consequence true. [P] See q^{t} she, whith^{r} this be not more truly prooved for that twoo greatest goodes divers in the^{m} selves can nev^{r} be. Th^{r}fore goodes that differs, One can not be that the oth^{r} is. For none of the^{m} can be p^{er}fect, when in both there lackes. Then that that is not p^{er}fecte, is playne can not be the greatest good, by no means th^{r}fore can they be greatest good that be dyvers. Wh^{r}fore we gath^{r} that bliss & God be the greatest good, wch makes that the greate Divinity is the greatest bliss. [B] Nothing ca^{n} be co^{n}cluded q^{t} I, nor in it self more true, nor by †reaason more stable, nor for god wo^{r}thyer. [P] In these causes as Geometricians be wont to doo, demo^{n}stra^{ti}ons p^{ro}pounded, They bring in somthing

wch they call πορίςματα. So will I give the somthing as a breefe gathering. For since men be blissed by getting of felicitie & felicitie is Divinitie, It co^{n}cludes, that by getting of Divinitie men be blessed, For as Iust men be made by getting Iustice, & wyse men by wisdom, So^{m} men getting Divinity, by lyke reason are made lykest to God. So ev^{r}y blessed man, is in a kinde

a God, but in nature one in p^{ar}ticipation many may be. [B] most fayre & precious is this wch yo^{u} call yor πορίςμα, or yor Collectio^{n}. [P] And so much is it the fayrer, that naturall reason it self p^{er}swades yo^{u} thus to ioyne the^{m}. [B] What of that, said I. [P] When blissednes co^{n}teynes many thinges in hit, whith^{r} be all the partes of this gatherd in one, as by varietie devided, co^{n}ioyned, or is ther so^{m} thing els, that fullfilles the fulnes of bliss, & to this all the rest is referd. [B] I wold thes thinges were explaned q^{t} I, as by a memoriall. [P] Dost thou not think blisfulnes good. [B] Yea, the greatest q^{t} I. [P] This all will grau^{n}te. For it is the only sufficiency, the only powre, rev^{r}ence, beauty, delyte. What tho? all these good thinges sufficiency, powre, all be but lyms of blissednes, be all thinges referd to good as to the Top? [B] I know q^{t} I what thou p^{ro}poundest to seeke, but what thou determynest to heare I desyre.

[P] Take this division of this sorte. Yf all these were partes of

blisse

44-Verso

bliss then should they differ in the^{m}sellves. For *th[is] is the nature of p^{ar}tes that divided they make a hole body, & all these thinges we have shewed to be one. Then they are not p^{ar}tes, or els bliss should seeme to be made of one p^{ar}te, wch can not be. [B] This doute I not, but that that remayns I attend. [P] For to the greatest, all the rest of goodes must needes be referd. For th^{r}fore sufficiency is desyrd, that good it is supposd, & powre in like ma^{n}ner so may we gesse, of revere^{n}ce[,] hono^{r} & delyte, for the somme of all desyrd thing[s] is good, That neyth^{r} in hit self nor in his lyke retayns any blisse that no man ought desyre. And co^{n}trary these that by nature be not good, if they seeme to be, as true good be desyrd. So is it, the greatest good, by right ought be beleevid, the grownd work & cause of all desyred. The cause for wch we wish ought, that must we desyre, as yf for helthes sake to ryde we desyre we seeke not more the †styrre of the exercise, than the good effecte of o^{r} helth. When than all thinges be desyrd for greatest good, we desyre not those thinges more than good it self. And that we grau^{n}t that all thinges be desyrd to obtayne bliss, So we co^{n}clude she is only to be sought: wh^{r}by it playnly appeeres that one only is the substance of that is good & blisfull. [B] I see no cause why any ma^{n} should doute heerof. [P] & God we have showed to be the only & alone good. So may we safely co^{n}clude that Godes substance is in that good & none oth^{r} co^{n}cluded.

**10. M.*

[P] *Al you togither come that take^{n} be*
Whome begiling Lust with wicked chanes hath bou^{n}d
dabeling the erthely myndz
here rest of Labor shal you have
here Open Sanctary for wretchis alone
Not al that Tagus with her golde^{n} sandz
doth give Or Hermus w^{t} her glitering shore
Or India^{n} dwelling †nire to hottische Circle
That †griny stone w^{t} Clirist doth mixe
So Clires the Sight, nor more the blindid mindz
Returnes into ther shades

what

45-Recto

What of al thes hathe pleased and delited
that erthe hathe kept in darkist Cave
The lustar that doth gide the heave^{n} and rule
the ruines darck of Soule forbidz
This Light he who Can decerne
beauty suche in Φebus beames denies[.]

*11. prose.

[B] **I graunt q^{t} I, for eche thing w^{t} stro^{n}gist reason linked is*[.] [P] *how muche woldz thou prise hit if the tru good thou couldst knowe*[?] [B] *At how infinite rate*[,] *for so shuld I obtaine to knowe what God wer*[.] [P] *And this w^{t} truest reaso^{n} I wyl expres if it be grauntid that afor was* sayd[.] [B] be *hit* so / [P] *have not we showed that those thinges that be desyrd of many, therfore are not p^{er}fett & good because they differ among the^{m}selves, so as where any want ther is of one thing to an oth^{r}, than can no playne nor resolute good com, but then is ther true good, when they are gathered in one forme & p^{er}formance that what suffisith may have powre, rev^{r}ence, hono^{r} & delyte, for w^{t}out all these be in one, a man hath nought that ought to be esteemd. [B] This is evident q^{t} I, & no man neede to doubte th^{r}of. [P] for those that when they disagree be not good, when they are one, must needes be so. but are not all these thinges made good by getting of a true unity[?] [B] Yes sure, said I. [P] but all that is good, dost thou suppose it good thorow the participating of that is so[?] [B] Yes. [P] Then needes it must be that that is only good, that is ev^{r} one. For the substance is the same of ech man, whose effectes naturally they have. [B] I ca^{n} not deny it. [P] All that is so, long must last & holde togith^{r}, as it is one, but must needes perish & decay, whan so it leaves to be, as in beastes we see, when they ingender, & be made of lyfe & body, then it is a Creature, but when this unitie makes a separa^{ti}on, then they are divided, perish & decay. This body allso when hit remayns in one forme & Ioyntes of lyms, then humay^{n} shape is seene, but if destract or p^{ar}tid in twoo they be, then they leave ther unitie wch made them be. In that sorte, all the rest

shall be

45-Verso

shall be playne to the serch^{r}, that every thing shall last while it is one, but whe^{n} it leaves that order, it perishith. [B] When I have co^{n}sidered many thinges, I find no oth^{r} thing. [P] Ys ther q^{t} I, any thing that naturally, leaving desyre of lyfe, wischith to co^{m} to ruine & an end[?] [B] In beastes themsellves that have som kynde of will *to fly or not, I fynde yf men co^{m}pell them not, they will not cast away their mynde of lasting & hye the^{m} to the way of destructio^{n}. For ech best I finde studys safety to keepe, & shu^{n}ith death & decay. I ca^{n} not tell what I may say of herbes of trees of rootes. I may doute. [P] And yet ther is no great cause when we see the trees & herbes revive agayne in ther fittist place, that as much as nature will p^{er}mitt they may not soone dry & dye. Som in feldes, som on hills doo spring, oth^{res} †marish beare, oth^{res} †stike to stone, som p^{ro}sper on barren sand, wch if any man pluck up to sett in oth^{r} place, they wither. So nature gives to ech that him beco^{m}s, & stryves that while they may remayne, they may not end. What shall I say? that som we see of the^{m}, as having turnd their top to earth, draw nourishm^{t} to the roote, & by their sap, spredes strength & bark. What, yea, that that is most soft as wer the marrow, is ev^{r} hyd in innermost rynde w^{t}out coverd by strength of som wood, but the utt^{r}most bark against the heavens weth^{r} as sufferer of harme is set a defende^{r}. Now how greate is natures dilige^{n}ce that all thinges be inlarged by most seede, wch all, no man is ignorant not only for a tyme of remayning p^{er}petually stryves to remayne. Those thinges that only have life, doo they not ev^{r} by a naturall instict desyre their own[?] Why does lightnes draw up the flame, & waight the earth doun=ward drawes, but that all these agrees in their place & in their own motio^{n}, And that agrees that ever is co^{n}served, As those thinges that discorde doth corrupte. Those thinges that of nature be hard as stones, they stick most fast to their own roote, & so resist

as easely

46-Recto

as easely they be not pluckt of. The fleeting thinges as ayre & wat^{r}, these easily be dep^{ar}ted, but quickly return fro^{m} whence they were drawen. but fyre resistith all separa^{ti}on. We doo not talk now of the volo^{n}tary motions of the soule of man, but of the naturall intent by nature given. As o^{r} meate we take w^{t}out great study, & breth we drawe in o^{r} slomber when we know it not. For in very beastes, the desyre of co^{n}tynua^{n}ce, not of their lyves pleash^{r}, but of their natures begyn^{n}ing †p^{ro}cdith, for oft tymes, o^{r} will imbracith death cause co^{m}pelling, wch nature dreades, & co^{n}trarywise desyre of making o^{r} lyk, wh^{r}by co^{n}tynua^{n}ce doth endure, o^{r} wills som tymes keeps us fro^{m} that nature desyres wh^{r}fore this love of o^{r} selfes p^{ro}ceedes not of a Creatures motio^{n}, but of a naturall intent. For godes p^{ro}vidence hath give^{n} to all thinges that be made the desyre, of remayning, that as long as they may, naturally they will byde. So needes thou nev^{r} doute that such thinges as naturally desyre an abode will shun destructio^{n}. [B] I co^{n}fesse it q^{t} I, For now I plainly see such thinges as doutfull I found. [P] that covetes ev^{r} to be one, that covetes to remayn & last. this being taken awaye, nothing can abyde[.] An unity th^{r}fore all desyre, And one we have showed that is only good. Since therfore Ech thing seekith the good, it is playne that is only the good that of all is desyred. [B] nothing q^{t} I, can trulyer be thought, for eyth^{r} all thing shall co^{m} to nought, & as wanting a head w^{t}out a guide shall †ruyne, or yf any thing ther be, to wch all hastes, that shall be the somme of all best. [P] O scholler myne q^{t} she, I ioye that I have fixd in thy minde one †m^{r}ke of meane to truth, and heerby mayst thou see that a little before thou sayedst thou knewest not. [B] What is that q^{t} I? [P] *[Wh]at was of all thing the end, for that is it that of all men is most sought **wiche by Caus we suppose the o^{n}ly good is hit* th^{r}fore we co^{n}fesse *that to get is all owre end.*

*[no catchword]

46-Verso

*11. Myter

[P] *Who so the trueth w^{t} deapest mynd doth serche*
And Sekes by no bywais awry to stray
Into him selfe returne the Light of inward my^{n}d
And Longe discours straining to a round
And teache his my^{n}d what so w^{t}out he seke
Layd up amo^{n}ge his treasure Let him kepe
Lately that wiche blacky Cloud hathe dimmed
that Lightar shal thou Shine Out
for not al Light fro^{m} mynd hathe drawe^{n}
the body Carrying a forgetful waight
Ther Stiks I trowe an inward Sead of trothe
Whiche kindelz best by Learnings belowes

for Axed why do you the right desire
If Instinct in thy hart ther wer not
If Platoes Musis tales the trueth
That Eache ma^{n} lernes
forgetting he reme^{m}bars[.]

*11. pr.

*12.pr.

[B] Than I, I agree well to Plato, for †twise thou hast reme^{m}bred me of it. First, whe^{n} memory I lost thorow bodyes syn, next, prest w^{t} sorowes burden. [P] Then she, yf the abovesaid thou hast regarded, thou wilt not be long ere thou reme^{m}ber that lately thou hast co^{n}fest thou knewest not. [B] Whats that thou meanest. [P] by what Raynes the world is guided, sayd she. [B] I remember it, & that my ignora^{n}ce co^{n}fessed shewes. Albeit I see what thou hast brought me, yet play^{n}lier of the to heare it I desyer. [P] A little before q^{t} she, Thou thoughtst ther was no doute but that the wo^{r}ld by god was ruled [B] neth^{r} now nor ev^{r} will I doute it, & what th^{r}fore be my reasons, in short I will tell yo^{u}. This world had nev^{r} co^{m} togeth^{r} into one form of so divers & co^{n}trarious p^{ar}tes w^{t}out one it

were

47- Recto

were that so divers thinges doth Ioyne, And being so knytt, the div^{r}sitie of their own natures amo^{n}g, th^{m}sellves disagreeing should uncouple & breake the^{m}, w^{t}out one it were that held that so he knytt. For so c^{r}tain an order of nature should not co^{n}tyane nor should show so many divers motions in ther place, tyme, woork, space & quality w^{t}out one it were alone that ev^{r} byding himselfe, disposeth their mutable varietye. What ev^{r} this is, wh^{r}by the made remayns & be wrought by usuall name of all men, God is calld. [P] Then she, Since this thou thinkst, I shall have but little labo^{r} that thou that co^{m}prehendst felicitie as an inhabiter should revere thy Cou^{n}trey. but let us looke on o^{r} own p^{ro}positions. Have we not set sufficiency in no^{m}ber of blisse, and so grau^{n}te that God it is, And to rule the world, he needith no oth^{r} help, for els if ought he needed, full sufficyncy he had not[?] [B] That must needes be. [P] Then by him self all he disposes alone, and god is he that only we have showed to be the good. by goodness th^{r}fore all he doth despose, for by himself he rulith all, who^{m} we have grau^{n}ted the only good. And he is the key & helm wh^{r}by this worldes molde stable & uncorrupt is kept. [B] I agree to this q^{t} I, and w^{t} a slender suspico^{n} I sawe afore what yo^{u} wold saye. [P] I beleeve it well, for evin now as I think more heedely to looke to truth, thou hast turnd thyne eye. And that I say is playne now, that thou w^{t} me may see. [B] Whats that[?] [P] When rightly we beleeve that god all Rules by goodnes order & that all thinges as I have taught yo^{u} by naturall instinct hyes to the hiest good. Can any man doute, that willingly they are so rulde, & turnes the^{m}selfes to the beck of the desposer, as Ruler of meetest & best agreeing[?] [B] It must needes be q^{t} I, for els it could not be a blessed raigne. yf it should be the yok of drawers back, not the *favo^{r} of the obeyeng. [P] And so nothing can co^{n}serve nature, that stryves to gaynesay his god

47-Verso

God. But what if he went about it, Can any thing ev^{r} p^{re}vayle against him who^{m} all men grau^{n}te by Lawe of bliss, the mightyest[?] [B] It should nought p^{re}vayle said I. [P] For ther is nothing that eyther can or may resist the greatest good. Then that is, the top of felicitie that stowtly rules & gently all disposith. [B] O How much q^{t} I, these thinges not only that are co^{n}cluded by great Reason, but thy wordes the^{m}selves much now delytes me, So as a man may be ashamd of him self that foolishly hath babled so much. [P] You have †hard er now sayd she[,] in fables how †Gyantes have clamard to the heavens, but the^{m} to as hit was meete, the gentle force hath deposd, but will yo^{u} have me make a co^{m}parison. Perchance thorow suche debate, som cleere sparkell of trouth shall leape out. Thy Iudgem^{t} hath made the suppose that no ma^{n} doutes but God is of all thing the mightyest. [B] no man will doubte th^{r}of, w^{t}out he be mad. [P] & he that Rulith all, Nothing ther is that doo he can not. [B] Nothing q^{t} I. [P] can god do †yll then? [B] No q^{t}I. [P] for yll is nothing, when he can not make it, that can doo all. [B] Do you dally w^{t} me q^{t} I, & wrap me in undooing laberinth of Reason, in wch thou entrest in, whence thou wentst out, & now goest out whence thou camst in.*So hast thou not thus wrapt a †Rondell of dyvine †si^{n}ceritie? For a little afore begy^{n}ing fro^{m} bliss, thou saydst she was greatest good wch only abode in the greatest god. Then thou saydst that god hi^{m}self was the greatest good & blisse, of who^{m} no ma^{n} was made blessed, but he that was lyke to him, And that thou gavest for a reward. Then thou saydst that the shape of good was the substance of god & bliss, & so didst saye, that he alone was greatest good, wch Naturally ech man desyrd and didst

dispute

48-Recto

dispute that god was he that ruld the univ^{r}salitie by the raynes of goodnes, & all thinges willingly did obey, And so ther was no evill in nature, And didst show how all thinges not by outward but one fro^{m} an oth^{r} lynking beleefe had ingraft †prooves and ther own. [P] Then she[,] we doo not sporte as godes gyfes the greatest doo require, that thing that of late we so much desyrd, for such is the shape of divine substa^{n}ce that neyth^{r} it slyppith to outward cause, nor inwardly doth take for him self any thing w^{t}out him, but as Parmenides sayth, A lyke co^{m}passe in Roundnes ech Circle caryes. Then if we have so well co^{m}past, that we have not gatherd o^{r} reasons out of the matter, but agreing w^{t} that that we have treated, ther is no cause then why thou shouldst doute, when thou hast lernt by Plato, that all talke should agree as neere of kyn to matter that we speak of.

**12. M.*

[P] *blist that may of Good*
The fo^{n}tain Clire behold
happy that Can Of waighty
Erthe the bo^{n}des to breake
The Tracian profit wons
his wives funeralz wailing
Wha^{n} w^{t} sorows note
The wavering trees he moved
And stedy rivers made
And †hind caused †Ioin
Unfearing Sides to Lion fierce
Nor hare did feare the Looke
Of Cruel dog so plesed w^{t} Song
Wha^{n} †ferventar desir the inward
brest more burnt
Nor Could the notes that al subdued
pacefie ther Lord
Of Ireful Godz Co^{m}planing
The helly house went to

there faining

48-Verso

Ther faining verse
Tuning to Sou^{n}ding Stringe
What he drew fro^{m} springs
The greatest of Mother Godz
What feable mone Could give
What doubled Love afourd
by Wailes and hel doth stur
And w^{t} dulce suite pardo^{n}
Of darkenes Lorde besiche
Wondar doth the thre hedded
Iailor amasid w^{t} unwo^{n}ted verse
Reve^{n}ging †Goddes of faultes
That wo^{n}tid Gilty feare
sorowing w^{t} teares bedewed the were
not Ixiones hed
The Whirling Whele did turne
And Lost w^{t} Longue thirst
Tantalus rivers skornes
The Vultur fild w^{t} notes
†Tityrus Livor tore not
At Last wailing Said the juge
Of Shady place we yeld
To ma^{n} we give his wife for †feere
Won by his Song
With this Law bou^{n}d be the gift
While in the †Tartar thou bidest
turne back thy Look thou must not
but who to Love gives Law
for greatest Law his Love he made
So night drawing to her ende
Eurydicen his Orφeus
Sawe, Lost, and Killed

This fable

*49-Recto [upper quarter]

this fable toucheth you
Who so doth seak to gide
To hiest day his mynd
for who in hely Shade
Wo^{n} ma^{n} his yies doth bend

What So he †*Chifist held*
I^{n} Vewing hel hathe Lost[.]
Et sic. *[]

*49-Recto [lower three-quarters]

*The fourth booke /

1\. pr.

Thus when Philosophy her stately looke & grave cou^{n}tena^{n}ce keeping, In mylde & sweete sorte had sung, Then I, not forgetting my late ingraven woe burst out to tell som p^{ar}t of my intent. [B] O, q^{t} I, Thou the guide of true light, such thinges as thy talke hith^{r}to hath utterd, by divine specula^{ti}on & reason thyne, are showed invincible. And though the same of late my iniuryes sorowe forgate, yet altogith^{r} of the^{m} I was not ignorant, but this was the self & greatest cause of all my woe, that when the Righter of all thing is good, eyth^{r} at all evills can be, or unpunished †pas. That how worthy of wonder it is co^{n}sider I pray yo^{u}, but to this a greater mater is added, For wickdnes Ruling & florishing, not only v^{r}tue wantes rewarde, but subiect to the feete of wicked men is troden downe & suffers payne that wicked folkes deserve. W^{ch} happening in a Raigne of him that all knowes, all *ma[y do,] & such a god that wills but only that is good, No man can but m^{r}vell & co^{m}playne.

[P] It should be worthy m^{r}vell q^{t} she, And horrible more than any mo^{n}ster, if as thou supposest in a house guyded by such a †m^{tr}, base vessells should be esteemed, & precious are despisd, but so it is not. For if such thinges be kept wch we of late co^{n}cluded, & be kepte togith^{r}, he being the maker of whose kingdom we

spake

49-Verso

spake, thou shalt knowe that ev^{r} good men be mighty, yll men, slaves & weake. And how Vice is ne^{r} w^{t}out punishm^{t}, nor v^{r}tue w^{t}out rewarde. And how prosperitie to the good

yll luck to evill betydes. And such lyke, wch may leaving quarrels, stre^{n}gthen the w^{t} steddy
soundnes. And for that thou haste seene the picture of true blisse, wch I shewed
the, and haste knowen where hit is placed, passing all those thinges that necessary
I think not, I will show the the way that home to thy house may bring
the, and stick such fethers in thy mynde, wh^{r}by thou mayst sore up on hye,
so as woe trode down, homedweller in thy cou^{n}try by my guyding, path & †Charyot mayst return.

1. M.

[P] *for Spedy quilles have I*
That fur above the pole do reache
Wiche wha^{n} my †flijnge mi^{n}d putz on
hating the erthe †despice hit
And hiar hies tha^{n} erthes Globe
and Cloudes behind me See
**And pas above the fiars top*
W^{t} swiftnis that the heave^{n}s heat
Until to Starry house hit co^{m}me
W^{t} Φebus †Sorteth way
And Soldiar made of Shining star
Cold Saturne doth felowe
Or wher the shewing night
The Circle Round doth make
and wha^{n} got ynough she hathe
The owtmost Pole he leves
And worthy made of hiest Light
Presseth the Waight of †spidy skie
he Lord holdz of kings the Septar
and Raines of world doth gide
And stable rules the Spidy Cours
Of all the noble Iuge
Hither if the way bak do bring the
Wiche now forgetting thou requirest

This wilt

50-Recto

This wilt thou Say my country is I knowe
hens Came I[,] here wyl I stay my step
And it of erthe hit please the

the darkenes Left to vewe
The gri^{m}*me Lookes that people dredeth so*
Of banissed Tirantz shalt behold

* *2. pr.*
[B] **Than I o Lord how great thinges dost thou promis*
nether doubt I but that p^{er}*forme thou canst*
hit, but stik not now at that thou hast begon.
[P] *First therfor thou must knowe q*^{t} *she that good*
men have ever power, Ivel men Lack ever
strength for good and yl being so co^{n}*trary*
Yf powreful be the first, the Last doth
shewe his Lack, but that your Opinio^{n}
may have more Credit by ether pathe I wyl
treade, and therby my propositio^{n}*s Co*^{n}*firme.*
Two thinges ther be by wiche the effecte
of eache mans doings apere[:] *wyl and power*
of wiche if ether Lacke nothing may
be p^{er}*formed, For Wyl wanting, No ma*^{n}
wyl go about that he wold not, and power
fayle, vain is wyl. So hit folowes that
wha^{n} *he wants that he wylz, no dout but power*
failes to get the desired. [B] *That is plain and*
can not be denied. [P] *And who*^{m} *thou seest*
†*optane that he wold*[,] *dost thou dout*
that he may not have the power[?]
In that he prevailes, In that man is able,
but weke must nides be, in that he may not[.]
dost thou reme^{m}*ber that in our Last arguments*
this was gathered that the intent of eache
ma^{n}*s wyl, thogh diversly distracted, is only to hie to blis?*

I reme^{m}ber it

50-Verso
[B] *I reme*^{m}*ber hit was so shewed,* [P] *dost thou*
Cal to mynd that blis is the greatest good
and So whan that is Soght al best is got[?]
[B] *I reme^{m}ber that well Inough q^{t} I, for that hold I fixd in mynde. [P] Th^{r}fore all good
men & yll stryve to co^{m} to the^{m} best by divers intentes. [B] So it is. [P] but most sure it

is they are made good men by obtayning good. but is it sure that good men doo allwayes obtayne that they desyre[?] [B] So it seemes. [P] but if yll men might obtayne good, they could not be yll. [B] So it is. [P] When they both desyre good, but the one gettes it, the oth^{r} not, It is c^{r}tain that good men be mighty & yll weake. [B] Who ev^{r} q^{t} I, doutes th^{r}of, neyth^{r} can co^{n}sider natures p^{ro}perty, nor sequele of Reason. [P] Then if twoo ther be that by nature requires one thing, one of the^{m} naturally does that & p^{er}forms, & the oth^{r} no way can do it, nor can agree to what nature will, & so to fullfill his intent doo but follow the fulfiller, wch of the^{m} *ij thinkest thou more of power? [B] Though I co^{n}iecture what yo^{u} wold, yet plainlyer I desyre to heare. [P] The motio^{n} of walking, yo^{u} can not deny but all men *ha[ve] nor does not doute that is not the feetes office. Yf any ma^{n} the^{n} that can go, & an oth^{r} to who^{m} the naturall p^{ro}pertie of the fete is wa^{n}ting, stryving w^{t} his Handes, stryves so to walke, wch of these *ij suppose yo^{u} more worth? [B] Perform the rest of that you will. For no man doutes but he is more of force that hath the use of nature, than he that wantes it. [P] But the greatest good said she, that is set before yll & good, the good desyre by naturall duty of v^{r}tue, the oth^{r} by a scatterd desyre, & stryve to get that wch is no p^{ro}per gift to such as will obtayne the greatest good. Doest thou think the co^{n}trary? [B] No q^{t} I, For that is playne that followes. For herby may we gath^{r} that I grau^{n}ted afore, good men to be mighty, & yll men weak. [P] Rightly hast thou discourst. And so as phisicians ought to hope, that it is a signe of a helthy & Resisting nature. But for that I see the redyest to und^{r}stan[d][,]

I will

51-Recto

I will heape up many reasons. Beholde how greate a weakenes is there appeers in vicious men that can not obtayne that to wch their naturall intent Leades & well nye co^{m}pells. And what if they be left of the greate & almost invincible help of his precedent nature, Consider how great a feblenes holdes wicked men. For neth^{r} can they gett light & vayne rewardes wch they ca^{n} not obtayne, but fayles in the Top of height. neth^{r} does good effect hap to the wretched, even the same that night & day they seeke. And yet in self same thing we see, the good mens strength excell. For as a man that walkes to that place whence chefely he wold co^{m}, being such as has no way beyond, woldst thou not think him best footeman, so shoulst thou think him mightyest that ca^{n} co^{m}p^{re}hend that end beyond wch no furder is, wh^{r}by it haps that who co^{n}trary is, the same be wicked & weake of all strength. For why doo they follow vice[,] leaving v^{r}tue behind the^{m}? For ignora^{n}ce of good? but what is more feeble than ignora^{n}ce blyndnes? but they know what follow they ought but their lust doth ov^{r}throw the^{m}, so doth inte^{m}pera^{n}ce the frayle men that in vice be delited, but wittingly & knowing do they leave that is good, And so bend the^{m} to vice? This waye, not only w^{t}out powre, but they leave to be. For they that forsake the co^{m}mon end of all thinges that be, They leave the^{m}selves to be. W^{ch} may seeme *str[range] to men, that evill men (that many be) we shall not say to be, but so the case standth. For they that evill be, I deny the^{m} not to be yll, but I deny that they be purely or simply. For as we so call a

Carcas

51-Verso

Carcas, a dead man, *symply we can not call him man. So vicious men we grau^{n}te the^{m} to be yll, but absolutely to be, that ca^{n} we not co^{n}fesse. For ther is that that keeps & retaynes natures order. Ther is that fayles fro^{m} that, & leaves that in their nature is grafted. But thou wilt say yll[,] men may doo, neth^{r} can I denye, but this powre to doo coms not of force, but of weaknes, For they can doo ill wch they should not doo, if they wold remayn in their creatio^{n} of good, wch possibilitie to doo, In not dooing shewes they can doo nothing. For yf as we have gathered afore, evill be nothing, when but only the yll they can doo, wicked men can doo nothing. [B] Thats playne. [P] And that you may understand what is the force of this powre, we have defynd afore that nothing is fuller of force than the greatest good, but that can not the wicked doo, but what man is it that thinkes man can doo all? [B] None but a mad man will so think. [P] And that the same can doo yll to? [B] Wold god they could not q^{t} I. [P] When then he is †mightest that ca^{n} doo all good, & †mightyest men in yll, ca^{n} not such thinges obtayne, then is it playne, that they can lest doo that be wicked. And so it haps, that rightly we have showed, all powre to co^{n}sist in thinges to be obtayned. And all such referd to greatest good, as to the top of natures best. but possibilitie of wicked acte ca^{n} not be refered to good, desyrd th^{r}fore it ought not be, & all powre is to be desyred, It followes th^{r}fore possibilitie of evill me^{n} is no powre, by all w^{ch}, the powre of good men plainly appeers & makes undouted the weaknes of wicked men, veryfyeng Platoes se^{n}tence to be true, that only wise men can p^{er}forme, that they desyre to doo, but wicked me^{n} use only that they will, but what they most desyre ca^{n} not obtayne. For they doo ce^{r}tain thinges, in wch delyting they suppose they have obtaynd the good that they desyre, but obtayne it they ca^{n} not

For reproch

*52-Recto

*[for] reproche nev^{r} coms to blisse[.]

52-Verso

[Blank]

*[53-Recto-56-Verso]

*57-Recto

*[Meter 2]

*This is before
in his due place

*See 2 Myter

**Thos wiche you se as Kings.*
Sit in the top of hiest Seat
Florishing w^{t} purple fayre
Invyrond w^{t} dreadful armes
With ireful looke that thretes
for hartz †yre scant drawing brethe
If any take from wicked men
Of false honor the cover
Within shal se ther Lordz
Straightnid gives to beare
hither Lust the^{m} drawes
here ire ther my^{n}dz afflictz
Who sturred raiseth stormes

Sorow or the take^{n} wers
Or Slippar hopes tourment
Wherfor whan One hed
So many tirantz beares
he doth not that he wold
prest w^{t} so wicked Lordz

*[no catchword]

*57-Verso

*The Third Booke

*53-Recto

*3 prose

*iij. prose

[P] See you not in what a great †slowe, wicked thinges be wrapt in & w^{t} how great a light, godlynes shynith, by wch tis playne that nev^{r} reward wantes to good, nor punishm^{t} to wicked folk. For it is no wrong, that of thinges don, that be ech reward for wch ech thing is don, as a Ru^{n}ner in a race has a guarland for wch he ran, in rewarde, but we have shewed how blisse is that self good, for wch all thinges be don. Then it followes that the only good is sett as the univ^{r}sall reward to men. And this fro^{m} good men can not be devided; For neth^{r} can he be Iustly cald a good man by right, that wantith true good. Th^{r}fore good co^{n}ditions can nev^{r} want rewarde. For though evill men afflicte the^{m}, a wise mans garland shall not fall nor wither. for oth^{r} mens wickednes can not pluck away the true hono^{r} fro^{m} honest myndes. For yf he reioyce at ought †rxd fro^{m} outward meane, Som oth^{r} man or he that gave it might take it awaye. but because Godlynes it self suffisith, Then shall he want reward, when he leaves so to be. Lastly, since all rewarde is th^{r}fore desyrd, because it is beleevid good, who can think an honest man, w^{t}out rewarde[?] but of what? of that that is fayrest & greatest. Reme^{m}ber this breefe that a little afore I gave yo^{u} to be the cheefest, & so co^{n}clude. When the greatest good is blisfulnes, they must needes be happy that are good, because they are so. And they that be happy, must needes be lyke to god. Th^{r}fore good mens reward is such as neyth^{r} any day drawes away, nor powre minish, nor **Ire* darken, but lyke to him they be, wch being true, no wise men may doute of the wicked mans inseparable payne. For where both good & yll, payne & reward be crosse one to an oth^{r}, it followes that such reward as haps to goodnes, the same must needes be of co^{n}trary sorte, for payne of wicked.

for as

53-Verso

For as sinceritie to the honest is rewarde, so to the wicked their unhappynes is their †plage, So as who ev^{r} is punisht must needes be wicked. Yf th^{r}fore they wold way well the^{m}selves can they suppose the^{m} voyde of payne, whose wickdnes in all ylls not only touchith the^{m}, but greevously infectes. See on th[']oth^{r} syde, such parte as is to the good, co^{n}trary, what payne doth follow the^{m}. I have taught yo^{u} afore that all that is, must be one, and that the only good is one. Then it followes, to what so that is[,] that seemes to be good. Then whosoev^{r} fayleth fro^{m} that good, he leaves to be, so that when evill they be, they leave to be that they were; but to prove that men they were, the forme of their humayne body †shewith, but turned into malice, they have left their humayne nature. And since that true pietie alone may lift up a man, it followes that who^{m} wickednes hath throwen downe fro^{m} state of man, hath cast him down beneth the merit of man, So it haps that who^{m} transformed thou seest w^{t} vice, thou mayst not suppose him a man. The violent robber of oth^{res} goodes is †farvent in his robberyes, swellith in coveting, & mayst call him woolflyke, feerce & co^{n}tentious, exercises his tongue in †bralles, evin lyke a dog. The secret lurker Ioyes w^{t} fraude to catche, And so is foxlyk, unte^{m}perate in Ire he †chafith, & men beleeve him a †lyar, but fearfull & flyeing, fearith & dredith that needes not. And he to deere is co^{m}pared. The sluggy & dullard languishith & lyke an Ass doth lyve. The light & unco^{n}stante man, changes his intentes, & differs so nought fro^{m} the byrdes, And is plunged in filthy & uncleane lustes. And is kept in the delyte of

his

54-Recto

his owne lewdnes. And so hit haps, that he that forsakyth honesty leaves to be a man, for not to be able to attayne a dyvine state, is tournid to the †bestly.

3. M.

[P] *Ulisses Captaines Sailes*
And Sailing Shippes in Sea
Eurus to †*Iland broght*
The Goddis †*fear Sitting*
As borne of Φebus Line
To her newe †*Gestz*
The Charmed Cup doth give
Wiche as in divers Sortz
†*herber rular gides her ha*^{n}*d*
This ma^{n} *the bores Snout do cover*
Another the †*Marmila*^{n} *lio*^{n}
With Tuske and paw indueth
This Like to the wolfe †*nu borne*
Wha^{n} *wepe he wold he* †*houles*
Another As Indian tigar
Walkes in his house as mild
Thogh fro^{m} *many evilz*
The winged Arcadian God
Pitijng the besiged Captaine
fro^{m} *gestz plague preserved*
Yet wicked Cup the Sailars
With mouthes supte up
And †*swin Changed Ceres corne*
for foode of Acorne chosen
To Lost me^{n} *naught remained*
Of body nor of voyce

*[no catchword]

54-Verso

Only ther mynd stabel above
Wha^{n} *the monstars suffar wales*
O hand to weke nor herbes of power
Thogh Limmes to Change
Hartz yet alter *[*may*] *not*[.]
Whithe in bides man strength
Hid in his towre
Thos venoms w^{t} *more fors*
Man fro^{m} *himselfe w*^{t}*drawes*
Who thogh the body not
The Soule w^{t} *woundz assailes*[.]

4. pr.

[B] I see q^{t} I, that vicious men have no wrong, tho they be said by p^{ro}perty of their mynde to beastes be transformed, tho in show they kepe the forme of humayn body. And yet I wold not have that the cruell & wicked mynde should be sharpnid by the fall of good men. [P] Neyth^{r} is it q^{t} she, as in convenyent place I will showe. And yet if that were taken away fro^{m} the^{m} that they are beleeved to have the wickedst payne, should be in greatest p^{ar}te releevid. For that that may p^{er}chance seeme impossible, hit must needes be that wicked men be unhappyer when they have fulfild their desyres, than if they could not get what they wish. For if a wretched thing it be, to wysh that is nought it is much more wretched to doo it. W^{t}out w^{ch}, the desyre of a wretched mynde, wold fall. Wh^{r}fore when ech man hath his own misery, Yt must needes be, that by tryple misfortune, they be vexed, who^{m} thou dost see have a will to do the worst. [P] I grau^{n}te it q^{t} I. And yet that quickly they might want this misfortune, I wish the^{m} deprived of

possibility

55-Recto

possibilitie to doo mischeefe. [P] They shall want it q^{t} she, sooner p^{er}chaunce than eyth^{r} thou woldest, or they themselves think they may. For neyth^{r} is any thing so long in the short mesure of o^{r} lyfe, that an immortall mynde may suppose to tarry to long, whose greate hope & hye woork of mischefe, oft is destroyde by an unlookt for & souden end, wch settes an end to their misery. For if iniquitie make men miserable, he must be more wicked that longer lastes, who^{m} most unhappy I should Iudge if their last death might not end their woe. For if we co^{n}clude the truth of wickednes misfortune, infinite must we suppose that misery that is everlasting. [B] Wonderful thinges q^{t} I, is this declara^{ti}on & hard to be grau^{n}ted, but I know the^{m} to well agree to such thinges as before have bene exprest. [P] Rightly dost thou think q^{t} she, and who so thinkes a hard co^{n}clu^{ti}on is made, it were reson he should showe, that ther hath bene som falshod in the p^{ro}positio^{n}, or that the tyeng of their argum^{t} bootith not for a necessary co^{n}clu^{ti}on, Or els all the abovesaid grau^{n}ted, ther is no cause to †cavill in the subsequent. For this that I saye, not only seemes not wonderfull, but by such thinges as are alledged, most necessary. [B] What q^{t} I. [P] I saye that happyer be wicked men whan they suffer punishm^{t}, than those who^{m} no payne of Iustice touchith. Neth^{r} mynd I now to speake of that ev^{r}y man thinkes, That wicked co^{n}ditions being corrected by revenge & brought to the right way by terro^{r} of their prison to oth^{r} men may serve for example to shun theyr faultes. But in oth^{r} sorte I suppose the wickd unhappy, tho ther were no cause of correctio^{n} to make them unpunished, nor no respecte of ensample. [B] What should this oth^{r} way be? [P] Have we not said afore, that good men be lucky & evill miserable? [B] So it is. [P] Yf th^{r}fore som goodnes chau^{n}ce to misery, is it not much more happyer for him than if his misery were alone by it self, w^{t}out any goodnes mixture. [B] So it seemes q^{t} I. [P] But

if to that

55-Verso

*But yf to that miserable man that wantes all good thinges, that evill be added to him to be above, is he not much more to be acco^{m}pted unhappy whose mysfortune is showed him thorow the participa^{ti}on of som good? [B] What els? [P] Th^{r}fore wicked men, when they are punisht, have som good Ioyned w^{t} it, that is Their punishm^{t}, wch for Iustice sake, is in it self good. And they whan they want their correctio^{n}, there is some thing besides of evill, wch is want of punishment, wch deserneably thy self hast co^{n}fest is the greatest yll Iniquitie can have. More unhappy th^{r}fore are wicked folkes, whan they want their punishm^{t}, than when they receave their iust reward. For greatest iniquitie is co^{m}mitted when Iust men be vexed, & wickd slip fro^{m} their reward. [B] Who can this denye? [P] Wh^{r}fore ech man must needes grau^{n}te, that all that is good, must needes be iust, & yll that is the co^{n}trary. [B] These be such thinges needes must follow the above co^{n}cluded. but I pray the q^{t} I, shall there be no soules punishm^{t} after the dead body. [P] Very greate q^{t} she, of wch som be used by bitter paynes, oth^{r} by a Pacifieng Clemency, but now my mynde is a little of these thinges to dispute. For this hith^{r}to we have don, that thou mightest knowe the unworthy powre of evill men is none at all, Evin such as thou co^{m}playnedst were voyde of punishm^{t}, that thou mightest see them nev^{r} want the payne of their wickednes. And that the liberty wch thou wisshest should be ended, thou mightest learne not to be long. And so much more unhappy, if longer[;] most unlucky, yf eternall. And then I sayd that wicked folkes were more miserable shu^{n}ning their Iust payne, than punisht w^{t} their right revenge. So follows it true w^{t} my opinio^{n}, That then they are greevid w^{t}

sorest

56-Recto

sorest punishm^{tes}, whan they are supposd less plagued. [B] Whan I co^{n}sider thy reasons said I, I can suppose nothing more true, but if I turne me to mans Iudgem^{t}, who is he to who^{m} not only these thinges will not seeme to be beleevid, but scarcly to be hard. [P] So it is q^{t} she, for they can not that have used their eyes to darknes, lyft the^{m} up to the light of a cleere trowth, & lyke they be to such byrdes whose sight the night dooth cleere & day darkens. For while they beholde not the order of thinges but their own affections, they suppose the liberty and lack of payne, for their faultes, the happiest. but now looke what the ev^{r}lasting *light makith. Yf to best thou doo apply thy mynde, thou shalt need no iudge to defer thy reward. Thou thy self hast ioyned the to the Excellency. Yf thou turn thy indevors to worsse, beyond thy self seeke no revenger. Thou thy self to worst hast throwen the, & lookest to heaven & clayey earth by fittes, when all outward thinges fayles the by thyne owne reason shalt p^{er}ceave, the differe^{n}ce between Sky & Claye, but the vulgar cares not for this. What tho, Shall we speake of such thinges now as shewes men most lyke beastes? What yf a man losing his sight hath forgotten that ev^{r} he had it, shall he suppose he lackes nothing of a mans p^{er}fec^{ti}on? shall we suppose these men, tho they see, to be blynde? They will not †leave so. But will w^{t} c^{r}tain grownd of reson know, that they are more unhappy that doo wro^{n}g, than those that suffer it. [B] I wold fayne know these reasons said I. [P] Thou dost not deny a wicked man is wo^{r}thy of all payne? [B] I deny it not. [P] You think to, they are unhappy that divers ways

are wicked

56-Verso

are wicked such as are worthy punishm^{t} therefore, no doute are miserable. [B] It agreeth well. [P] Yf th^{r}fore thou satest as a Iudge, on who^{m} woldst thou inflict the payne? eyth^{r} on him that made or suffered the wro^{n}g? [B] I doute not but that I wold satisfy the sufferer by the punishm^{t} of the Acter. [P] Then wretcheder is the maker than the Receavo^{r}. [B] It is reason. [P] For this & many oth^{r} causes all hangyng on one roote, hit appeers that synne of his owne nature, makes men wretched. And that iniury is not the receavers misery, but the givers. but Orators doo oth^{r}wise. They go about to move co^{m}misera^{ti}on of the iudges for the^{m} that have co^{m}mytted some greate & cruell thing. When rath^{r} a Iuster co^{m}misera^{ti}on ought to be had of such as be not brought by Irefull accusers, but by such as the^{m}selves beemones & takes co^{m}passio^{n} of, as tho they wold bring the sick to the phisician, & cut of the disease by the false punishm^{t}, by wch eyther the endevo^{r} of the defendors should coole, or if it should proffit the^{m}, must be turned into the forme of the Accusation. But wicked men, yf they see any but a small clift where v^{r}tue is to be seene, where wicked vice they may put of by paynes cruelty, under coulo^{r} of reco^{m}pensing v^{r}tue[,] will not call this cruelty, but will refuse their defendors labo^{r}, & give the^{m}selves wholly to the accusers & Iudges, so as wise men have no place left them for hate. For who but a very foole will malice a good man[?] And who but he that lackes reson will not hate the yll? For as the bodyes sicknes, so is vice the myndes disease, evin as we suppose that sick men deserve not hate but co^{m}misera^{ti}on, so ought they not be p^{er}secuted but pitied whose mynde[,] than all sicknes bytterer, Iniquitie hath beseeged.

*In continuation in the duplicate

of the fourthe book
*what bootes

*57-Recto-57-Verso

*58-Recto-63-Verso

*64-Recto

**4. M. of ye iiijth*

booke /

[P] **What boutes hit make so great strife*
And w^{t} thy hand thy dethe procure
If dethe you seake she draweth ny
Agrijng not abides the winged horse
Who^{m} Serpent, Lio^{n}, Tigar, beare and †*bore*
W^{t} bite do Seake w^{t} blade your selves pursue

That properties agre not but do difar
Ar they the Cause of wicked strife and war
And perische wold with weapon divers
No Iust meane of Cruelty ynough
Fit †*mede woldest thou give desartz?*
Of right the good do Love[,] *the yl bemone*[.]

5. prose

[B] Than I began, I se q^{t} I, what felicitie or misery it is, that is sett in the desertes of *hone[st] & wicked men, but in co^{m}mon fortune I see, but little good or yll to be. For no wise man wold rath^{r} choose to be †exule, poore, dispisde, than riche[,] rev^{r}enced, mighty, & florishing abide in his own Citie. For then more plainly & w^{t} better witnes, is the p^{ro}p^{er}tie of wisdom seene, when the happines of Rulers be as it were skatterd amo^{n}g such peeple as be strau^{n}gers, when cheefely †geayle, Lawe & oth^{r} tormentes for due punishm^{t}, rath^{r} p^{er}tayne to wicked Citizens for who^{m} they were first ordeynd. but whe^{n} these be turnd in wry sorte, & wickedes payne doo presse good men, & yll doo snatch reward fro^{m} v^{r}tue, I wonder much what may seeme the reaso^{n} of so uniust a co^{n}fusio^{n}, & doo desyre of the to know, for lest wold I †m^{r}vell therat, if I beleeved all thinges were mixt by cha^{n}cing luck now, God the guide, my doute increasith, wch when oft tymes he gives to good delytes, to evill, hard haps, somtyme agayne, He gives yll cha^{n}ce to good, & grau^{n}tes the yll their wish. w^{t}out there could a cause be founde, what hit should be that makes a difference fro^{m} chau^{n}cing
haps

64-Verso

haps. [P] It is no wonder q^{t} she, if any thing rash & confou^{n}ded be belevid when orders reason is unknowen. but thou, allthough thou knowest not the cause of so greate an order, yet because a good guyder the world tempers, doubte thou not all thinges rightly orderd be.

*5. *Myter of y^{e}*

....th booke

iiij

[P] **Yf man know not how stars*

the Arcture next by hyest pole doo slyde
*Nor why *Bootes slow glydes by ye wane*
And sluggy flames in Sea doo dip
When her swift rysings to soone p^{er}forms
Of hyest heavens ye Lawe will muse
Of fulled Moone the hornes whytenid
Infected w^{t} ye bounds of darkest night
And such as w^{t} her shyning face were shaded
Dymmed Pheba those stars discover
A co^{m}mon Error folkes assayles
And brasen tymbrells stryke w^{t} many strokes
None musith that y^{e} †Southest wynde
w^{t} hurling wave †astones ye shore
Nor that ye hardenid snowy ball by cold
By fervent heate of sonne resolves
For Ready is ye cause of y^{is} be seene
but hydden causes whyrls ye mynd
Such as o^{r} Age scarce knowith lyke
And vulgar fleete at souden †gase
Let cloudy faultes of Error give his place
And wonders sure be seene shall ceasse.

So it is

65-Recto

*6. prose.

[B] So it is, sayd I. but since thy office it is to unfold the cause of hidden maters, & expresse reasons hid under shade, I besech the, to looke on this, & for that this miracle doth most vexe me teache it me. [P] Then she, smyling a little, You call me to a matter that all men chefely seek, to who^{m} †scacely suffisith to taste alone. for it is such a mater that one doute †cut of, inummerable oth^{r}s as Hydras Heades increase, neth^{r} ev^{r} will ther be an end unles a lyvely fyre of the mynd doo bynde it. For in this mater, we inquire of the purenes of Providence, of the successio^{n} of Chaunce, of hapning Luckes, of the knowledge & p^{re}destina^{ti}on of god, & of o^{r} free will, wch of how greate burden all these be, thy self canst waye, but because this is som portio^{n} of thy medecin to know these thinges, tho we be wrapt in a strayte lymite of tyme, yet we will stryve somwhat to determyne. For if thou delyte in a musicall song, thou must differ a little thy delyte, while I doo tune in order the Reasons knyt togith^{r}. [B] As please yo^{u} said I. [P] Then as begy^{n}ning of an oth^{r} theme, thus she disputed. The creatio^{n} of all thinges & the disposing of mutable natures, & what ever by any meane is mooved, getes the cause order & forme of godes mynde stabilitie. And this sett in the top of her **Purenes*, appoyntes a soundry ma^{n}ner for ech actio^{n}, wch order when it is beheld in the very cleerenes of divine und^{r}standing, is named **Provide^{n}ce*, but whe^{n} it is referd to those thinges that hit moovith & disposeth[,] of the Au^{n}cientes it is called **Desteny*, wch easely shall appeer *[ ] divers, yf a mans mynde will see the efficacy of both. For p^{ro}vide^{n}ce is godes pleash^{r} appoyntyd by him that all rulith & all disposith, but Desteny is the disposing of causes Ioynd to remooving causes, by the wch Provide^{n}ce knittith all thinges by her orders. For Provide^{n}ce includith all, whith^{r} they be divers or infinite, but desteny devideth ev^{r}y thing according to her motio^{n}, distributing it to place, to forme, & tyme,

that this

65-Verso

that this deviding of te^{m}porall order Ioynd to the divine Pleash^{r} may be made p^{ro}vide^{n}ce, but that Ioyning, being severd & devided into tymes, that is **Fate*. W^{ch} tho they be sondry, yet they de=pend one of any oth^{r}. For fatall order p^{ro}ceedith of Provide^{n}ce purenes. For as a Craftes man co^{n}ceaving in his mynde the forme of a woork, causeth him to end & that wch he hath plainly & †p^{re}ntly forseene, he ordrith by tymes Rule: So god by his p^{ro}vide^{n}ce singularly & stable disposith all thinges to be don, but by desteny so devided, aboundantly & in his due reason workes it. Whith^{r} desteny be exercised by familiar Spirites that serves for godes p^{ro}vide^{n}ce, or whith^{r} the fatall work be knytt by the soule alone, or Nature serving in p^{ar}te therto, or celestiall co^{r}ses of the heavens, or by Ange = licall powers, or by sondry industry of Spirites, or by som of these or by all, This is most playne, that the forme of all thinges unmoveable & simple is **Provide^{n}ce*. But desteny is of such thinges as the Divine Cleerenes disposith to be don, & makith the mooving lynk & orderly Rule. So followes it that all that subiect be to **Fate*, be under Rule of *†*Provid.* under who^{m} **Fate it self* down layes. But som thinges there are by Provide^{n}ce appoy^{n}ted that doo exceede **Fates Force*, those thinges they be wch fixed stably next to divinitie, exceed the **Nature* of fates mutabilitie. For as of all **Circles* the inmost that turnes the^{m}selves about one Rounde, comes neerest to the **Purenes* of the †midst, And as a steddy stay of all that rolles about, doth circuite the same, but the uttmost by wyder bredth rolled the more hit goes fro^{m} the undivided midst of the poy^{n}te, So much the more hit is spred by larger spaces, but whatsorev^{r} drawith neer & acco^{m}panith the midst, & w^{t} his purenes is ruled, ceasith to be stopt or overrun:

w^{t} lyke reaso^{n}

66-Recto

w^{t} lyke reason, that furdest goes fro^{m} the first intent, is wrapt in straighter knotes of **Fate*. And so much the freer is any man fro^{m} the same, as neerest he doth drawe to the orderers wheele. And yf he stick to the ev^{r}during eternall mynde, wa^{n}ting change, he goith above **Destenyes* necessitie. For as Reason is to understa^{n}ding, & that that is made, to that that is, And as tyme to **Eternity, & Circle* is to the middest poynte, So is the order of fate changeable, co^{m}pared to the stable purenes of **Provide^{n}ce*. For desteny moovith heaven & skye, tempers the elem^{tes} among the^{m}selves, & turnes the^{m} thorow diveres changes, & such thinges as be bred & dye, renewes *<u>such</u> by lyk generatio^{n} of frutes & seedes. This knittes actions, Fortunes of men by an indissoluble lynk of causes, wch since they co^{m} all fro^{m} the begy^{n}ing of an un = cha^{n}ging p^{ro}vide^{n}ce, Yt must needes be that oth^{r}wise than so, they can not cha^{n}ge. For so thinges be well ordered, yf the ev^{r}lasting purenes of godes mynde doth p^{re}scibe an unturning order of causes, but this Rule byndith in thinges mutable, & rashly fleeting, by his owne steddynes, Wherby altho to yo^{u} that ca^{n} not co^{n}sider the order of thinges, they seeme co^{n}fuse, & †iombled togith^{r}, yet he that is cause of all good, directes all thing to hit. For ther is no man how wicked soev^{r}, that for yll sake, will doo ought so, who^{m} tho as I have told yo^{u} afore, in seeking good, an yll erro^{r} hath turned, yet the order that co^{m}s fro^{m} the roote of all good, turnes no man fro^{m} his begy^{n}ning. but what thou wilt saye, can be a greater co^{n}fusio^{n} or a woorsse, than that

adv^{r}sitie

66-Verso

adv^{r}sitie & p^{ro}speritie happens to good men, & alyke to evill doth hap, both wisht & hated. Doo men lyve of such integritie of mynde, that it must needes be that they be wicked or good, that be supposed so? For in this we see divers Iudgem^{tes} of men vary, who^{m} som thinkes worthy rewarde, oth^{r} suppose deserve punishm^{t}, but let us grau^{n}te, that one man may descerne the good & yll men. Can he look upo^{n} the inward te^{m}per of the mynde, as well as of the body[?] The wonder is not unlyke to him that knowes not why to men of wholle bodyes, somtymes to these sweet thinges please, som oth^{r} delyte in sowre, why sick men, som be helpt by Remities, som oth^{r} cured by corrosives, but this a **Phisician* that knowes the mean of his helth & sicknes togith^{r} w^{t} his te^{m}p^{er}, nothing wonders at *ther at. What oth^{r} thing is the myndes helth, than sincerity[;] what the sicknes, but vice? Who oth^{r} is eyth^{r} keep^{er} of good, or ov^{r}thrower of yll, than the directo^{r} and Phisician of o^{r} mynde, god himself, who when he lookes out of the glasse of his hye Provide^{n}ce, knowith what for ech man is best. And that he knowes is best, that he gyves him. And this is the greate miracle of Destenyes order, when it is treated by a skyllfull p^{er}son, at wch the ignorant woonder. And that I may somwhat touche what mans Reason may co^{m}p^{re}hend of godes depth, in that mater

that thou

67-Recto

that thou supposest to be most Iust, & keeps greatest equalitie & it seemes all to be different fro^{m} him that knowith what Provide^{n}ce is. And as o^{r} frend Lucan sayde, the wynners cause pleased God, the †w[o^{n}] overs Cato. For in this world what so thou seest be don beyond hope, is the rightest order of all. And p^{er}vers is the co^{n}fusio^{n} of opinio^{n} her self. but if a man have †so much ma^{n}ner that he will agree both of divine Iudgm^{t} & humayne, yet is he of his myndes strength so weake, as if any adv^{r}sitie hap him, he will leave to prise ynnoce^{n}cy, by who^{m} he could not keepe Fortune. For the wise giver sparyth him who^{m} he knowes adv^{r}sity will him spayre, so as he will not suffer him labo^{r} in payne, for ought behooves him not. An oth^{r} man ther is univ^{r}sally v^{r}tuous, holy, & next to god. This man the divine p^{ro}vide^{n}ce Iudgith a wicked thing w^{t} adv^{r}sitie to afflict, so that he will not suffer him be vext w^{t} bodely disease: For as an excellenter than my self sayde, **A good man, his v^{r}tues doo inhabite him*. So it co^{n}cludes, that good men have all thinges to rule, that abou^{n}ding iniquitie might be ruyned. To oth^{r} men he destributes c^{r}tain mixtures according to the qualitie of the mynd: Som men he stingith lest they should ov^{r}flow into greate felicity, others he tosses w^{t} adv^{r}sitie, that he may establish their myndes v^{r}tue, by patie^{n}ce use & exercyse, oth^{rs} som to much fear that beare they might, som oth^{r} to much despise that carry they can not. These men he leades by woe to know the^{m}selves.

som oth^{r}

67-Verso

Some oth^{r} deserve an honor.^{ble} name w^{t} price of glorious death. Som oth^{r} have shewed a sample to the rest, †uniniurible of payne, And so doo shew to wicked men, O how unwon v^{r}tue is, wch how rightly & in order & for their good to who^{m} it hapt they have bene don, ther is no doute. For evin that eyth^{r} sorowfull or desyred haps to the wicked folkes, p^{ro}ceedes of like cause. And as for the wicked, no man wonders, for thinking the^{m} worthy all yll: whose punishm^{t} both †feares oth^{r} fro^{m} faultes, & breedes their amendem^{t} on who^{m} it is imposd. prosperous thinges serve for greate argum^{t} that they be good, but what ought men iudge of such felicitie? when they see them the servantes of the wicked, In wch mater so^{m}tyme they seem to have a dispensa^{ti}on, for that som mans nature is so headstrong & Rash, that neede of necessities cause, may make him fall into a mischeefe, who^{m} the p^{ro}viding of mo^{n}ny got, might serve for Remedy, but when he looke[s], his fyled co^{n}science w^{t} faulte, & w^{t} himself disputing of his fortune, p^{er}cha^{n}ce fearith that the losse should be sorowfull, of that the use was delytefull. He will change th^{r}fore his co^{n}di^{ti}on, and whyle his luck feares to lose it, he will leave his wickednes. Unworthy gotten felicitie throwes downe som men to deservid Ruine. som men have leave to punish, that they might inure. good men, & punish the yll. For as no league ther is between the wicked & good, So can not the evill amo^{n}g the^{m} selves agree. What els, when ech man disagrees, ther vices being sondry, & often doo such

thinges

68-Recto

thinges, wch they so discerne they ought not doo, after don they be. So haps it oft, that godes p^{ro}vide^{n}ce wo^{r}kith a miracle, that evill men, make yll men good. For when they see that they suffer harm the^{m}selves by evill men, abhoring such †Actors, retourne to v^{r}tues frute, while they study to be unlyke such as they hate. For it is godes only powre, to make of evill good, when using the^{m} as they ought, drawes fro^{m} the^{m} som effect of good. For Order keeps ech thing, so as what so doth leave his assigned way of order, the self same tho it hap to an oth^{r}, falles in Rule, lest in Providences kingdom, Rashnes should p^{re}vayle. Hard for me it is these thinges that touche god, as all the rest, describe. For neyth^{r} doth it beco^{m} man to co^{m}prhend all shapes of his woorkes, or by tongue or wit expresse. only this may suffise[,] that we p^{er}ceave that God the maker of all nature, disposeth so of all as directes it to the good. And while he hyes to keepe such thinges in order as he made, he dryves all evill out of the boundes of his kingdom, by the order of a Fatall necessitie. So it followes that such thinges as we beleeve the Earth to have plenty, if we look upon the directio^{n} of Provide^{n}ce, we shall see ther is no yll at all. but now I see the burdned w^{t} waight of questio^{n}, & wearyed w^{t} lenghth of Reasoning, to expecte the sweetnes of som verse. Take th^{r}fore a draught wh^{r}by refresht thou mayst trye stronger furder to go.

If wary

68-Verso

*6. *Myter.*

of ye iiijth booke

[P] **If wary alone of thundring God ye Lawes thou wilt*
w^{t} purest mynde beholde
of hyest heaven ye top doo vewe,
there Planets w^{t} Iustest league of all
agreement old doo keepe

The sonne styrd up by Ruddy fyre
Phebas †frosy axill tree ne letts
Nor that beare that on ye top of world
A ru^{n}ning Course doth bend
that never other stars wet behold
Dround under western depth is touched
*and seketh not wth flames the Sea to hit
*Ever w^{t} equall turne of tyme
Hesperus showes ye later shades
And Lucifer retourns y^{e} †fayest day,
So enterlaced Loove renewes
the Eternall courses all
So Iarring warr fro^{m} starry sky made outlaw
*the Elementz all accord tempars
In equal Sort that Striving
Moisteurs to droughtes turnes give way
That the Coldz kipe faithe w^{t} flames
And hanging fire upward bend
And hevy erthe w^{t} waight bow downe
by selvesame Cause in milddist springe
The flowring yere his Savors yeldz
hottist So^{m}mer Cor^{n}e dothe ripe
And fruitful Autu^{m}ne apples beares
Dripping Showres Wintar moistz
*This temp^{er} feedes and brings fourth
what so lyfe in world doth brethe

The same

69-Recto

The same snatching makes & plucks away
by the Last Gasp ending spring
The maker hye meane while sitts
Ruling bends of all ye Raynes
king & lord spring and fyrst
Lawe[,] and wyse, of Iust ye Iudge,
And such by styrring as he rayses[,]
Backdrawing stayes, and wandring keeps,
For but returning rightest lynes
again he bent to bowing wheels
the Order that now stable keeps
disseverd all fro^{m} spring wold faynte,

such is ye co^{m}mon Love of all,
that w^{t} returne for end of good be kept
In other sortes endure they could not,
*unles agayne by Love *returnd*
*back to the cause *them made the *bond.*

*7. prose.

[P] Doo yo^{u} see now what all these thinges we have told may get? [B] What is that said I. [P] that all fortune may be good. [B] And how may that be? [P] Attend said she, when every fortune eyth^{r} plesing or hard be made eyth^{r} to exercise & reward the good, or to punish & correcte the yll. It is evident that all is a good cause that eyth^{r} is manifest to be iust or p^{ro}ffitable. [B] I p^{er}ceave this reaso^{n} to be most true. And if I co^{n}sider eyth^{r} p^{ro}vide^{n}ce or fate, that yo^{u} have afore tolde[,] yor opinion leanith[,] I p^{er}ceave[,]

to steddyest

69-Verso

to steddyest ground, but let us set her yf please yo^{u} amo^{n}g such as we have supposed to be out of mens opinio^{n}s. [P] What is that said she? [B] For the co^{m}mon speche of men deceaves itself, & oft supposith mens Fortunes hard. [P] Will ye have me a little draw neere to the vulgarest opinions? [B] As it please yo^{u} said I. [P] Doo yo^{u} not suppose that to be good that avayles, & such thing as exercises or correctes good th^{r}fore is it good? [B] What els? [P] but these belong to those wch eyther virtuous, †Iarre against adv^{r}sitie, or strayeng fro^{m} vice takes v^{r}tues waye. [B] I can not deny it. [P] May the co^{m}mo^{n} peeple denye that the rewarde is not good, that good men have? [B] No. For it must needes be the best. [P] And what of all the rest? will the co^{m}mon sorte think that that is not best, that tho it be sharp, yet lymites wicked men by iust payne? [B] Yea, q^{t} I, I think that to be the most misery of all. [P] Let us beware lest following the co^{m}mon opinion we doo somthing unawares. By this that we have grau^{n}ted, we co^{n}clude that worsse is the state of the^{m} that be eyth^{r} in the possibilitie, or in the advance or obtayning of v^{r}tue, And yet byde in their iniquitie. [B] This is true said I tho no ma^{n} dare co^{n}fesse it. [P] Wh^{r}fore said she, So ought not a wise man beare w^{t} greefe, Fortunes †wrestell, as it becoms not a stro^{n}g man to be mooved, when a battell begynes. For the hardnes is argumt for bothe, eythr to inlarge his glory, or to confirm his witt whrby we call it force that stycking to his owne strenght

*is not

70-Recto

[Blank]

*70-Verso-71-Verso

*72-Recto

is not won by wo. For you cam not to us in the advancemt of vertue, to make us ovrflow wt delites, or drownd in pleashr, but that we should make a sharp battell against all Fortune, And that neythr the sowre oppresse you, nor pleasant corrupt you, the middle waye wt steddy force maynteyne you. For who so beneth this or beyond goes has but felicities contempte, no †travells rewarde. For in yor hand it is what fortune you will frame you. For what so seemith sharpest eythr inures, correctes or punishith.

*70-Verso [upper third]

**7. My.*

of ye fourth

booke

[P]†*Twis five yeres wratheful Atride made*
With †*Φrisians ruines war*
The unchast bed of brother so revenged
he[,] *while hoissing Sailes to Grecians ship he gave*
With wische and bloud the windes †*apeced*
dispoiled of fathers Care the cruel priest
his daughtars †*throte of life deprived*
Ulysses Waild his Lost peers
Whom bloudy Poleφemis in his Large den
Gulped downe unto his Cruel †*panche*
And furius yet wt his †*yeles hed*

his Ioy repaid with woful teares his owne
**hardy Labors his hercules did grace*

*71-Recto [upper third]
he Ce^{n}taures proude did tame
Of skin the Lio^{n} †flead
With certain shaftes the birdz did hit
Snatched Aples fro^{m} the Looking drago^{n}
his Left ha^{n}d peaced with golde^{n} metal
Cerberus with thre fold †Cheain doth drawe
A Victor he is said to set the Lord for meat
To Cruel forefoted bests
Hidra killed by venom †sered
Achelous streame w^{t} firy Looke
drowned under the shore his Shamed face
Antius he strake undar Libians Sa^{n}des
**Cacus Apesed Eva^{n}dars wrothe*

*71-Verso [upper third]
And Shuldars thos wiche †hy heaves shuld pres
The bore the Same with †folme did marke
The Last Labor †heave bearing w^{t} nek unbowed
the heave^{n} decernes for Labors pane
forward go that Stro^{n}ge be wher hiest way
Of gretest †Sample bides
Why Sluggardz baks do you turne
The erthe won the heavens he
**gives*[.]

*this is y^{e} end of y^{e}
Fourth booke

*72-Recto

72-Verso-73-Recto

[Blank]

73-Verso

*The Fourth booke
these are written with
the hand of queene
Elizabeth ———

73A-Recto-73A-Verso

[Blank]

74-Recto

The *fift Booke /.

1. pro.

Thus spake she & tournd the co^{r}se of talke to treate & dispatche c^{r}tain oth^{r} thinges. [B] Then I told her, Right was her exhorta^{ti}on, but worthyest of all her autoritie. but this I have found by experie^{n}ce true, that lately yo^{u} told me of providence, how she was wrapt in divers oth^{r} matteres, but I ask, whith^{r} there be any at all, or whith^{r} chaunce be. [P] Then she told me, I hye to p^{er}forme my dett, and shew the the way to bring the to thy Cou^{n}try. And tho these thinges for knowledge be most proffitable. Yet be they somwhat strayeng fro^{m} the path of o^{r} Intent. And so must we use it, lest wearyed by the †bye Crookes, thou mayst not be *hable to endure the †Io^{r}ney to right way. [B] I feare not that said I, for place of quiet I shall have most, to know such thinges as most delyte me. And when all the ma^{n}ner of the disputa^{ti}on hath bene playne of greatest assura^{n}ce, no cause I have to doute of the rest. I will obey thy will q^{t} she, & thus began. [P] Yf any man defynes chau^{n}ce to be a hap that lightes by rash motio^{n} & by no knot of causes, then I grau^{n}te ther is no chau^{n}ce, And see it a vayne voyce that nought signifies. For what place can there be left for Rashnes, wher God in order all kepith. For it is a true sayeng, That of nought, nought is made, agaynst wch none of the old wryters could gayn say, tho they did not suppose there were any founda^{ti}on Layde by him that all made, but that all were subiect to som materiall cause as tho the nature of all reason made it. but if ought there be springes of no cause, it must needes be, it is made of nothing. And if this ca^{n} not be so, neth^{r} is it possible for any such chau^{n}ce to be, as we have above †rehrest. [B] What then q^{t} I? Ys there nothing that may be rightly called cha^{n}ce or Luck, or is ther any such, tho vulgar peeple knowes not, to who^{m} such name p^{er}tayns? [P] Aristot. myne q^{t} she[,] in his Phisickes hath defynd it in a neere Reason to breefenes & trouth. [B] How so q^{t} I. [P] As oft q^{t} she, as any thing is don for any cause what ev^{r},

that haps

74-Verso

that haps beside the intent of him that did it, that is called Chau^{n}ce, as if a man digging up his grounde for cause of tylling should fynde turnd up a waight of golde. This is beleevid ever to hap by chau^{n}ce, but it coms not of nought, For it hath his own p^{ro}per occa^{ti}on, of wch the happing & unlookt for luck seemes to have wrought this hap. For if the plow man had not harrowed his ground, & yf the layer up had not there hid his mo^{n}ny, gold there had not bene found. These be the causes of happing Chaunce, because it coms of meeting & agreeing causes, not from the Doers Intent. For neyth^{r} did he that hid it, nor he that plowde it, mynde to have found it there. but this agrees, that made him fynde it, because the oth^{r} hid it. Th^{r}fore it is lawfull to defyne Cha. to be a thing unlookt for, & a hap growing of such thinges as for an oth^{r} intent *[is] be don. But order it self that goes on w^{t} an †unshu^{n}ning turne, that it is, that makith causes agree & meete, W^{ch} co^{m}ming fro^{m} the fountayne of provide^{n}ce disposith all in their place & tyme.

*1. M.

[P] *Neare the Craggs of Achemi^{n}as Rock wher turned*
to folowars
brestz the flying wariar dartz doth throw
fro^{m} one springe Tigris eke Euφrates arise
Strait by waters parted †Soundred be
Who met and in One Cours reclaimed
The Streame that Eache depthe drew agries
Let top Sailes miet and †trunches by Curra^{n}t draw^{n}e
and mixed waters fil the changing Cours
And Suche falz as be^{n}ding erthe hath Skattered
A running Ordar of falling Gulfe Ordars
So what so Seame by Slaking ranes to Slip
Chanchis †bit yet indures and by a Law goes on[.]

I mark

75-Recto

*2. prose.

[B] I mark it said I, & as yo^{u} say, so agree[,] but in this co^{r}se of agreing causes, is there any lib^{r}ty in o^{r} will, or does a fatall chayne co^{n}strayne the motions of mens myndes? [P] There is one said she, For neth^{r} shold there be a naturall Reason, but that there were an arbitrable lib^{r}ty, For that

that naturally can Reason Rule, that hath Iudgem^{t}, by wch all by hit selfe discernes. Then it knowes both what to shun & wish. He desyres that he wisshith, & shuns that he thinkes meete to flye. wh^{r}fore to such as reaso^{n} have, a lib^{r}ty of willing or denyeng is, but in all, I suppose not alyke. For to celestiall & divine substances there is a playne iudgem^{t} & uncorrupted will, & a stro^{n}g powre ready to p^{er}form the desyred. And needes it must be that humayn soules be freer when they keepe the^{m}selves in the co^{n}templa^{ti}on of godes will, & lesse when they slyde to bodyes Care, & lest of all, when they are †lymed w^{t} earthly lyms. But it is the greatest bondage, when they give^{n} to vice hath fallen out of the possessio^{n} of their own Reason. For when they throw theyr eyes fro^{m} light of hyest truth to base & darkest maters, straight dymed by ignora^{n}ce cloude, are vext w^{t} slayeng affections, wch increasing, & agreing unto, they heape that bondage that to the^{m}selves they bring, And are in a state captived by ther own lib^{r}tie, wch he beholding that sees all fro^{m} the first, & vewes the sight of his own providence, all destenyes he desposith, agreing to their merit, all thinges beholdes & heares[.]

*2. M.

[P] **Cleere Phebus w^{t} purest light*
The honnyed mouth of Homer sings,
Who yet ye deepe bowells of Earth and sea
**W^{t} weake Sight of beames †pears not*[.]
Not So of the Great world the framar
Gainst him that al from hy doth view
No waight of earthe may resist
Not night w^{t} darkist Clouds Gainsays
In moment stroke his mynd all Sees
What wer what be what shal bifall
Who^{m} Sole alone for that he al espies
truly the may †Sole Call[.]

Lest I should

75-Verso

3. pro.

[B] Lest I shold be co^{n}founded w^{t} a harder doute, I pray yo^{u} tell me what this is I do co^{n}iecture. [P] q^{t} she[,] what most troubles the[?] [B] me thinkes it a crosse mater & in it self disagreing, that God all knowes, & yet ther should be a free will. For if god all forsees, nor beguilde can nev^{r} be, it must needes follow that his p^{ro}vidence hath seene, must be.

Then yf fro^{m} the begy^{n}ning, not o^{n}ly mens deedes, but their Cou^{n}sells & wills he hath aforknowen, no free will should be. For neth^{r} can any man doo, nor will, but that that his divine never fayling p^{ro}vidence knowes. For yf such thinges as be foreseene might be turned, then shold ther not be any assured foresight of that shuld happen, but shold breede an unc^{r}tain opinio^{n}, wch to beleeve of god, I iudge iniquitie. For neth^{r} do I allow that reason by wch som men beleeve, they can lose the knot of this questio^{n}. For they say, that that shall not hap only because god has foreseene it, but co^{n}trariwyse because it was sure to hap, th^{r}fore the divine p^{ro}vid. knew it, & th^{r}fore it is necessary that this shold fall to the co^{n}trary parte. For, because they are foreseene, that makes not that they shall hap, but because they must be, they are foreseene, As tho this were the co^{n}tention, whith^{r} the cause of ech thing be the foreknowledge of necessitie that so it should be, or the foreprovidence of God that makes necessitie. But we will stryve to make it playne, how the order of causes is such that necessary must be the hap of that that chau^{n}ces, altho we doo not see aforehand the neede of that hapes. For if a man sytt, of necessitie he must know that he syttes. and co^{n}trarywise, whith^{r} the opinio^{n} be right that because he sittes, th^{r}fore of necessitie he must sitt. In both ther is a necessitie, in the one of sytting, in the oth^{r} of truth. but it followes not that th^{r}fore he sittes, because the opinio^{n} was true that he did so, but the opinio^{n} is rath^{r} true because he sat afore. So when truth is on both sydes, ther is a necessitie of both. The

lyke

76-Recto

*The lyke we must reason of provide^{n}ce & thinges to co^{m}. For altho they be foreseene because they shall hap, They hap not yet bicause they are foreseene. Yet of necessitie they must needes eyth^{r} hap foreseene by god, or *provided for chau^{n}ce, wch is ynough to kyll the libertie of o^{r} will. but how out of reason is it, that the hap of te^{m}porall thinges, should be said the cause of eternall foresight? For what is it els but to think that God th^{r}fore foresees that that is, because it should hap, than for to think that such thinges should hap, the divine p^{ro}vide^{n}ce to be the cause. Besides, when I knew any thing to be, it must needes be that that was. So whe^{n} I know what shall be, It must needes be that so it shall be, & so it should follow that the chau^{n}ce of that that is foreseene can not be shund. Lastly, yf any man think awry of that that is, not only that is not a knoledge, but is a false opinio^{n}, furr diffrent fro^{m} the trouth of knowledge. So as, yf any thing so shall hap that of hit ther is no c^{r}tain nor necessary hapening, who can know aforehand that that must needes hap? for as the knowledge it self is †mixt w^{t} falshed, so needes must be the same that of her is gatherde. For that is the cause, †why science wantes falshed, because it must needes be of necessitie, such thing as true knowledge must co^{m}p^{r}hend. What then? How doth god foreknow these unc^{r}tain thinges. For if he p^{er}ceave happing chau^{n}ces, that can not be shund, if it be possible that such thinges happens, than he is deceaved, wch not o^{n}ly is iniquitie to think but as yll to speak. but if he knowes that they shall be such as they shall, in eyth^{r} knowing they shall hap, or not chau^{n}ce, what a foreknowledge is this, that co^{m}p^{re}hendes nothing sure nor c^{r}tain? for what makes mater, or why should we esteeme this mocking p^{ro}phey of Tiresse[:] **What I shall say, †or shall be, or shall not.*

Why should

76-Verso

Why should divine p^{ro}vid. excell humayne opnio^{n}, if it Iudge unc^{r}=tainties as men doo? whose sequele is unc^{r}tain. And if w^{t} him the surest fou^{n}ten of all thinges, no unc^{r}taintie can abyde, such is the hap of those thinges, that undoutedly he knowith shall hap. Wh^{r}fore th^{r} is no lib^{r}ty in mans Cou^{n}sels nor actes, wch godes mynd that all foresees w^{t}out falshodes erro^{r} tyes & co^{n}strayns to one end. W^{ch} once co^{n}cluded, what a fall shall hap then to humain cause, is playne. For in vayne rewardes to good & payne to yll be set to who^{m} no volu^{n}tary & free motio^{n} of the mynde is due. And that should seeme most wicked of all other, that now is deemed Iustest[:] Eyth^{r} wicked men be punisht, or the good rewarded, who^{m} no self will turnes the^{m} to eyth^{r}, but a c^{r}tain necessitie of hap co^{m}pels them. So neyth^{r} should th^{r} be vice nor v^{r}tue but rath^{r} a mixt & *unseparable co^{n}fusio^{n} of merite, Wh^{r}by *(,than wch nothing can be wickedlyer imagyned,) when all order of maters is led by p^{ro}vid. & nothing lawful for mans determinations, hit co^{n}cludes that all o^{r} faultes be turnd to the Autho^{r} of all good. so should th^{r} be no reaso^{n} of hoping ought, or of intreating, for what should any man hope or sue for, yf an unturning necessitie co^{n}straynd all thinges that we *wish. so should the co^{n}v^{r}sa^{ti}on we have amo^{n}g men, & co^{m}fort of god, be taken away, wch is of hope & prayer. For thorow price of true humilitie, we deserve the unestimable inclina^{ti}on of godes grace, being the only meane men seeme w^{t} god to speake, & Ioynd to his unexpressible light by meane of o^{r} prayer, evin afore we obtayne yt, wch if we beleeve the necessitie of thinges to hap, shall seeme to have no stre^{n}ghth, wh^{r}by we may styck & cleave to the †Prince of all thinges, And so of necessitie, mankynde, as a little afore thou hast told, shall

co^{n}sume

77-Recto

consume disseverd & disioynid fro^{m} his own fountayne.

**3. M.*

[B] *What disagrijng Cause the bond of al things breakes*
What God suche wars twixt two trothes makes
That what so coupled singly agree
The selfsame mixt must be disioyned
but discord none among the truthes befals
And Certain Sure unto the^{m}selves do stik
but mynd Opprest by blinded Limmes
Can not by flame of †overwhelmes Light.
The smal knots of al things finde
but why w^{t} suche desire doth true mynde seake
The hide^{n} Cause of thinges serche Out
Knowes he that †gridely to knowe he wyls
Why strives he to knowe agane the †had?
If ignorant he be, why blinded things seakes he
for who that wischith that knowes not,
Or who foloweth that he wotz not
Or how may he finde or found knowe
Suche forme of wiche he knowes not shape
And wha^{n} he viewes the hyest mynd
The Chief and al togither may he get
but now the mynde hid in Limmes Cloudes
hath not of al forgot his owne
And thogh the partz be lost retaines the hed
Who evir Seakes the trueth to knowe
Of nether Sort is rightly Called
for nether al doth knowe nor ignorant of al
but top of al retaining †kipes by whos ov^{r}vew
fro^{m} hy the seen draweth that bettar he may
The partz forgot the kept reioninge[.]

This is an

77-Verso

4. pr.

[P] This is an old quarrel q^{t} she, of p^{ro}vid., veheme^{n}tly handed by Tully, when he devided desteny, & a thing by the much & long sought, but yet not by any of yor sufficient nor c^{r}tainly found out, whose cause of darknes is for that the motio^{n} of mans Resons can not attayne the purenes of godes foreknowledge, wch yf she might by any meanes imag[i]ne, no doute at all were left, wch yet I will atte^{m}pte to expresse & make playne, if I had once dispatcht the thinges that first thou movest: For I ask, why dost thou think the reason of men that wold expresse it, is not sufficyent? wch for that hit supposith the prescience not to be the cause of necessitie to haps, th^{r}fore thinkes that free will is †let thorow the foresight. For whe^{n}ce dost thou drawe thy argum^{t} of the necessitie of haps, but supposing they are foreknowen, they must needes hap. Yf th^{r}fore the forek^{n}wledge doo †ad no necessitie to that followes, as thou thy self co^{n}fest, what cause is ther then, that o^{r} volu^{n}tary haps should be co^{m}peld to the sure end of causes. For Argum^{tes} sake, mark what wold follow. Then should we agree ther were no prescience. Are they co^{m}pelled to a necessitie, because they hap by o^{r} own free will? [B] No. [P] let us reson that he have free will, & yet that it makes no necessitie, then yt remaynes that o^{r} free will is wholle & †sownde, but thou will saye, foresight tho it bring no necessity that thinges must hap, yet it is a token that such thinges may hap. And by this meanes tho there were no foreknowledge, yet necessary end of

thinges shold

*78-Recto

*78-Verso

*of thinges shold be, For every lyke showes what it is, but doth not make that it showes. Wh^{r}fore we co^{n}clude that so^{m} thinges hap of necessitie, so that the foreknowledge seemes to be a foretoken of the necessitie, or els if it were no foreknowledge, hit could not be the signe of that wch is not. Now yo^{u} have the co^{n}clu^{ti}on evident by a fyrme reson, wch is not drawen out of signes & argu=

mentes that be farr fro^{m} the mater, but of co^{n}venient & necessary causes. but how haps hit that those thinges doo not chaunce that be foreseene shall be? as tho we did beleeve that such thinges should not hap, wch the divine p^{ro}vid. hath foreknowen shall hap, but rath^{r} this doo we think, tho they doo chaunce, no necessitie of nature hath made them so to be, wch heerby thou mayst easely see, for we beholde many thinges while they be don, subiect to o^{r} sight, evin as such thinges we †looke[,] that †Car men shold doo in draweng & turning of those he guydes, and so of all oth^{r} maters, but doth any necessitie co^{m}pell this? [B] no. For in vayne should be the end of art, yf all thinges co^{m}peld were mooved. [P] such thinges th^{r}fore when they are don, wante a necessitie to co^{m}pell the^{m}, the same afore than be don, w^{t}out necessity must be wh^{r}fore som thinges ther be that haps, whose end is free fro^{m} all necessitie, for I suppose no man will saye, that those thinges could nev^{r} hap wch he hath seene to be don, th^{r}fore these thinges fore knowen have there

haps *fre[e]

79-Recto

haps free. For as knowledge bringes no necessity to doo, so foreknowledge co^{m}pels nothing to be don, but thou wilt saye, This is douted, whith^{r} ther can be any foreknowledge of that that necessarily must not hap. For that seems to disagree. Dost thou think that necessitie must needes follow such thinges as are foreseene? Yf th^{r} be no necessity, it can not be foreknowen, & so nothing can be co^{m}p^{r}hended by knowledge but it must be c^{r}tain. and yf we beleeve unc^{r}tain haps to be none, but such as c^{r}tain knowledge hath foreseene, it is playne that that is the darknes of o^{r} opinio^{n}, not the trouth of o^{r} knowledge. For els oth^{r}wise than truth is, thou shouldest think, & have a beleefe awry fro^{m} the integryte of true knowledge, of whose erro^{r} this is cause, that men suppose all thinges that they knowe to be deryved of the force & nature of the causes them selves, wch wholly is co^{n}trary. For all that is knowen, is co^{m}prehended not according to his worth, but according to the knowers powre. For as by this short example it is playne, that the †circuite of a body is knowen div^{r}sly by sight, & div^{r}sly by touche, for when hit remaynes above, does fro^{m} thence behold all w^{t} beames cast abrode, but when kept in his own circle, & so bound in about the co^{m}passe of his owne motio[n], he circles Rowndnes w^{t} his own partes **parceaveth* so. Man himself is beheld in div^{r}se sortes, by sense, Imagina^{ti}on, reson & und^{r}standing, for sense Iudgith of the figure that is set in his materiall subiect. Ymagina^{ti}on lookes upo^{n} her forme, w^{t}out her matter. but Reason ov^{r}passith this & wayeth her show wch remaynes in all thinges by any univ^{r}sall co^{n}sidera^{ti}on, but understandinges eye lookith hyer. For ascending to the largenes

of the u.

79-Verso

of the univ^{r}salitie, lookes upo^{n} her symple forme, w^{t} the pure myndes insight. In wch this is most to be co^{n}sidered for the upp^{r}most force of understanding, includith the inferio^{r} but the lower can nev^{r} Ryse up to the hyar. For neth^{r} is sense ought worth w^{t}out his subiect, or Ymag.^{on} behold univ^{r}sall formes, or Reson, co^{m}p^{r}hend the simple forme, but under=standing as looking fro^{m} above, co^{n}ceaving the right forme, Iudgith aright of all thinges that be under, & in that sort co^{m}p^{re}hendes it as knowen to none oth^{r}. For hit knowith the univ^{r}sality of Reaso^{n}, the shape of ymagi^{on}. & senses matter, nor using reason imagina^{ti}on nor sense, but orderly by one twynkell of the mynde, all ov^{r}lookith. Reson allso when hit beholdith all thinges can not comp^{re}hend by ymag^{o}n. nor using sense, such thinges as be to be ymagened & to be felt. For this is hit, that defynes the univ^{r}salitie of ev^{r}y mans conceyte. A man is a Resonable *ij footed Creature, wch tho it be an univ^{r}sall knowledge, yet no man is ignorant but hit hath sense & Imag^{on}. wch no man co^{n}siderith by imaga^{on}. or sense, but by a reasonable co^{n}ceyte. For tho Imag^{on}. tooke her begyning of seeing, & forming figures, yet tho sense were away, it respectith all sensible thinges, tho w^{t} a sensible & imaginary reason. Do you not see then how in knowing all, they rath^{r} use their own p^{ro}pertes than of thinges knowen, & that by reason, for whe^{n} all Iudgem^{t} remaynes in the acte of the Iuger, it must needes follow that ev^{r}y man p^{er}forms his work not by oth^{r}s powre but his own.

Once in ye porch

*78-Recto

**4. M.*

[P] *Ons in the porche wer broght in me^{n}*

Of obscure line and old the wer
Who Sens and Image out of †lest notes
In mens myndz ingraven believe
As Oft haps the running stile
In †Sea paper Leve
Some printid Lettars stik
That marke have none at all
but if the mynd by her owne raigning
Expres by motions naught
Save only patient Lies
Subiect to bodies markes
And Vain the †fourmes
Glaslike of all doth make
†Whenche this that in our my[n]d raignes
Knowelege of al discernes
What power all beholdz
Who the knowe[n] devides
And knowing eache way
Now lifts on hie the hed
That falz to Lowest thinges
Than gathering in hit selfe
With †truethe fals rebukes
This is the making Cause
Wiche muche more mightiar is
Tha[n] suche as only material markes
Receaves with her owne prints
but yet a passio[n] doth begin and sturs
The myndz fors while body lives
Wha[n] ether Light the yies doth hit,
Or So[u]nd in ear doth strike
Tha[n] sturred strengh of my[n]d
What figures w[t]in hit holds
Ioinded Like he Cals
**Applies them to the outword knowe[n]*
And fancies mixe to formes
That hide[n] rest w[t]in[.]

For yf in feeling

*80-Recto

5. prose.

[P] For yf in feeling bodyes, the motions that be made outwardly affecte the senses p^{ro}perties, & that the bodyes passio^{n} doth go afore the strength of the doers mynde, wch p^{ro}vokes the myndes actions, & styrrith in meane while the quiet fansyes that inward remaynes, Yf in sensible bodyes I saye the mynde is not afflicted w^{t} passion but by viole^{n}ce †shewith the same that the body makes, how much more those thinges wch are most voyde of bodyes affections in discerning, follow not outwardly they cast afore them, but doth p^{er}forme the actio^{n} of the mynde. by this reson, many knowledges have given place to divers & differing substa^{n}ces. For o^{n}ly sense dep^{ri}ved of all oth^{r} knowledge *wantes to lyving thinges that have no motio^{n}, as the sea shells & such oth^{r} as by cleaving to Rockes, be nourished. but Imag.^{on} seems only an affec.^{on} in creatures that move & have desyre to shun or seek. But mans reson is o^{n}ly p^{ro}p^{er} to him-self, as und^{r}standing to god, so as that knowledge exceedes all oth^{r} that by her own nature not o^{n}ly her own, but *know^{t} the rest of knowledges subiect to her. but what if sense be taken fro^{m} reson, & Imag.^{on} lost, shall we saye there is no thinge univ^{r}sall that generally Reson hath to looke unto? For that that is sensible & Imaginary that can not be univ^{r}sall, For eyth^{r} true is the Resons iudgm^{t} & sense to be nothing worth, or because it knowes that many thinges be subiect to sense, & Imag.^{on}, th^{r}fore vayne shold the co^{n}ceyte of Reson be, wch because it is sensible & singuler, co^{n}siders yet an univ^{r}salitie above it. besydes, yf Reason gayne sayi^{n}g, aunswers, that she sees what is sensible, what Imaginary in the reson of all that co^{m}p^{re}hendes, yet she can not aspire to the knoledge of that only, for that her scie^{n}ce can not exceed the bodyes shape. but we must beleeve of the knoledge of all thi^{n}ges w^{t} a steddyer & p^{er}feter Iudgm^{t}. In this co^{n}trov^{r}sy th^{r}fore, we that have both powre of resoning, Imagining & feeling, shall not we more allow the cause of reson? It is evin lyke as mans Reson doth *[ ] think how it may looke upo^{n} godes understandi^{n}g of outward thinges, w^{t}out it self doo know it. For thus yo^{u} dispute, yf such thinges as seem not to have c^{r}ten & necessary sequels, the same can nev^{r} be foreknowen surely to hap

80-Verso

surely to hap, th^{r}fore there is no p^{re}science of such thinges, wch if we beleeve to be, then should there nothing hap of necessitie. Yf th^{r}fore, as we be p^{ar}takers of reson, so we had the iudgem^{t} of godes will, as we iudge that imag^{o}n. & sense ought to give place to Reson, so shold we deeme it most Iuste that humayne reson should submit hit self to godes mynde. Let us th^{r}fore lyft up o^{r} selves into the Top of his und^{r}standing. For there reson shall beholde that in hit self it ca^{n} not see, that is, how those thinges that have not c^{r}ten & sure endes, yet shall he see the^{m} assured, & a determynid aforeknoledge. And that is not opinio^{n}, but an included purenes of the hyest knoledge that is shut in no lymites.

*5. *M.*

[P] *In how many shapes pas beastes*
on ground
Of wiche of bodies Long dust some turnes
Withe fors of brest co^{n}tinued trace doth trail
Some whos swiftnis wings the windz do part
And strait the bredth of Largist Skie doth pas
Some on ground ther steps to print †reiois
Or †grinny fildz to pas or woodz to haunt
Whos formes thogh thou see difar far
*Yet downe face thers ther dullid sencis *[ ]*
Ma^{n}kind alone his hed upward bendz
At eas doth stand w^{t} body Clad and erth Lookes on
This figure warns but for the Clays deceat
*that thou w^{t} lifted Looke that heaven aspiri^{n}g upcast thy *h[ed]*
On hy thy mynd shuldst raise Lest overwaid
thy body made aloft thy mynd shuld
Lowar sit[.]

For that th^{r}fore

81-Recto

*6. pr.

[P] For that th^{r}fore, as a litle afore I showed all that is knowen, not of her own nature, but of the nature of such thinges as are co^{m}p^{r}ehended is knowen, Let us looke now as much as beco^{m}s us, what is the state of the divine substa. that we may the better know, what is the knoledge th^{r}of. It is the co^{m}mon Iudgem^{t} of all that lyve by Resons Rule that god is ev^{r}lasting. Let us co^{n}sider what is eternitie, for this shall show us both godes nature, & his knowledge. Eternitie ys th^{r}fore an unending, wholle & p^{er}fet possess.^{on} of lyfe, wch more cleerly appeers by the co^{m}parison of te^{m}porall thinges, for what so lives in tyme, that p^{re}s^{n}t fro^{m} past, goos on to the following. And nothing is ther appoy^{n}ted in tyme, that altogeth^{r} can co^{m}p^{re}hend the whole co^{m}passe of his lyfe. For if he knows not the morrow & the yestarday hath lost & in this p^{re}s^{n}t lyfe move oth^{r}wise ye lyve than in that cha^{n}ging & tran^{n}sytory moment, Then that that suffers change of tyme, altho it were as †Arist. thinkes of the *wo[r]ld that nev^{r} hit began, nor ev^{r} shall end, & that the lyfe th^{r}of shold stretch to the endlesnes of tyme, yet could yt not be such that rightly ev^{r}lasting may be Iudged. For albeit he could at once co^{m}p^{re}hend well the whole co^{m}passe of o^{r} lyfe, *<u>yet that that shall com, & hath not</u> yet chau^{n}ced, can he nev^{r} attayne. Then it follows, that whatsoev^{r} co^{m}p^{re}hendes & possesses the wholle fulnes of endles lyfe, to who^{m} neth^{r} any thi^{n}g co^{m}ming is absent, nor any thing past is *chau[nged that] rightly eternall showed, & must needes be that p^{re}s^{n}t w^{t} himself, wholly his own may ev^{r} stand, & hath in his p^{re}s^{n}ce the infinitenes of the wavering tyme. Wh^{r}foore they have not rightly don, who when they herd that Plato thought this world nev^{r} to have had begy^{n}ing

nor ev^{r} to

81-Verso

nor ev^{r} to receave end, supposed that by this meane the world should be made eternall, lyke him that is eternall: For it is an oth^{r} thing that Plato meanes to attribute to the world, meaning of a lyfe that might guide him to be eternall. An oth^{r} thing it is that o^{n}e wholle lyfe p^{re}s^{n}t should co^{m}p^{re}hend the p^{re}s^{n}ce of the the^{n} unending lyf, wch is manifeste to be the p^{ro}perty of godes mynde, for he himself ought not to be iudged au^{n}cienter than that he made, for qua^{n}tytie of tyme, but rather for the p^{ro}p^{er}ty of his owne pure nature, for the infinite motio^{n} of te^{m}porall thinges doth but co^{n}terfet the p^{re}s^{n}t state of the untourning. And when it can not neth^{r} picture it nor equall it, abydes unremoved by his co^{n}stancy, & by the wekenes of that is p^{re}s^{n}t, doth weaken it self into the infinite qua^{n}tity of that shall be & was. And when he ca^{n} not possess the whole fulnes of his own lyfe in that p^{ar}te that he nev^{r} leavith to be, he seems to cou^{n}terfet that that he ca^{n} neth^{r} fulfyll nor expresse, bynding himself to any kinde of rep^{re}senta^{ti}on of this that is small[,] slyding & mome^{n}tary, wch because hit bearith som ymage of the ev^{r}lasting p^{re}s^{n}ce, to who^{m} so ev^{r} it haps, this good it does, that he seems so to be. but because hit ca^{n} not last, hath taken an endles Io^{r}ney of tyme. And so he makes, that by going he co^{n}tynues lyfe whose fulnes he ca^{n} not co^{m}p^{re}hend in byding. *[T]h^{r}fore yf we wold gyve right names to matter, following Platos Rule, we should name god Eternall, & the world p^{er}petuall, because th^{r}fore all Iudgem^{t} co^{m}p^{r}hendith according to the nature of such thinges to wch he is subiecte, to god th^{r}fore all is eternall, & lyke is ev^{r} his state his science ov^{r}passing all motio^{n} of tyme, remaynith in the Purenes of his own

82-Recto

of his owne p^{re}s^{n}ce, co^{m}p^{r}hending the infinite space of that is past *<u>& shall</u>. And all co^{n}siderith in his own †pure knoledge as don now they were. Wh^{r}fore if thou woldest way his foreknoledge by wch he all und^{r}=standith, thou woltst Iudge that he hath not afore=knowledge of thinges to co^{m}, alone, but rightlyer a science of nev^{r} worn co^{n}tynua^{n}ce. Wh^{r}fore we must not call it foresight, but p^{ro}vidence wch being set ov^{r} all thinges, yea in the meanest, vews the^{m} all as out of the very top & spring of all. Why dost thou ask th^{r}fore why necessaryly thinges must needes be, that by godes light be ov^{r}lookt? when not men the^{m}selves make all thinges necessary because they see them. For does thy Looking on, make any necessity for such thinges to be, as thou dost behold? [B] No. [P] And if we durst co^{m}pare togither divine & humayne p^{re}s^{n}ce, evin as yo^{u} see c^{r}tain thinges at this instant, so he eternally all beholdes. wh^{r}fore this divine foreknoledge cha^{n}gith not the naturall p^{ro}p^{er}ty of thinges, but looks of such thinges as are p^{re}s^{n}t that they shall hap in tyme neth^{r} does he co^{n}found the Iudge.^{mtes} of causes but o^{n}ly w^{t} the vew of his mynde, *know^{t} what needes must be, & what shall not hap as yo^{u} whan yo^{u} see a man walke upo^{n} the ground, & does behold the sonn aryse in skye, tho at once, both ye vewe, yet yo^{u} see that the one is volu^{n}tary, & the oth^{r} yo^{u} Iudge necessary. So th^{r}fore godes looke beholding ech thing, doth not p^{er}turbe their p^{ro}p^{er}tyes, tho p^{re}s^{n}t to himself they be all, yet by tymes dista^{n}ce they are to co^{m}. So hit co^{n}cludes, that this is not opinio^{n}, but rath^{r}, knowledge

sticking

82-Verso

*knoledge sticking to truthe, when he knowes any thing that shall be, then he is sure that of necessitie it must be. heere yf yo^{u} say that god seith that that shall happen it ca^{n} not be then but it must hap, & that that ca^{n} not chose but to cha^{n}ce, that must fall out of necessitie. And so wold yo^{u} bynde me to needes name[?] I must co^{n}fesse that it is a mater of soundest troth, but such one as no ma^{n} ca^{n} attayne to, but must have an Insight of divinity. Th^{r}fore I will a^{n}swere that one thing if it be referd to godes knoledge, is of necessyty, yf it be wayde in his own nature, is free & absolute. Th^{r}fore there are *ij necessities, the one playne as that it must needes be that men be mortall, the oth^{r} is co^{n}ditionall, as if thou knoest a ma^{n} doth walke, it must needes follow that he goes, for it ca^{n} be no oth^{r}wise but that that a ma^{n} *know^{t} is playne, but this, yf, drawes not of co^{n}seque^{n}ce the oth^{r} that is playne & simple. For such a necessity o^{r} own p^{ro}p^{er} nature makes not, but the Ioyning of that. Yf for no necessitie co^{m}pels a ma^{n} to go, but willi^{n}gly he walkes, tho when he steps he must go. So yf p^{ro}vid. sees any thing p^{re}s^{n}t, that must needes be, tho it have no necessyty of nature so to be, And god as p^{re}s^{n}t beholdith all such thinges as following shall happ to p^{ro}ceede of free will, All these thinges referd to the divine sight be necessary for the state of godes knoledge, but co^{n}siderd by the^{m}selves, they differ nothing fro^{m} the absolute lib^{r}ty of nature her selfe. All thinges th^{r}fore doutles be made, wch god himself foreknowes shall be, but som of these p^{ro}ceedes of free will, wch tho

by being

83-Recto

by being they hap, yet they lose not their owne nature, for afore they hapt, they might have fortuned not to hap. What yf they be not necessary when they hap necessarily by the state of godes science? this is the differe^{n}ce, that evin as these thinges that I p^{ro}pou^{n}ded afore, the son rysing, & the ma^{n} going, wch whyle they are a doing, ca^{n} not but be don, yet the one afore it hapt, was of necessity, the oth^{r} not so. so those thinges that p^{re}s^{n}t god beholdes, are in lyke sorte, but of the^{m} som hapes by causes necessity, the oth^{r} by the powre of the doar, wh^{r}fore we have not saide amisse that so^{m} be necessary in respecte of godes knoledge, oth^{r} if they be by the^{m}selves co^{n}sidered, be unlosed fro^{m} necessities knot: For evin as all that is playne to o^{r} senses, yf ye refer it to Reson, it is univ^{r}sall, if to hit self that is don, it is singuler, but thou woldst saye, yf in my powre it be set to cha^{n}ge my purpose, I will make voyde p^{ro}vid. whe^{n} p^{er}cha^{n}ce I shall cha^{n}ge that she foreknew. I will a^{n}swere the, I grau^{n}te that thou mayst cha^{n}ge thy p^{ur}pose, *but because the ev^{r}p^{re}s^{n}t troth of p^{ro}vid. beholdith that eyth^{r} thou may doo, or whith^{r} mayst *tho[u] [must], [or] whith^{r}soev^{r} thou turnest the, shalt thou nev^{r} shun his divine foreknoledge, as thou canst not fly the sight of his p^{re}s^{n}t eye tho thou be turned by thy free will to soundry actions. what? woldst thou say. shall divine scyence be cha^{n}ged by my dispo^{ti}on, that wha^{n} I will this or that she shall seeme to chaunge the turns of her knoledge? O no. For godes looke foreru^{n}nith all that shall be, & †wryes to the

p^{re}s^{n}ce of

83-Verso

p^{re}s^{n}ce of his own knoledge, & back callith, not alterith as thou supposest the varyeties of his knoledge, now this now that, but in a mom^{t} steddy he †p^{re}ventes & co^{m}p^{r}hendes thy sundry changes, wch p^{re}s^{n}ce that all co^{m}p^{r}hendes sees he hath not got of the hap of such thinges as shall cha^{n}ce, but is p^{ro}ceeded out of his purenes, Wheron is co^{n}cluded that ye hast told afore, how unwo^{r}thy it were, that the cause of godes science shuld p^{er}forme haps, for the force of his knoledge by a p^{re}s^{n}t und^{r}sta^{n}ding, co^{m}p^{re}hendith all. Appoyntes to all a meane & owes nothing to the co^{m}ming, wch being true ther Remaynes a sure lib^{r}ty of will to mortall folkes. For neyth^{r} lawes be wicked, that doo p^{ro}pounde rewarde & payne yf o^{r} wills were freed fro^{m} all necessity. There lastith also a vewer of us all the foreknowing god, whose ev^{r} p^{re}s^{n}t et^{r}nitie of sight agreith w^{t} the following p^{ro}p^{er}ty of o^{r} Actions. And so dispensith to good reward, to yll their desertes, neyth^{r} in vayne doo we put trust in god, neth^{r} of small price o^{r} prayers, wch being truly

made, can nev^{r} fall in vayne. Avoyde vice th^{r}fore, prise v^{r}tue,
yor myndes lift up to true hopes, & settle yor hu^{m}ble prayers
in hyest place, For yo^{u} *[] a g[reat] necessitie,
yf you will not yo^{r}self beguyle, when yo^{u}
*yo^{r}self beholde afore the eyes of that iudge that all desernes.

*Fift Booke

[Two Unnumbered Pages]

83A-Recto-83A-Verso

[Blank]

*84-Recto-99A-Verso

Appendix I
Two Variant Copies of the Computation of Days

[First Variant Copy]

7-Recto

*The Computation of the dayes and houres in wch your Matie began and finished y^{e} translation of Boethius.

*Your Matie began your translation of Boethius the tenth day of October 1593 and ended it the fift of November than next Immediatly. following which were fyve and twenty dayes in all.

*Out of wch xxv. dayes are to be taken fowre Sondayes, three other *hollyday[es] and six dayes on which your Matie †rwd abrode to take the ayre. And on those dayes did forbeare to translate, amounting togither to thirtene dayes.

*Which xiij being deductid from xxv remaynith then but twelve dayes.

*And then accompting twoo houres only, bestowed every day one w^{t} an other in the translating. The computation fallith out. That in fowre and twenty houres your Matie began and ended your translation.

7-Verso-8-Recto

[Blank]

8-Verso

*Computation of the nomber of
dayes and houres in wch your ~
Matie began and ended the translatio^{n}
of Boëthius ·
At Windsor ·

9-Verso

*15 November 1593
A note of the dayes and
houres, in wch her Matie
finished her translation
of Boethius, de consolatio
ne Philosophiae.

[Third Variant Copy]

10-Recto

*The Queenes Matie being at Windsor in the xxxvth yeere of her Raigne, upon the xth of October *1593, began her translation of *Boethius de consolatione Philosophie*, and ended it upon the eight of Novembre then next following, wch were xxx^{ty} dayes:

*Of wch tyme there are to be accompted xiij dayes, parte in Sondayes and other holy dayes, and parte in her Ma^{jie} ryding abrode, upon wch her Matie did forbeare to translate,

*So that xiij dayes being deducted from xxx^{ty}, Remaynith
*17. dayes. xvij dayes, In wch tyme her Matie finished her translation.

*And in those xvij dayes, her Matie did not exceede one houre and a half at a tyme, in following her translating:

*Whereby it apperith that in xxvj houres or theraboutes, her Matie p^{er}fo^{r}med
*26. houres the wholle translation.

10-Verso-11-Recto

[Blank]

11-Verso

*November 1593
Note of y[e] tyme wherin her
Ma[tie] began and ended her
translation of Boethius

*[ ]

11A-Recto-12-Verso

[Blank]

Appendix II
Fragmentary Second Draft of Book I

[Fragmentary Second Draft of Book I]

100-Recto
*Fair Copie of part
of the First
Book:

[no title]

[Meter 1]
Rymes that my growing study once perfourmd
In teares alas compelld wofull staves begyn
My muses torne, behold what writ I shall indite
where true wofull verse my face wt dole bedews.
These at Least no terror might constrayne
that fellows to our mone, our way they shuld refrayne.
The glory once of happy greeny youth,
Now fates of grunting age my comfort all.
unlookt for age hyed by mishap is com.
And sorrow bids his tyme to add withall
unseasond hory heares upon my head are pourd
And loosed skynn in feeble body shakes
Blessid death that in sweetest yeeres refrayns
But oft calld comes to the wofull nights.
Ô wt how defe eare she from wretched wryes
And wayling eyes, cruel, to shutt denyes.
while guilefull fortune wt vading goods did shyne
My life well ny the dolefull houre bereued
whan her false Looke a cloude hath changed
My wretched Life thankles abode protracts.
why me so oft my frends have you happy cald,
who fallith downe, in steddy step never strode.

[Prose 1]

While of all this alone in sylence I bethought me, and fearefull co^{m}playnte in stilice office I ment, over my head to stand a woman did appeere of stately face w^{t} flamming eyes of insight, above the common worth of men, of fresh coulo^{r} & unwoon strenghth, though yet so olde she were, that of o^{r} age she seemid not to be one. her stature such as skarce coulde be desernd: for som while she skanted her to the common stature of men, Straigte she seemd w^{t} croune of head the heavens to stryke, And lyfting the same up hyar, the heavens themselves she entered, beguiling the sight of lookeres on. Her weedes she ware of smallest thrides parfitt for fyne

100-Verso

fyne woorkmanship & lasting substance, as after by her self I knew, was by her handes all wrought, whose forme, as to smoky images is wont, a certain dymnes of despised antiquitie over whelmed. Of these weedes in the lowest skyrtes Π, In the upper syde a Θ was read, all woven, And between both †tres., ladder wyse, certain steps marked, by wch from lowest to hyest Element ascent ther was: yet that self garment the handes of violent men had torn, And peeces such as get they coulde, away they stole. Her right hand held a booke, the left a scepter. Who whan she spyed poetes muses standing by my bed, & to my teares inditing woordes, somwhat mooved, inflamed w^{t} glowing eyes. [P] Who suffred quoth she, these Stages harlottes approche this sick man, wch not only wolde not ease his sorow w^{t} no remedies, but w^{t} sweete venom nourish them. These they be that w^{t} baren affections thornes, destroye the full eares of Reasons frute, and mens myndes w^{t} desyres inured, not frees. But if of vayne man, as vulgar wontes, yor allurementes had deprived me, w^{t} lesse greefe had I borne it: for by such o^{r} woork had got no harm. but this man have you touched, who^{m} Stoik & Academik study brought out. Gett you away Sirens sweete till end be seene; To my Muses leave him for cure & helth. To this the checked raball w^{t} looke down caste w^{t} wo, w^{t} blush confessing shame, dolefull out of doores they went. but I whose sight drownde in teares was dymde, coulde not know what she was of so imperious rule: And setling my eyes on grounde, what she wolde more doo, in silence I attended. Than she drawing nar on my bedsyde, sett down: And vewing my Looke of heavy woe, & w^{t} my dole to the earth throwne down, in verses these of my myndes *payne, complaynith thus:

[no catchword]

101-Recto

[Meter 2]
[P] O in how hedlong depth
the drownid mynde is dym,
And Losing light her owne,
to others darknes drawne,
As oft as driven w^{t} earthly flawes
The harmefull cares to hyest grow.
Once this man free in open felde
used the skies to †vew
Of Rosy forme the light beheld
Of frosty moone the planetes sawe
And what star els runs wonted course
Bending by many circles this man had †woo^{n}n
by nomber to know them all.
Yea, causes ech whan roring wyndes
the Seas perturbes,
Acquaynted w^{t} the spirit
that Rolles the stedy world.
And why the star that fallz
To the hesperias waters
from her reddy roote
doth rayse her self:
who that gives the springes
milde houres, their temp^{er}
That w^{t} Rosy floures
The earth bedecks.
who made the fertile automne
at fullest of the yeere
Abounde w^{t} grapes
all swollen w^{t} rypest frutes.
he wonted to serch & fynde
*t . . causes of hidden nature,
down he is, of
myndes light bereft

w^{t} brused neck, by
overheavy chaynes
A bowed lowe Looke
by waight bearing
Dryven, alas, the
Selly earth beholde.

But fytter

101-Verso

[Blank]

102-Recto

[Prose 2]

[P] *But fytter tyme q^{t} she: for medicin than complaynte. Than fixing on me her steddy eyes, Art thou the same q^{t} she, who once nourished w^{t} my mylk, w^{t} o^{r} foode art growne to strenght of manly mynde? on who^{m} we bestowed such weapons as if thou hadst not cast away, had saved the w^{t} invincible strength. Doest thou me knowe? why art thou du^{m}m? Is it shame or wonder makes the silent? But whan she spyed me not only still, but woordles & du^{m}m, on my brest gently Layde her hand, & sayd Ther is no danger, he is enterd in a Lethargie, A common disease of mynd distract. He hath a little forgotten himself, his memory will retourn whan first he hath rememberd me: And that he may, a little let us wype his eyes overdymmed w^{t} cloude of erthly thinges. Thus speaking, my eyes flowing w^{t} teares, folding her garment, she dryed:

[Meter 3]
Than night overblowen, the darknes left me,
And former strength unto my eyes retournd.

As whan

102-Verso
As whan the heavens astund w^{t} headlong Wynde
And Pole amongest ye cloudy mists,
The forme is hid, and in ye heavens no stars appeers
from hye the night on Earth is spred,

The same yf Boreas sent from his Thracian Den
  Doth stryke and opens the hidden day
shynes out, and w^{t} his soudain Light Phoebus shaken
  w^{t} his beames strykes all Lookers on.

[Prose 3]

No otherwise mistes of my woe dissolved, to heaven I reached, & raysde my mynde to know my Curars face. Then whan on her I rolde my eyes & Looke I fixed, My nursse I sawe, in whose retired roomes in my youth I dwelt, [B] And lo, q^{t} I, Art thou com to the solitarines of our exile? O Pedagogue of all vertues fallen from the highest step, Shalt thou w^{t} me be tormented to, w^{t} false crymes? [P] Shall I q^{t} she, scholler myne, the leave, and not to ease thy burden, wch for my sake thou bearest, in easing thy labo^{r} w^{t} following of thy payne? It ill becoms Philosophy to *leave alone an Innocentes Waye. Shall I dreade my own blame?

*and as the

103-Recto-104-Verso

[Blank]

105-Recto

*END

*105-Verso

Appendix III
Fragmentary Second Draft of Book IV

[Fragmentary Second Draft of Book IV]

58-Recto

The fourth booke.

*1 prose

Thus when Philosophy her stately looke & grave co^{n}tena^{n}ce Keping, in myld & sweete sorte had sung. Then I, not forgetting my Lat[']ingrande wo, burst out to tell som parte of my intent. [B] O q^{t} I, thou the guide of true light, such thinges as thy talke hith^{r}to hath uttered, by divine specula^{ti}on & Reason thyne, are showed invincible. And though the same of late, any Iniuries sorow forgate, yet alltogith^{r} of the^{m} I was not ignorant, but this was the self & greatest cause of all my woe. That when the Righter of all thing is good, eyth^{r} at all evills can be, or unpunished pass. That how wo^{r}thy of wondar it is. Consider I pray yo^{u}: But to this a greater mater is added, For wickednes Ruling & florishing, not only vertue wantes reward, but subiect to the feete of wicked men, is troden down, and suffers payne that **wicked folkes* deserve, wch haping in a raigne of him that all knowes, all made, and such a god that willes but only that is good. No man can but m^{r}vell & co^{m}playne. [P] It should be wo^{r}thy m^{r}vell q^{t} she & horrible more than any mo^{n}ster, yf as thou supposest in a house guyded by such a †m^{r}, base vessells should be esteemed, & precious despised. But so it is not. For if such thinges be kepte wch we of late co^{n}cluded, & be kepte togith^{r}, he being the Maker, of what Kingdom we spake. Thou shalt knowe that ev^{r} good men be mighty, yll men, slaves & weak. And how vice is nev^{r} w^{t}out punishm^{t}, nor v^{r}tue w^{t}out reward. And how prosperitie to the good, yll luck to evill betydes. And such lyke, wch may, leaving quarrelles, strenghthen the w^{t} steddy soundnes. And for that thou hast seene the picture of true blisse, wch I shewed the, & hast knowen whence it is placed, passing all those thinges that necessary I think not, I will shew the the waye that home to thy house may bring the, & stick such fethers in thy mynd wh^{r}by thou mayst sore up on Hye. And so woe trode downe, homedweller in thy cou^{n}trey by my guyding, path & charyot, mayst retourn.

*1 Myter
[P] For speedy quilles have I
that fare above ye Pole doo reach,
wch whan my flyeng mynd putts on
hatyng ye Earth despises it,

And hyes hyar

58-Verso

And hyar hues that Earths Globe
and Clouds behynd me see,
And pass above ye Feerce top
w^{t} swiftnes that ye heavens seate,
Untill to starry house hit com,
wch Phoebus sortith waye,
And souldiour made of shynning star
Saturne doth Followe,
Or where ye shewing night
the Circle round doth make
And whan got ynough he hath
the uttmost Pole he leaves,
and worthy made of hyest light
Pressith the Wayght of speedy skye,
he lowe, holds of kings ye scepter,
and Raynes of World doth guyde,
And stable rules ye speedy Course,
of all, the Noble Judge,
Hither if ye way back doo bring the
wch now forgetting thou requirest
This wilt thou saye my Cou^{n}try is I know
Hence cam I, here Will I stay my step,
And if of Earth hit please the
the darknes left, to vew,
The gry^{m}me lookes that peeple dreedith so

of bannisht tyrants, shalt beholde.

*2 prose

[B] Than I, O Lord, how greate thinges dost thou p^{ro}mise, neyth^{r} doute I but p^{er}form thou canst it. but stick not now at that thou hast began[.] [P] Fyrst th^{r}fore, Thou mayst knowe q^{t} she, that good men have ev^{r} powre, & evill men lack ev^{r} strength, for good & yll being so co^{n}trary. Yf powrefull be the fyrst, the last doth shew his lack. But that yor opinio^{n} may have

more credit

59-Recto

more Credit by eyth^{r} path I will treade, & th^{r}by my p^{ro}posicions co^{n}fyrme. Twoo thinges ther be, by wch the affecte of ech mans dooinges appeers, will, & powre. Of wch if there lack, nothing may be p^{er}formed: For will wanting, no man will go about that he wolde not. And powre fayle, vayne is will. So hit followes, that whan he wantes that he Wills, no doubte but powre fayles to get the desyred. [B] That is playne, & can not be denyed. [P] And who^{m} thou seest obtayne that he wolde, dost thou doubte that he may not have the powre? In that he p^{er}vayles, in that man is hable, but Weak must needes be, in that he may not. Dost thou reme^{m}bar that in o^{r} last argum^{tes} this was gathered, that the intent of ech mans will, though div^{r}sly distracted, is only to hye to blisse. [B] I reme^{m}ber it was so shewed. [P] Dost thou call to mynde that blisse is the greatest good? And so whan that is sought, all best is got? [B] I reme^{m}ber that well ynough q^{t} I, For that holde I fixt in my mynde. [P] Th^{r}fore all good men & yll stryve to co^{m} to the best by divers Intentes. [B] So it is. [P] But most sure it is, they are made good men by obtayning good. But it is sure that good men doo allwayes obtayne that they desyre? [B] So it seems. [P] But if Yll men might obtayne good, they could not be yll. [B] So it is, [P] whan they both desyre good, but the one gettes it, the oth^{r} not. It is c^{r}tain that good men be mighty, & yll, Weak. [B] Who ev^{r} q^{t} I, doutes th^{r}of, neyth^{r} can co^{n}syder natures p^{ro}p^{er}ty, nor sequele of Reason. [P] Then yf twoo ther be that by Nature requyres one thing, one of the^{m} naturally does that & p^{er}forms. The oth^{r} no way can doo it. Nor can agree to what Nature will. And so to fullfill his intent does but follow the fullfiller. W^{ch} of the^{m} ij thinkest thou more of powre? [B] Tho I co^{n}iecture what yo^{u} wolde, yet plainlyer I desyre to heare. [P] The motio^{n} of walking, you can not denye but all men have, nor does not doubte that is not the feetes office. Yf any man then that ca^{n} go, & an oth^{r} to who^{m} the naturall p^{ro}p^{er}tye of the feete is wanting, stryving w^{t} his handes, stryves so to walke. W^{ch} of these ij suppose yo^{u} more worth? [B] p^{er}form the rest of that yo^{u} will. For no man doubtes but he is of more form that hath the use of Nature then he that wantes it. But the greatest good sayde she, that is set before yll & good, the good desyre by naturall duety of v^{r}tue, the oth^{r} by a scattred desyre, & stryve to gett that w^{ch}

no p^{ro}p^{er} gyft

59-Verso

no p^{ro}p^{er} gyft to such as will obtayne the greatest good. Dost thou think *th[e] co^{n}trary? [B] No q^{t} I, for that is playne that followes. For heerby may we gather that I grau^{n}ted afore, Good men to be mighty, & yll men, Weak. [P] Rightly haste thou disco^{r}sed, and so as phisicians ought to hope, that it is a figure of a healthy & resisting Nature. But for that I see the readyest to und^{r}stand, I will heape up many reasons. Beholde how greate a Weakenes is ther appeeres in vicious men, that can not obtayne that, to wch their naturall intent leades & well nye co^{m}pells. And what if they be left of the greate & almost invincible help of his †preceder nature? Consider how greate a p^{r}oblemes holdes wicked men. For neyth^{r} can they get light & vayne rewardes wch they can not obtayne, but fayles in the top of height, neth^{r} does good effect hap to the wretched, evin the same that night & day they seeke. And yet in self same thing we see the good mens strength exceld. For as a man that walkes to that place where chefely he will com, being such as has no waye beyond, woldest thou not think him best foote man. So shouldest thou think him mightyest that can co^{m}rehend that end, beyond wch no farder is. Wherby it hapes that who co^{n}trary is, the same be wicked & weake all strength. For why doo they followe vice, leaving vertue behinde them? For ignorance of good? but what is more feeble than Ignorance blyndnes? But they knowe what follow then ought? But their lust doth ov^{r}throw them. So doth inte^{m}pera^{n}ce the frayle men, that in vice be delyted. But wittingly & knowing doo they leave that is good, & so bend them to vice? This waye not only w^{t}out powre, but they leave to be.

For they that forsake the co^{m}mon end of all thinges that be, they leave the^{m}selves to be, wch may seeme straunge to men, that evill men (that many be) we shall not saye to be. But so the case standith. For they that evill be, I deny the^{m} not to be yll, but I deny that they be purely or simply. For all we call a Carcas, a dead man, simply we can not call him man. So vicious men we grau^{n}te they to be yll, but absolutely to be, that can we not co^{n}fesse. For ther is that keepe & retaynes natures order. Ther is that fayles fro^{m} this, & leaves that in theyr nature is grafted. but thou will saye

60-Recto

wilt saye: yll men may doo. Neth^{r} can I deny but this powre to doo coms not of force, but of weakenes. For they can doo yll wch they should not doo, if they wolde remayne in their Creatio^{n} of good, wch possibilitie to doo in not dooing shewes they can doo nothing. For yf, as we have gathered afore, evill be nothing, when but only the yll, they can doo, Wicked men can doo nothing. [B] That is playne. [P] And that yo^{u} may understand what is the force of this powre, we have defynde afore, That nothing is fuller of force, than the greatest good. But that can not the wicked doo. But what man is it that think man can doo all? [B] None but a mad man will so think. [P] And that the same can do yll to. [B] Wold god they could not q^{t} I. [P] Whan then he is mightyest that can doo all good, & mightyest men in yll, can not such thinges obtayne. Then is it playne that they can lest doo that be wicked. And so it haps that rightly we have shewed, all powre co^{n}sist in thinges to be obtayned. And all such referd to greatest good, as to the Top of Natures best. but possibilitie of wicked acte can not be refered to good, desyred th^{r}fore it ought not to be, and all powre is to be desyred. Yt followes th^{r}fore, possibilitie of evill men is no powre. By all w^{ch}, the powre of good men plainly appeeres, & makes undouted the weakenes of wicked men, veryfyeng Platoes sentence to be true. That only wyse men can p^{er}form that they desyre to do. but wicked men use only that they will. but what they most desyre, can not obtayne. For they doo certain thinges, wch delyteing, they suppose they have obtayned the good that they desyre, but obtayne it they can not. For reproche nev^{r} coms to blisse[.]

*2. Myter.

[P] Those wch you see as kings

Set in top of hyest peak,
Flourishing w^{t} purple fayre
Envyroned w^{t} dreadfull Armes,
w^{t} Irefull looke that threats
for harts Ire scant drawing breth,

Yf any

60-Verso

If any take from Wicked men
of false honor ye Coovre,
within shall see their Lords
straightenid †guyves to beare,
Hither lust them drawes,
here Ire their mynds afflicts,
who styrred, raysith stormes,
sorrow, or ye taken weaves.
Or slipper hopes torment
wherfore whom one head
So many tyrants beares,
He doth not that he Wold,
Prest w^{t} so wicked Lords.

3. pr.

[P] See yo^{u} not in how greate a showe, wicked thinges be wrapt in, & w^{t} how greate a light, godlynes shynith. By wch it is playne, that nev^{r} reward wantes to good, nor punishm^{t} to wicked folke. For it is no wrong that of thinges don, that be eche rewarde, for wch eche thing is don, As a Runner in a Race, has a garland for wch he ran in rewarde. [B] But we have shewed how blisse is that self good, for wch all thinges be don. Then it followes that the only good is sett as the univ^{r}sall rewarde to men and this from good men can not be devided. For neyth^{r} can he be iustly called a good man by right, that wantith true good. Th^{r}fore good conditio^{n}es can nev^{r} want rewarde. For tho evill men afflicte them, a wise mans garland shall not fayle nor with^{r}. For oth^{r} mens wickdnes can not pluck awaye the true hono^{r} fro^{m} honest myndes. For if he reioyce at ought receavid from outward meane, som oth^{r} man or he that gave it, might take it awaye. But because Godlynes it self suffisith then shall he want reward, when so he leaves to be. Lastly, Since all rewarde is th^{r}fore desyred, because it is beleevid good, who can think an honest man w^{t}out rewarde? but of what? Of that that is fayrest

& greatest

61-Recto

& greatest. Reme^{m}ber this breefe that a little afore I gave yo^{u} to be the cheefest, & so conclude. When the greatest good is blissfullnes, then must needes be happy that are good, because they are so. And they that be happy, must needes be lyke to god. Therfore good mens rewarde is such as neyth^{r} any daye drawes awaye, nor powre minish, nor Ire darken, but like to him they be. W^{ch} being true, no wise man may doubte of the wicked mans inseparable payne: For when both good & yll, payne & rewarde be crosst one to anoth^{r}, hit followes that such rewarde as hapes to goodnes the same must needes be of co^{n}trary sorte, for payne of wicked. For all sinceritie to the honest is rewarde, So to the wicked their owne unhappynes is their plague, So all who ev^{r} is punisht, must needes be wicked. Yf th^{r}fore they wold waye well themselves, can they suppose the^{m} voyde of payne, whose wickednis in all ylles not only touchith them, but grevously infectes? See on the oth^{r} syde, such parte as is to the good. Contrary, what payne doth follow the^{m}. I have taught yo^{u} afore that all that is, must be one, and that the only good is one. Then hit followes, what so that is, that seems to be good. Then whosoev^{r} faylith fro^{m} that good, he leaves to be. So that when evill they be, they leave to be that they were. But to proove that men they were, the forme of their humayne body shewith, but turned into malice, they have left their humayne nature.

And since that true pietie alone may lift up a man, It followes that who^{m} wickednes hath throwen downe from state of man, hath cast him downe beneth the merite of man. So it hapes that who^{m} transformed thou seest w^{t} vice, thou mayst not suppose him a man. The violent Robber of otheres goodes, is fervent in his Robberyes, swellith in coveting & mayest call him woolfelyke, feerce & co^{n}tentious, exercises his tongue in bralles, evin lyke a dog. The secret Lurker Ioyes w^{t} fraude to catche, and so as foxlyke, untemperate in yre he chasith, & men beleeve him a lyar, but fearfull & flyeng, fearith & dreadith that needes not, And he to deere is co^{m}pared. The sluggy & dullard languishith, & lyke an Asse doth lyve.

The light

61-Verso

The light & unco^{n}stant man, changes his intentes, & differs so, nought fro^{m} the byrdes, & is plunged in fylthy and uncleane Lustes, And is kept in the delyte of his own Lewdnes, And so *[ ] it haps that he that forsaking honesty, leaves to be a man, for not to be able to attayne a divine state is tourned to the beastly.

*3. Myter.

[P] Ulisses Captaines sayles
And sayling ships in Sea
Eurus to Iland brought:
The Goddess fayre sitting
As borne of Phoebus Lyne,
To her new guests
the Charmed Cup doth give:
w[ch] as in divers sortes
herbs Ruler guides her hand,
This man the Bores †Snowte do cover
An other y[e] †Marmican Lyon
w[t] tusk and pawe induith
This lyke to y[e] wolf new borne
whan weepe he wold, he howles,
An other as Indian Tigar
walkes in his house as mylde,
though from many Evills
the winged Arcadian God
Pityeng the beseeged captaine,
from Guests plague preservid,
Yet wicked Cup the Saylars
with mouthes supt up,
And Swyne changed, Ceres corne,
For foode of Acorn chosen,
To Lost men naught remayned

of body

62-Recto

of body nor of Voyce.
Only theyr mynde stable above
whom the monsters suffer wayles.
O hand to weake, nor herbes of powre,
though Lyms to change,
Harts yet alter may not
within bydes mans strength
hyd in his Towre.
Those vennoms w[t] more force
Man from himself w[t]drawes,
who though y[e] body not
The Soule w[t] wounds assayles[.]

*4. prose.

[B] I see q^{t} I, that vicious men have no wro^{n}g, tho they be sayde by p^{ro}p^{er}tie of their mynde, to beastes be transformed, tho in show they keepe the forme of humayne body. And yet I wolde not have that the cruell & wicked mynde should be sharpnid by the fall of good men. [P] Neyther is it q^{t} she, as in convenyent place I will showe. And yet if that were taken away from them, that they are beleevid to have, the wickedst payne should be in greatest parte releeved. For that that may p^{er}chaunce seeme impossible, hit must needes be that wicked men be unhappyer when they have fulfilled their desyres, then yf they could not gett what they wish. For yf a wretched thing hit be, to wish that is naught, It is much more wretched to doo yt: w^{t}out w^{ch}, the desyre of a wretched mynde wold fall. Wh^{r}fore whan ech man hath his own misery, It must needes be that by tryple misfortune they be vexed who^{m} thou dost see have a will to doo the worst. [B] I grau^{n}te it q^{t} I, And yet that quickly they might want this misfortune, I wish them deprived of possibilitie to doo in mischeefe. [P] They shall want it q^{t} she, sooner p^{er}chau^{n}ce than eyth^{r} thou Woldest, or they themselves think they may. For neyth^{r} is any thing so long in the short measure of o^{r} lyfe, that an immortall mynde may suppose to tarry to long. Whose greate hope & high work of mischeefe, oft is desroyed by an unlookt for & souden end, wch settes an end to their misery. For yf iniquitie make men miserable, he must be more wicked that longer lastes, whom most unhappy I should Iudge, yf their last death might not end their woe. For yf we co^{n}clude the truth of wickednes misfortune, infinite must we suppose that misery that is ev^{r}lasting. [B] Wonderfull thing q^{t} I, is this declara^{ti}on and hard to be grau^{n}ted, but I knowe they to well agree to such thinges as before have bene exprest. [P] Rightly dost thou think q^{t} she, and who so

62-Verso

and who so thinkes a hard co^{n}clu^{ti}on is made. It were reason he should shew that there hath bene som falshode in the p^{ro}posicion, or that the tyeng of their argumente booteth not for a necessary co^{n}clu^{ti}on. Or eles all the abovesaid grau^{n}ted, there is no cause to Cavill in the subsequent. For this that I saye, not onely seems not wonderfull, but by such thinges as are alledged most necessary. [B] What? q^{t} I, [P] I saye that happyer be wicked men whan they suffer punishm^{t}, than those who^{m} no payne of Iustice touchith. Neyther mynde I now to speake of that every man thinkes, That wicked conditions being corrected by revenge, & brought to the right way by terro^{r} of their prison, to oth^{r} men for example to shun their faultes. But in oth^{r} sorte I suppose the wicked unhappy, tho there were no cause of correctio^{n} to make them unpunished, nor no respecte of ensample. [B] What should this oth^{r} waye be? [P] Have we not sayde afore, that good men be lucky, & evill miserable? [B] So it is. [P] Yf oth^{r} fore som goodnes chau^{n}ce to misery, Is it not much more happyer for him than if his misery were alone by ytself w^{t}out any goodnes mixture. [B] So it seems q^{t} I. [P] But if to that miserable man that wantes all good thinges that evill be added to him to be alone, is he not much more to be acco^{m}pted unhappy, whose misfortune is shewed him thorow the participa^{ti}on of som good? [B] What els? [P] Therfore wicked men, whan they are punisht, have some good Ioyned w^{t} hit, that is, their punishment, wch for Iustice sake, is in it self good. And then when they want their correction, there is som thing besydes of evill, wch is, want of punishment, wch desernably the self hast confest is the greatest yll Iniquitie can have. More unhappy th^{r}fore are Wicked folkes, when they want theyr punishm^{t}, than whan they receave their Iust rewarde. For greatest iniquitie is co^{m}mytted, when Iust men be vexed, & Wicked slyp fro^{m} their rewarde. [B] Who can this denye? [P] Wh^{r}fore ech man must needes grau^{n}te that all that is good, must needes be iust, And yll, that is the co^{n}trary. [B] These be such thinges needes must follow the above co^{n}cluded. But I pray the

Quoth I

63-Recto

q^{t} I, shall ther be no soules punishm^{t} after the dead body? [P] Very greate qt she, of wch som be used by better paynes, oth^{r} by a pacifieng Cleme^{n}cy. But now my mynd is a little of these thinges to dispute, For this eith^{r} we have don, that them mightest knowe, the unwo^{r}thy powre of evill men is none at all, evin such as thou co^{m}play=nedst were voyde of punishment, that thou mightest see they nev^{r} want the payne of their wickednis. And that the libertie wch thou wisshedst should be ended, thou mightest learne, not to be long. And so much more unhappy, if longer, most unlucky, yf eternall. And they I sayde that wicked folkes were more miserable, shu^{n}ning their iust payne, than punisht w^{t} their right revenge. So followes it true w^{t} my opinion. That they are greevid w^{t} sorest punishm^{tes}, when they are supposed lesse plagued. [B] Whan I co^{n}sider thy reasons sayd I, I can suppose nothing more true, but yf I turne me to mans Iudgem^{t}, who is he to who^{m} not only these thinges will not seeme to be beleevid, but skarcely to be †hard. So it is q^{t} she. For they can not that have used their eys to darknes, up to the light of a cleere truthe. And like they be to such byrd whose sight the night doth cleere, & daye darkenes. For while they beholde not the order of thinges, but their own affections, They suppose the libertie & lack of payne for their faultes, the happiest. But now Looke what the ev^{r}lasting light makith. Yf to best thou doo apply thy mynde, thou shalt neede no Iudge to defer thy rewarde. Thou thy self hast Ioyned the to the Excellency. Yf thou turn thy

indevores

63-Verso

indevores to worsse, beyond thy self seeke no Revenger. Thou thy self to worst hast throwen the, & lookest to heaven & Clayen earth by fyttes. when all outward thinges fayles the, by thyne owne reason shalt thou p^{er}ceave the differe^{n}ce between Skye & Claye. but the vulgar cares not for this. What tho? Shall we speake of such thinges now as shewes men most lyke beastes? what if a man Loosing his sight hath forgotten that ev^{r} he had it, shall he suppose he lackes nothing of a mans p^{er}fection? Shall we suppose these men, though they see, to be blynde? They will not leave so, but will w^{t} c^{r}tain ground of reason, know that they are more unhappy that doo wrong than those that suffer it. [B] I wold fayne know these Reasons said I.

[P] Thou dost not denye, a wicked man is wo^{r}thy of all payne. [B] I deny it not.

[P] You think to, They are unhappy that div^{r}s wayes are wicked, such as are wo^{r}thy punishm^{t} th^{r}fore, no doute are myserable. [B] Yt agreith well. [P] Yf th^{r}fore thou satest as a

Iudge, on who^{m} woldst thou inflicte the payne, eyth^{r} on him that made or suffred the wro^{n}g? [B] I doute not but that I wold satisfie the sufferer by the punishm^{t} of y^{e} †Acto^{r}. Then wret = cheder is the maker than the Receave^{r}: [B] It is Reason, [P] for this & in any oth^{r} causes all hanging on one roote, hit appeeres that synne of his own nature, makes men wretched, And that misery is not y^{e} Receavores misery, but the gyveres. But Orators do oth^{r}wise. They go about to move co^{m}misera^{ti}on of the Iudges, for they that have co^{m}mytted som greate & cruell thing, when rath^{r} a iuster Co^{m}misera^{ti}on ought to be had of such as be not brought by Irefull Accuseres, but by such as themselves bemones & takes co^{m}passion of, as though they wold bring the sick to the phisician & cutt of the disease by the false punishment, by wch eyther the indevo^{r} of the defenderes should roole, or if it should p^{ro}ffit the^{m}, must be turned into the forme of the Accusation. But wicked men, yf they see any but a small Clyft where verture is to be seene, where wicked vice they may putt of by paynes Crueltie, under coulo^{r} of reco^{m}pensing vertue, will not call their Crueltye, but will refuse their defendors Labo^{r}, & give themselves wholly to the Accuseres & Iudges, So as wise men have no place left then for hate. For who but a very foole will malice a good man? And who but he that lackes reason, will not hate the yll. For as the bodyes sicknes, So is vice the myndes disease, evin as we suppose that sicke men deserve not hate, but co^{m}misera^{ti}on, So ought they not be p^{er}fected but pitied, whose myndes (than all sicknes bitterer), Iniquitie hath assayled.

*What boutes

Appendix IV
A Third Draft of Book IV, Meter 2

[Book IV, Meter 2]

52-Recto

**2. M.*

Those wch you see as kings
Sit in y^{e} top of hyest seate
Florishing w^{t} purple fayre,
Envyrond w^{t} dredfull armes
w^{t} Ireful Looke that threats
for hartes Ire scant drawing breth
Yf any take fro^{m} wicked men
of false honor ye Covre
w^{t}in shall see theyr Lordes
straygħtenid †gyves to beare
hither Lust them drawes
heere Ire their myndes afflicts
who styerid Raysith stormes
Sorow or the taken †weares
or slypper hopes tourm^{te}
wherfore when one head
So many tyrants bears
he doth not that he wold
prest w^{t} so Wicked Lords[.]

Textual and Explanatory Notes

Computation of Days and Hours

Location Designations	Reference Designations	Notes
1-Recto-1-Verso	––	these small sheets contain a partial listing of the English translations of the *Consolation of Philosophy*; this listing is a late addition to the items collated into the MS; the listing was probably prepared and inserted at the time of binding
3-Recto-5-Recto	––	these sheets contain a brief *Vita* of Boethius; the *Vita* is a late addition to the items collated for the MS; this *Vita* was probably prepared and inserted at the time of binding
7-Recto-8-Verso	––	the variant copy of the Computation that appears on 7-Recto has been moved to Appendix I (First Variant Copy); this is the first, in the order of appearance in the MS, of the three variant copies collated into the MS
9-Recto	––	this is the second, in the order of appearance in the MS, of the three variant copies of the Computation; this variant appears to be the earliest inscription; it prefaces the translation here because "first-draft versions" of all elements in the translation appear in the body of this edition

Location Designations	Reference Designations	Notes
1	The Queenes	although this 9-Recto inscription of the Computation appears in the MS after the 7-Recto version (see Appendix I, First Variant), and before the 10-Recto version (see Appendix I, Third Variant), it was probably inscribed first, as evidenced by its multiple crossings out and corrections; the beginning date of translation, 10 October 1593, agrees with the other two variants; the date of 8 November as the concluding date for the translation agrees with the third variant but not with the second
5	Of w^{ch}	all three variants agree that Elizabeth I left thirteen days free of translation; this second variant and the third variant leave the particular days unspecified
6	[w^{ch}]	this word is inscribed above the line as part of a whole phrase, "in wch her"; this phrase has been crossed out, but the "w^{ch}" seems to be needed to complete the phrase "in her," which appears below it, in the text; it is possible that the correction was crossed out when the original inscription should have been crossed out
9	So	the number of days, seventeen, devoted to translation specified here agrees with the third variant, but not with the first, which specifies twelve days
note	17 dayes	this note is inscribed in a later hand, in the left-hand margin, preceding the tenth line of text
11	And	this second variant, in the order of appearance in the MS (but first in order of inscription), allows "either twenty-six or twenty-seven hours" for translation; the first variant allows twenty-four, and the third variant allows twenty-six

Location Designations	Reference Designations	Notes
note	[2]6 hours	this note is inscribed in a later hand, in the left-hand margin, preceding the fourteenth line of text; the "2" is obscured in the binding
15	The number	this information appears only in this variant; it probably refers to the number of pages [88] in the Latin text either used by the amanuensis during the translating process or consulted by Bowyer when he compiled the Computation of Days
9-Verso	--	see Appendix I, Third Variant, and the explanatory notes for 9-Verso
10-Recto	--	see Appendix I, Third Variant, and the explanatory notes for 10-Recto
11-Verso	--	see Appendix I, Third Variant, and the explanatory notes for 11-Verso

The Queen's Translation of Boethius's *De Consolatione Philosophiae*

Book I

	Location Designations	Reference Designations	Notes
	Book I		
	rubric	[Book One]	there is no rubric for Book One; all the other books have rubrics
Meter 1			
	rubric	*1. Myter.*	Elizabeth I's hand
	1	*Righmes*	almost all of the meters are inscribed in Elizabeth I's hand (for exceptions to this general rule, see the notes for IV Meter 2; IV Meter 5; IV Meter 6; and V Meter 2); with few exceptions, most prose passages are in the non-italic hand of amanuenses; unless otherwise noted, italic type in the edition signifies entries in Elizabeth I's hand
Prose 1			
	1	*While*	Elizabeth I's hand continues throughout Prose 1
	38	*vres*	an odd abbreviation; probably "verses" is intended (see the note below for I Prose 4, line 67, for a similar, odd abbreviation)
Meter 2			
	rubric	*2. Myter.*	Elizabeth I's hand
Prose 2			
	1	*but*	Elizabeth I's hand continues throughout Prose 2
Meter 3			
	rubric	*3.Myt.*	Elizabeth I's hand

	Location Designations	Reference Designations	Notes
Prose 3			
	1	*No*[*w*]	Elizabeth I's hand continues into line 18 of Prose 3
	18	Have	a "first" amanuensis's non-italic hand begins with this word; this is the first of what appear to be the hands of three amanuenses: (1) this initial amanuensis; (2) the "second" amanuensis, who is the primary amanuensis for most of the first-draft inscription of the text (see the note below for information on I Prose 4, line 10); and (3) the amanuensis of the fragmentary second- and third draft inscriptions of the text (see Appendix II, Appendix III, and Appendix IV)
	31	Cauni	Elizabeth I retains the Latin genitives for these three names; most proper names are Anglicized in the MS
	32	[. . .]	torn page; L. *pervetusta* [ancient; very old]
	38	despi[sed]	frayed right margin; the end of the word is obscured
Meter 4			
	rubric	*4.Myter.*	Elizabeth I's hand
Prose 4			
	1	*Knowest*	Elizabeth I's hand continues into line 10 of Prose 4
	10	w[ch]	a "second" amanuensis's hand, identified in Pemberton's Introduction (xi) as that of Thomas Windebank, begins with this word, at the end of prose 4, line 10; this is the hand of the primary amanuensis, and it will continue throughout most of the MS

	Location Designations	Reference Designations	Notes
	54	[basenis] Wickednes	"Wickednes" first was inscribed in the primary text and then underlined; "basenis" then was inscribed above; perhaps we see evidence here of Elizabeth I's use of the underline to indicate a translation that should be revisited and perhaps corrected later; "basenis" was inscribed above by the amanuensis, perhaps as a correction, but the underlined word was never crossed out below (see the note below for V Prose 1, line 41)
	67	tres	"[let]tres" was intended (see Appendix II, where the abbreviation seems to have been interpreted as "[let]tres" in the fragmentary second-draft inscription of this book) (see the note above for I Prose 1, line 38 for a similar abbreviation); [L. *litteris*]
	71	*Canius*	amanuensis's italic hand
	72	*Caius*	amanuensis's italic hand, for all three units of the name; "C" appears, but "G" obviously was intended
	73	*Yf I had*	amanuensis's italic hand
	74	co^m^play[n]	torn page
	79	*Yf ther*	amanuensis's italic hand
	95	[of]	hole in manuscript
	103	[. . .]	torn page; possibly "there" was inscribed
	105	*Obey thy God*	amanuensis's italic hand
	108	*Symmacus*	amanuensis's italic hand

	Location Designations	Reference Designations	Notes
Meter 5			
	rubric	*5.Myter.*	Elizabeth I's hand
	catchword	[no catchword]	no catchword appears
	41	*O now*	the whole line is obscured, and some tears or holes occur along the line; this damage is due to repeated folding along the line; only this meter appears on this sheet, and the following sheet is blank; perhaps this is an indication of the separation and subsequent return of a sheet prior to the collation of the MS; some the sheets do not evidence folding, and the majority that do, the folding varies: some into thirds, some into halves and then again into quarters
	47	*the stable*	following this final verse of Meter 5, the lower quarter of the sheet remains blank
	19-Verso		
	note	The First Booke	this note is written sideways, right-to-left, from the right-hand margin; 19-Verso has two quarter-page fragments affixed, right-to-left, in its lower half; this note appears on the upper of the two quarter-page fragments
Prose 5			
	1	wo[es]	this word, and particularly its ending, are obscured by discoloration of the top of the sheet
Meter 6			
	rubric	*6.M.*	Elizabeth I's hand

	Location Designations	Reference Designations	Notes
	1	[*sm*^{e}]	an odd abbreviation, unique in the MS; *hevy Cancer* (June 21 and following) brings summer, so the abbreviation probably indicates the season, "summer"
	22	*seest suffer*	these two words are inscribed below, and to the right, of the primary line of text; a caret above them seems to indicate that they should be inserted at the end of line 22; the word *seest* is difficult to interpret because the letter "s" is inscribed almost like an "f"
	21-Recto [bottom half]-22-Verso [top quarter]		
		A serious problem seems to have occurred at this point in the inscription of the MS sheets. The top half of 21-Recto presents the final verses of Meter 6, inscribed on the sheet as a block of text; the bottom half of 21-Recto presents the opening verses of Meter 7, inscribed on the sheet in two columns.	
		Two blank sheets, 21-Verso-22-Recto, then separate the opening and the ending verses of Meter 7.	
		The final eight verses of Meter 7 are inscribed at the top of 22-Verso, in two columns. A line is drawn across the sheet under the inscription of these closing verses of Meter 7. Beneath the line, the inscription of Prose 6 begins.	
		In this edition, all of Meter 7 has been moved to its proper sequential position in the text, following Prose 6.	

	Location Designations	Reference Designations	Notes
Prose 6			
	--	6.pr.	Prose 6 begins on the bottom three-quarters of 22-Verso, following the final verses of Meter 7; in this edition, Prose 6 has been moved to its proper sequential position, following Meter 6; as noted above, Meter 7 has been moved to follow Prose 6
	29	may a man	the final letters of *may* and *man*, the "y" and the "n" look very much alike in this phrase
	[23-Verso]	--	23-Verso contains two page-fragments affixed to the sheet, with the larger fragment above, the smaller fragment below; the page-fragments are described below; both fragments are badly damaged
	page-fragment upper edge above 46	-------	the first of the two page-fragments on 23-Verso is affixed here, with frayed edges at the top (just above line 46, which is the first line of text on the fragment) and at the bottom (just under line 61, which is the last line of text on the fragment); it is a half-page fragment
	46	[. . .]	word obscured by discoloration of the page-fragment; L. *vices* [changes *or* vicissitudes]
	48	thy hoste	underlined in MS; no correction is indicated
	49	great[est]	the final letters of this word are obscured by discoloration at the top of the page-fragment

	Location Designations	Reference Designations	Notes
	57	[. . .]	the word is obscured by an ink blot; L. *induantur* [possibly *in-dued*]
	page-fragment lower edge below 61	--------	a frayed edge marks the bottom of the first page-fragment
	page-fragment upper edge	--------	another frayed edge marks the top of the second page-fragment; this second fragment is the shorter of the two page-fragments
	catchword	Dym cloudes	on this badly-damaged quarter-page fragment, the catchword for Meter 7 has been preserved
	note	The fyrst	this note is written sideways, right-to-left, from the right-hand margin
	page-fragment lower edge	--------	a frayed edge marks the bottom of the second page-fragment
	21-Recto [bottom half]		
		--	as noted above, Meter 7 has been moved from its position in the MS (between Meter 6 and Prose 6) to its proper sequential position, here, following Prose 6
Meter 7			
	rubric	7.m.	verses 1–24 of Meter 7 are inscribed on the bottom half of 21-Recto in two columns, with verses 1–10 to the left and verses 11–24 to the right
	22-Verso [top quarter]		

	Location Designations	Reference Designations	Notes
		--	the remaining verses of Meter 7 appear on the top quarter of 22-Verso, in two columns, with verses 25–28 to the left and verses 29–31 to the right
	note	here endith	this note appears, following the inscription of Meter 7, in the right-hand margin of the sheet, just above a line drawn to separate the final verses of Meter 7 from the opening lines of Prose 6
	line following 31		
		-------	in the MS, a line is drawn across the width of 22-Verso to separate the final verses of Meter 7 from the opening lines of Prose 6
	22-Verso [bottom three-quarters]-		
	23-Verso	--	Prose 6, inscribed on these sheets, has been moved to its proper sequential position in the text, following Meter 6 and preceding Meter 7
	24-Recto	--	a badly frayed blank sheet, affixed to a blank whole-page, is preserved here; the reason for its preservation cannot be discerned
	24-Verso	--	a badly frayed blank sheet, affixed to a blank whole-page, is preserved here; a watermark appears at the center of the sheet; few watermarks appear on sheets in the MS
	25-Recto	--	two lines were inscribed at the top of this sheet, but then crossed out; otherwise, the sheet is blank

Book II

	Location Designations	Reference Designations	Notes
Prose 1			
	4	*hit*	corrected in Elizabeth I's hand
	5	*shaped*	corrected in Elizabeth I's hand
	13	*bifal*	corrected in Elizabeth I's hand
	19	*hath*	corrected in Elizabeth I's hand
	26	*hatest*	corrected in Elizabeth I's hand
	30	*p*^{re}*nt*	this word (*present*) is abbreviated similarly throughout the MS
	35	*wisched*	corrected in Elizabeth I's hand
Meter 1			
	rubric	*1.Myter*	Elizabeth I's hand
	4	won ma^{n}	underlined in the MS; no correction is indicated
Prose 2			
	20	[to]	a "to" may have been omitted here; a "to" seems necessary to complete the sense of the passage
	31	Paul	Aemilius Paulus
	27-Recto		
	catchword	[no catchword]	no catchword appears
	35	thressholl	the final word on 27-Recto is repeated as the first word on 27-Verso; as noted, there is no catchword at the bottom of 27-Recto
	39	*desirest*	corrected in Elizabeth I's hand
Meter 2			
	rubric	*2. Myter.*	Elizabeth I's hand
	18	[*ove*^{r}]	orthography unclear; possibly "over" was intended
Prose 3			
	4	*florist*	corrected in Elizabeth I's hand

	Location Designations	Reference Designations	Notes
	4	*over*	corrected in Elizabeth I's hand
	4	*Retorik*	amanuensis's italic hand
	4	th[e]y	letters obscured at the binding edge
	7	. . . .	the text stops midway in line 7; line 7 then continues as a series of dots
	8	~ / ~ / ~ /	a series of waves and back-slashes are entered from the beginning of line 8 to its midpoint, where the text recommences
Meter 3			
	rubric	*3. M.*	Elizabeth I's hand
Prose 4			
	21	*thinges*	corrected in Elizabeth I's hand
	41	*ther*	corrected in Elizabeth I's hand
	56	*hit*	corrected in Elizabeth I's hand
	57	*hit*	corrected in Elizabeth I's hand
	58	*getting*	corrected in Elizabeth I's hand
	59	*her*	corrected in Elizabeth I's hand
	63	*hit*	corrected in Elizabeth I's hand
	64	*wold*	corrected in Elizabeth I's hand
	66	*w[t]*	corrected in Elizabeth I's hand
	68	*by*	corrected in Elizabeth I's hand
Meter 4			
	rubric	*4 Myter*	Elizabeth I's hand
Prose 5			
	46	exclama[[ti]]on	the superscribed abbreviation appears to have been omitted in this word
	50	[no]	the right-hand margin of the page is torn

	Location Designations	Reference Designations	Notes
	51	outwar[d]	the right-hand margin of the page is torn
	59	[yo(u)]	the right-hand margin of the page is both obscured by discoloration and torn
	60	humayn[e]	the right-hand margin of the page is torn
Meter 5			
	rubric	*5. M.*	Elizabeth I's hand
	8	*serche*	L. *sericus* (adj.) silken; *sericum* (n.) silk; Elizabeth could have read *serum* as *sericum* and translated it as *serche*
	27	*O who the*	the final four verses of this meter are written sideways, right-to-left, in the left-hand margin; they are separated from the text by a line drawn top-to-bottom along the left-hand edge of the text
Prose 6			
	1	*What*	Elizabeth I's hand continues into line 12 of Prose 6
	12	that	amanuensis's non-italic hand begins with this word
	26	Bucidides	Busiris, king of Egypt
	32	*disagreing*	corrected in Elizabeth I's hand
	34	*good*	corrected in Elizabeth I's hand
	34	*wiche*	corrected in Elizabeth I's hand
	46	who[m]	object of the verb "acco[m]panyes"
Meter 6			
	rubric	*6. M.*	Elizabeth I's hand
Prose 7			
	2	*pride*	corrected in Elizabeth I's hand
	12	*Creatures*	corrected in Elizabeth I's hand

	Location Designations	Reference Designations	Notes
	12	*knowe*	corrected in Elizabeth I's hand
	14	drynes	partially (the final "s") corrected in Elizabeth I's hand
	14	*distended*	corrected in Elizabeth I's hand
	34	*have*	corrected in Elizabeth I's hand
	41	*outward*	corrected in Elizabeth I's hand
	42	*twixt*	corrected in Elizabeth I's hand
	42	*infinitie*	corrected in Elizabeth I's hand
	42	*and*	corrected in Elizabeth I's hand
	42	*ending*	corrected in Elizabeth I's hand
	60	*gial*	corrected in Elizabeth I's hand
Meter 7			
	rubric	*7. Myter*	Elizabeth I's hand
Prose 8			
	1	*but*	Elizabeth I's hand continues into line 11 of Prose 8
	11	in	amanuensis's non-italic hand begins with this word
	19	fellow sure	underlined in the MS; no correction is indicated
Meter 8			
	rubric	*8. Myter*	Elizabeth I's hand
	27	*O happy*	the final four verses of this meter are written sideways, right-to-left, in the left-hand margin; they are separated from the primary inscription of the meter by a line, drawn top-to-bottom along the meter's left-hand edge; a caret preceding "*O happy*" corresponds to a caret at the end of the primary inscription of the meter, indicating where the four verses are to be added, or read

	Location Designations	Reference Designations	Notes
	note	Here endes	this note is written at the bottom left-hand corner, in linear fashion, just below the verses that are written sideways above
	35-Verso		
	note	The second Booke	two quarter-page fragments are affixed, from right-to-left, across the bottom of this sheet; the top fragment contains this note, written right-to-left, from the right-hand margin

Book III

	Location Designations	Reference Designations	Notes
	rubric	thrid	*sic.*
Prose 1			
	13	bese[c]h	the "c" is omitted in the MS
Meter 1			
	rubric	*1. Mytre*	Elizabeth I's hand
Prose 2			
	5	in	the final word on 36-Recto is repeated as the first word on 36-Verso; it does not appear in the catchword in the MS
	21	of	the final word on line 20 is repeated as the first word on line 21; on line 20, "of" is inserted as a caret-addition ("partaking of") inscribed above a crossed-out word at the end of line 20
	21	fo[r]	the right-hand margin is torn

	Location Designations	Reference Designations	Notes
	37	no sure	probably meaning: *surely not*; a rhetorical response made by Philosophy to her own question
	38	*covetz*	corrected in Elizabeth I's hand
Meter 2			
	rubric	*2. Myter*	Elizabeth I's hand
	14	*and*	verses 14 and 15 are written sideways, right-to-left, in the right-hand margin; they are separated from the primary inscription of the meter by a line, drawn top-to-bottom, along the meter's left-hand edge; a caret preceding "*and furius*" corresponds to a caret between verses 13 and 16, indicating where the two verses are to be added
Prose 3			
	rubric	3.pr.	rubric is penciled in by a later hand
	1	yo[ur]	the right-hand margin of the page is torn
	16	[any]	word obscured by hole in page
	22	[]	hole torn in page, perhaps as a result of an attempted erasure; possibly "that" had been inscribed
	24	coms	grammatically, verb should agree with "co^{m}playntes"; "come" probably was intended
	32	[nor]	inscribed above line in a later hand, without caret
Meter 3			
	rubric	*3. M.*	Elizabeth I's hand

	Location Designations	Reference Designations	Notes
Prose 4			
	2	the[n]	hole torn in page, perhaps a result of an attempted erasure (see the note for Prose 3, line 22, above, which refers to the same tear, but on the reverse side of the sheet)
	31	N[ow]	obscured by a large ink blot
Meter 4			
	rubric	4. Mytre.	rubric is penciled in by a later hand
Prose 5			
	rubric	5. Prose	rubric is penciled in by a later hand
	17	garde[s th]at	obscured by a large ink blot
	30	*harme*	corrected in Elizabeth I's hand
Meter 5			
	rubric	*5. M.*	Elizabeth I's hand
	6	A |	a vertical line is drawn top-to-bottom along the right-hand margin of the text; an "A" inscribed at the end of line 6, just to the right of the text, but to the left of the line, indicates that an omitted verse should be added there
	6	| A	another "A," inscribed to the immediate right of the vertical line, corresponds to the "A" to its left; this second "A" marks the verse to be added; the verse is inscribed, in linear fashion, to the right of the vertical line, at line 6
Prose 6			
	rubric	6. prose.	rubric is penciled in by a later hand

	Location Designations	Reference Designations	Notes
	5	*be praised*	corrected in Elizabeth I's hand
	6	*laude*	corrected in Elizabeth I's hand
	6	*hit*	corrected in Elizabeth I's hand
Meter 6			
	rubric	*6. M.*	Elizabeth I's hand
Prose 7			
	Rubric	7. prose.	rubric is penciled in by a later hand
Meter 7			
	rubric	7. Myter	rubric is penciled in by a later hand
Prose 8			
	rubric	8. prose	rubric is penciled in by a later hand
	2	*whither*	corrected in Elizabeth I's hand
	14	*marvel*	corrected in Elizabeth I's hand
	16	*soudan*	corrected in Elizabeth I's hand
Meter 8			
	rubric	8. Myter	rubric is penciled in by a later hand
	catchword	[no catchword]	no catchword appears
Prose 9			
	rubric	9 Prose	rubric is penciled in by a later hand
	1	*Hitherto*	Elizabeth I's hand continues through line 12 of Prose 9
	13	Dost	amanuensis's non-italic hand begins with this word
	34	none	underlined in the MS; no correction is indicated
Meter 9			
	rubric	*9. M.*	Elizabeth I's hand

	Location Designations	Reference Designations	Notes
Prose 10			
	19	*Prince*	amanuensis's italic hand
	24	[to]	written "ot"
	28	have	verb should agree with "fath^{r}"; confusion could derive from some equivocation between "think that the fath^{r} has taken" and "think the fath^{r} to have taken"
	72	th[is]	an ink blot slightly obscures the last two letters of this word
Meter 10			
	rubric	*10. M.*	Elizabeth I's hand
Prose 11			
	rubric	11. prose	rubric is penciled in by a later hand
	1	*I*	Elizabeth I's hand continues into line 6 of Prose 11
	6	have	amanuensis's non-italic hand begins with this word
	30	to fly	underlined in the manuscript; the underline probably indicates a problem in translation (between the ideas of "willing" and "flying"); in this instance, there are two underlines in the text, which occurs nowhere else in the translation; the upper is under the phrase "to fly" only; the lower extends from an "ing" of will[ing] to the end of "to fly"; that "ing" has been crossed out, which might indicate at least a partial correction in response to this underline

	Location Designations	Reference Designations	Notes
	80	[Wh]at	the first two letters are legible, but badly obscured by an ink blot
	81	*wiche*	ten words are added here in Elizabeth I's hand
	83	*that*	seven words added here in Elizabeth I's hand
	catchword	[no catchword]	no catchword appears
Meter 11			
	rubric	11. Myter	rubric is penciled in by a later hand
Prose 12			
	rubric	11.pr.	the first rubric, inscribed in the amanuensis's hand as Prose 11, mislabels the passage
	rubric	12.pr.	a later rubric, penciled in by a later hand; corrects the mislabeling to Prose 12
	38	favo[r]	underlined in the MS; no correction is
	58	So hast thou not	underlined in the MS; the "not" appears as an addition above the line, but it does not appear in the main line of the text; it is possible that the underline was responded to, in this instance, by the addition of the "not" above the line of text
Meter 12			
	rubric	*12. M.*	Elizabeth I's hand
	49-Recto [upper quarter]		

	Location Designations	Reference Designations	Notes
	--	the final eight verses of Meter 12 are inscribed on the upper quarter of 49-Recto; the opening of Book IV occupies the lower quarter	
	59	[]	an obscure abbreviation follows *Et sic*; possibly "*Et sic. iij*" was intended

Book IV

	Location Designations	Reference Designations	Notes
	49-Recto	--	the final verses of III Meter 12, occupy the upper quarter of 49-Recto
	49-Recto [lower three-quarters]		
	rubric	The fourth	the inscription of Book IV begins after the first quarter page of 49-Recto, and it fills the lower three-quarters
Prose 1			
	12	ma[y do]	torn page
Meter 1			
	rubric	*1. M.*	Elizabeth I's hand

	Location Designations	Reference Designations	Notes
	7	And	verses 7 and 8 are written sideways, right-to-left, in the right-hand margin; a line drawn top-to-bottom along the right-hand edge of the meter separates the primary inscription from the two verses in the margin; a caret at the end of verse 6 indicates where the two verses are to be added; no corresponding caret accompanies the two verses in the margin
Prose 2			
	rubric	*2.pr.*	Elizabeth I's hand
	1	*Than*	Elizabeth I's hand continues through line 29 of Prose 2
	30	I	amanuensis's non-italic hand begins with this word
	40	ij	two, in Roman numerals
	42	ha[ve]	torn page
	45	ij	two, in Roman numerals
	75	str[range]	torn page; possibly "strange" was intended
	79	symply	underlined in MS; no correction is indicated
	52-Recto	––	
		Inscribed on 52-Verso, there are:	
		(1) the single, concluding line of Prose 2 at the top, followed by	
		(2) a copy of Meter 2, in the italic hand of an amanuensis.	
		The lower one-third of the sheet remains blank. The inscription of Meter 2, in the amanuensis's italic hand, has been moved to Appendix IV (A Third Draft of IV Meter 2).	

	Location Designations	Reference Designations	Notes
	52-Recto	[for]	an ink blot obscures this word; it is possible that the "for" from the catchword was repeated, and then became obscured
	53-Recto-56-Verso	––	these sheets contain the translation of IV Prose 3; an inscription of Meter 2 in Elizabeth I's hand (57-Recto) has been moved to precede Prose 3, to replace the inscription of Meter 2 found there in the amanuensis's italic hand; the amanuensis's inscription has been moved to Appendix IV
Meter 2			
	57-Recto	see the note for line 1, below	
	rubric	[no rubric]	no rubric appears for Elizabeth I's inscription of this meter
	note	This is before	this note, inscribed in linear fashion in the left-hand margin, indicates that Meter 2, inscribed here in Elizabeth I's hand, appears earlier in the MS, but inscribed in the amanuensis's italic hand (following Prose 2, on 52-Recto)
	note	See 2 Myter	this note, penciled in at the right-hand margin by a later hand, directs the reader to the proper sequential position for Elizabeth I's inscription of Meter 2, at 52-Recto
	1	*Thos*	
		This meter is inscribed in the primary text (among the first-draft inscriptions) in an amanuensis's italic hand, on 52-Recto.	

	Location Designations	Reference Designations	Notes
		"First-draft" inscriptions of Elizabeth I's translation appear in the body of this edition. Therefore, Meter 2, inscribed in the amanuensis's hand, has been moved to Appendix IV (A Third Copy of Book IV, Meter 2), and replaced here, among the first-draft inscriptions, by Elizabeth I's "first-draft" inscription.	
		The orthographic peculiarities in the amanuensis's inscription, which has been moved to Appendix IV, are consistent with those of the amanuensis who inscribed the fragmentary second-draft revisions of Book I and Book IV.	
		Elizabeth I's inscription of Meter 2, affixed in the MS to the bottom of 57-Recto, is followed, interestingly, by the fragmentary second-draft inscription of Book IV, 58-Recto-63-Recto (see Appendix III).	
		Thus, it appears that the sequence in which the three copies were inscribed (as indicated by orthographic similarities and differences) is as follows: 1) Elizabeth I's Meter 2 (57-Recto) was inscribed first; 2) Meter 2, the replacement copy (52-Recto), was inscribed next; 3) Meter 2, in the fragmentary reworking of Book IV, was inscribed last.	
		(See also the notes for: IV Meter 5; IV Meter 6; and V Meter 2; these meters, along with IV Meter 2, are the meters that evidence either full or partial inscription in hands other than that of Elizabeth I.)	
	catchword	[no catchword]	following the catchword, the lower one-third of this sheet is left blank
	57-Verso		
	The Third	this note is the only inscription on this sheet; it is written sideways, right-to-left, in the right-hand margin, on the lower half of the sheet	
	53-Recto	—	Prose 3 proceeds from here

	Location Designations	Reference Designations	Notes
Prose 3			
	rubric	3. prose	rubric is penciled in by a later hand
	rubric	iij. prose	this rubric, unique in the manuscript, is centered on the sheet, inscribed in the amanuensis's non-italic hand
	23	*Ire*	corrected in Elizabeth I's hand
Meter 3			
	rubric	*3. M.*	Elizabeth I's hand
	catchword	[no catchword]	no catchword appears
	31	[*may*]	the word is obscured in the MS, or possibly crossed out
Prose 4			
	45	But	the final word on 55-Recto is repeated as the first word on 55-Verso
	83	light	possibly "law" would be more accurate; L. *lex*
	56-Verso		
	note	In continuation	this note is penciled in by a later hand, in linear fashion, in the lower left-hand corner of the sheet
	56-Verso		
	[catchword]	what bootes	this catchword anticipates the opening words of Meter 4, which follows later, on 64-Verso.
	57-Recto-57-Verso	--	these two sheets contain: (1) Meter 2 in Elizabeth's hand (57-Recto) and (2) a marginal note (57-Verso); they have been moved to precede Prose 3, inscribed on 53-Recto and following

	Location Designations	Reference Designations	Notes
	58-Recto-63-Verso	--	
		A fragmentary revision of Book IV, complete from the beginning of Prose 1 (58-Recto) through the conclusion of Prose 4 (63-Verso) is inserted into the MS here. The first-draft inscription of the translation, from Meter 4 onward, then follows, from the top of 64-Recto.	
	64-Recto	--	the first-draft inscription of Book IV resumes here
Meter 4			
	rubric	*4. M. of*	Elizabeth I's hand; the rubric for this meter is inscribed in a slightly expanded form
	1	*What boutes*	see the note above, for 56-Verso [catchword]
Prose 5			
	2	hone[st]	the last two letters of the word are obscured by crossings out
Meter 5			
		This is the only meter that is exclusively in the hand of an amanuensis. Perhaps Elizabeth I's inscription of the meter was misplaced or lent out and never recovered; the amanuensis may have attempted here to reconstruct the translation, which could explain its unusual, "truncated" state (see also the notes for: IV Meter 2; IV Meter 6, and V Meter 2).	
		The hand that inscribed this meter is consistent with that of the amanuensis who inscribed the fragmentary second-draft revisions of the translation (see Appendix II and Appendix III).	
Meter 5			

	Location Designations	Reference Designations	Notes
	rubric	*5. Myter of*	Elizabeth I's hand; the rubric for this meter is inscribed in a slightly expanded form; Elizabeth I's translation of this meter greatly abbreviates the Latin original, which is inconsistent with her usual practice of literal translation
	1	*Yf man*	the orthographic peculiarities seen in this inscription (such as the repeated use of the abbreviation "y^{e}" for "the") are consistent with those of the amanuensis who inscribed the fragmentary second-draft inscriptions of Book I and Book IV (see Appendix II and Appendix III)
	3	*Bootes*	Boötes
Prose 6			
	rubric	6. prose	rubric is penciled in by a later hand
	20	*Purenes*	amanuensis's italic hand
	21	*Provide*^{n}*ce*	amanuensis's italic hand
	23	*Desteny*	amanuensis's italic hand
	23	[ ]	torn page
	32	*Fate*	amanuensis's italic hand
	44	*Provide*^{n}*ce*	amanuensis's italic hand
	46	*Fate*	amanuensis's italic hand
	47	*Provid.*	amanuensis's italic hand
	47	*Fate it self*	amanuensis's italic hand
	49	*Fates Force*	amanuensis's italic hand
	50	*Nature*	amanuensis's italic hand
	51	*Circles*	amanuensis's italic hand
	52	*Purenes*	amanuensis's italic hand
	59	*Fate*	amanuensis's italic hand

	Location Designations	Reference Designations	Notes
	62	*Destenyes*	amanuensis's italic hand
	64	*Eternity & Circle*	amanuensis's italic hand
	66	*Provide*^{n}*ce*	amanuensis's italic hand
	69	such	underlined in the MS; the word that follows *proceding* has been crossed out; no further correction is indicated
	98	*Phisician*	amanuensis's italic hand
	100	ther	underlined in the MS; no correction is indicated
	126	*A good man*	amanuensis's italic hand
Meter 6			
	--	--	this meter shows an unusual alternation between Elizabeth I's hand and that of her amanuensis (see also the notes for: IV Meter 2; IV Meter 5; and V Meter 2)
	rubric	*6. Myter. of*	Elizabeth I's hand; the rubric for this meter is inscribed in a slightly expanded form
	1	*If wary*	
		This meter begins with the words "*If wary*," written in Elizabeth I's hand; these words have been crossed out and replaced above with the same words in the amanuensis's italic hand, which continues through line 18.	
		The hand that inscribed this meter is consistent with the orthographic peculiarities of the amanuensis who penned the fragmentary second-draft inscriptions of Book I and Book IV.	

	Location Designations	Reference Designations	Notes
	12	*and seketh not*	this entire verse is added, as a correction in Elizabeth I's hand, above a line that has been crossed out below it; the first two words are underlined by Elizabeth I in the MS; no further correction is indicated
	13	*Ever*	amanuensis's italic hand resumes with this word
	19	*the Elementz*	Elizabeth I's hand resumes here and continues through line 29; the words "*All things*" were crossed out in the line and replaced above by "*the elementz all*," inscribed in Elizabeth I's hand
	30	*This*	amanuensis's italic hand resumes with this word
	47	*returnd*	corrected in Elizabeth I's hand
	48	*them*	corrected in Elizabeth I's hand
	48	*bond*	corrected in Elizabeth I's hand
Prose 7			
	rubric	7. prose	rubric is penciled in by a later hand
	69-Verso		
	catchword	is not	Prose 7 is interrupted following this catchword at the bottom of 69-Verso; the catchword anticipates the continuation of Prose 7 on line 34, at the top of 72-Recto

	Location Designations	Reference Designations	Notes
	70-Verso-71-Verso	--	these three sheets contain Meter 7; each sheet presents a portion of the meter inscribed on a quarter-page fragment affixed to the top third of each sheet: (1) 13 lines on 70-Verso, (2) 13 lines on 71-Recto, and (3) 9 lines plus a note on 71-Verso; Meter 7 has been moved to its proper sequential position in the text, following the concluding lines of Prose 7, on 72-Recto
	72-Recto	--	the concluding 9 lines of Prose 7 are inscribed on the top third of 72-Recto; this short closing passage has been moved to its proper sequential place in the text, ending Prose 7
	70-Verso [upper third]		
		--	see the note above for 70-Verso-71-Verso
Meter 7			
	rubric	*7. My.*	Elizabeth I's hand; the rubric for this meter is inscribed in a slightly expanded form
	13	*hardy*	the entry stops at mid-page, following this verse, and continues on the following sheet (71-Recto)
	71-Recto [upper third]		
		--	see the note above for 70-Verso-71-Recto
	26	*Cacus*	the inscription stops at mid-page, after this verse, and continues on the following sheet, 71-Verso

	Location Designations	Reference Designations	Notes
	71-Verso [upper third]		
		--	see the note above for 70-Verso-71-Recto
	35	*gives*	the entry stops at mid-page
	note	this is	Book IV ends at mid-page; this final note is inscribed, beginning at mid-line, just under the final verses of Meter 7
	72-Recto	--	this misplaced continuation of Prose 7 has been moved to follow 69-Verso
	73-Verso		
	note	The Fourth	this note is written sideways, right-to-left, on the upper of two quarter-page fragments, affixed to the lower half of the sheet

Book V

	Location Designations	Reference Designations	Notes
	title	fift	*sic.*
Prose 1			
	10	hable	an unusual spelling for "able"
	41	[is] be	"be" is underlined on the text line and "is" has been inscribed above; possibly the word "be" was questioned and then corrected to "is"; "be" was not crossed out (see the note above for I Prose 4, line 54)
Meter 1			
	rubric	*1. M.*	Elizabeth I's hand

	Location Designations	Reference Designations	Notes
Prose 2			
	rubric	2. prose	rubric is penciled in by a later hand; left-hand margin torn
Meter 2			
	rubric	2. M.	rubric is penciled in by a later hand; left-hand margin torn
	1	Cleere	the first three verses of Meter 2 are in the amanuensis's non-italic hand (see also the notes for: IV Meter 2; IV Meter 5; and IV Meter 6)
	4	*W*^{t} *weake*	Elizabeth I's hand begins with this word
Prose 3			
	31	The	the final word on 75-Verso is repeated as the first word on 76-Recto
	34	provided	underlined in the MS; no correction is indicated
	58	*What*	amanuensis's italic hand (for the entire line)
	72	unseparable	underlined in the MS; no correction is indicated
	73	(,than	parentheses and commas both appear together in the MS; commas probably preceded an upgrade to parentheses
	78	wish	underlined in MS; above this word, "wish was reinscribed, but then crossed out; "wish" is not crossed out in the primary line
Meter 3			
	rubric	*3. M.*	Elizabeth I's hand

	Location Designations	Reference Designations	Notes
Prose 4			
	78-Recto	--	Meter 4 is inscribed on this sheet; Meter 4 has been moved to its proper sequential position in the text, following Prose 4
	78-Verso	--	Prose 4 continues here
	27	of	the final word on 78-Recto is repeated as the first word on 78-Verso
	catchword	fre[e]	torn page
	72	*parceaveth*	amanuensis's italic hand
	79-Verso		
	92	ij	two, in Roman numerals
	78-Recto (see above)	--	Meter 4 has been moved to this position from 78-Recto in MS
Meter 4			
	rubric	*4. M.*	Elizabeth I's hand
	35	Applies	the three final verses of Meter 4 are inscribed sideways, bottom-to-top, and left-to-right, in the right-hand margin; they are separated from the text by a line drawn top-to-bottom along the right-hand edge of the meter; no caret has been provided to indicate where the three verses should be added
	80-Recto	--	Prose 5 follows from here
Prose 5			
	9	<u>wantes</u>	underlined in MS; perhaps questioning the translation of L. *cessit*; no correction is indicated
	14	know[t]	the superscripted "t" probably represents "-eth"

	Location Designations	Reference Designations	Notes
	27	[]	this word is difficult to decipher; possibly either "mis" or "not" was intended ("mans Reason doth [mis or not] think")
Meter 5			
	rubric	*5. M.*	Elizabeth I's hand
	10	[]	torn page
	14	*h*[*ed*]	right-hand margin torn
Prose 6			
	rubric	6. pr.	rubric is inscribed by a later hand
	15	wo[r]ld	"r" omitted; possibly to be superscripted; space was left between "wo" and "ld"
	19	yet that	phrase underlined in MS; the "shall com, &" has been inscribed above the line, which might represent a correction in response to the underline
	22	chau[nged that]	tear in the MS (along a fold line); only the first letters of the word are legible
	48	[T]h^{r}fore	tear in page
	54	& shall	underlined in MS; no correction is indicated
	72	know^{t}	the superscripted "t" probably represents "-eth"
	79	knoledge	the final word on 82-Recto is repeated as the first word on 82-Verso
	89	ij	two, in Roman numerals
	93	know^{t}	the superscripted "t" probably represents "-eth"
	124	but because	underlined in the MS; no correction is indicated

	Location Designations	Reference Designations	Notes
	125	tho[u]; [must]; [or]; [?]	holes in the MS along a fold line; the emendations suggested here are speculations
	151	[]	hole the in MS along a fold line
	153	yo^{r}self beholde	underlined in MS; no correction is discernible
	83-Verso		
	note	Fift Booke	the text ends some inches above the bottom of 83-Verso; this note is inscribed below the text, right-to-left, from the right-hand margin
	84-Recto-99-A-Verso		
		--	these sheets contain translations made by Elizabeth I that are not part of the translation of the *Consolatio*

Appendix I
First Variant of the Computation of Days

Location Designations	Reference Designations	Notes
7-Recto	The Computation	this is the first of three variant inscriptions of the Computation; it was inscribed in a "third" amanuensis's hand (a careful and highly legible hand, consistent with the hand that also inscribed the Fragmentary Second Draft inscriptions of Book I and Book IV); this is probably the final (third) inscription of the Computation, as indicated by the care shown in its inscription
1	Your Ma[tie]	10 October 1593 appears as the beginning date in all three variants; this variant gives 5 November as the concluding date, whereas the other two give 8 November as the concluding date
4	Out	all three variants agree that Elizabeth I left thirteen days free from translation; this variant is the only one that specifies the particular days left free and the purposes for which those thirteen were left free
4	hollyday[es]	tear in the MS, along a fold line
8	Which	
9	And	this variant allows two hours per day for translation; the other two allow one-and-one-half hours; this variant allows twenty-four hours total for the completion of the translation, whereas variant two allows twenty-six or twenty-seven hours and variant three allows twenty-six hours
8-Verso		

Location Designations	Reference Designations	Notes
note	Computation	the note appears on the lower of two quarter-page fragments affixed to the top half of 8-Verso; the note is written sideways, right-to-left, from the right-hand margin; the lower half of 8-Verso is blank
9-Verso		
note	15 November	this note is written sideways, right-to-left, from the right-hand margin, on a quarter-page fragment affixed lengthwise, just below the center of the sheet

Third Variant of the Computation of Days

Location Designations	Reference Designations	Notes
1	The Queenes	the beginning date of 10 October 1593 agrees with the other two variants; the concluding date of 8 November agrees with the second variant, but not with the first; fewer corrections appear here than in the 9-Recto version; this is probably the second of the three variants to be inscribed
2	1593	underlined in the manuscript
6	Of w[ch]	as in the second variant, the particular days are unspecified
9	So	this third variant agrees with the second variant in assigning seventeen days to translation
note	17. dayes.	this note is inscribed in a later hand, in the left-hand margin, at line 10

Location Designations	Reference Designations	Notes
11	And	this third variant allows one-and-one-half hours per day for translation; this agrees with the second variant, whereas the first variant allows two hours per day
13	Whereby	a total of twenty-six hours is allowed for translation in this third variant; the first variant allows twenty-four; the second variant allows either twenty-six or twenty-seven
note	26. houres	this note is inscribed in a later hand, in the left-hand margin, at line 14
11-Verso		
note	November	this note is written sideways, right-to-left, from the right-hand margin, on a quarter-page fragment affixed lengthwise, just below center page
[ ]	a downward spiral flourish of the amanuensis's pen follows the note	

Appendix II
Fragmentary Second Draft of Book I

	Location Designations	Reference Designations	Notes
	100-Recto		
	note	Fair	this note is penciled in at the top left-hand margin, by a later hand
Prose 1			
	32	payne	the inscription ends with this line, at mid-page; the bottom half of the sheet is blank
	catchword	[no catchword]	no catchword appears
Meter 2			
	31	t . . causes	"sondry" appears in the first-draft inscription of the text; L. *varias*; the reason for this omission cannot be discerned
Prose 2			
	1	But	the text begins at mid-page; the top half of the sheet is blank
Prose 3			
	9	leave	text terminates after this line, at mid-page; this line is the last line of the text inscribed on 15-Verso, in the first-draft inscription; it is followed by the catchword: "and as"
	note	and as the	these three words are penciled in as a "catchword" by a later hand; they appear, inscribed in linear fashion in the left-hand margin, following the termination of Prose 3; they are the first three words of the text that should continue at this point (see the opening words on16-Recto in the primary inscription of the translation)

	Location Designations	Reference Designations	Notes
	105-Recto		
	note	END	this note was inscribed at a later date on an otherwise blank sheet, probably to mark both the end of the *Consolation* translation and the end of the MS
	105-Verso	[ ]	a note on the cost of wool is inscribed on the top quarter of this otherwise blank sheet; it is dated 1661

Appendix III
Fragmentary Second Draft of Book IV

	Location Designations	Reference Designations	Notes
Prose 1			
	rubric	1 prose	rubric is penciled in by a later hand
	11	*wicked folkes*	amanuensis's italic hand
Meter 1			
	rubric	1 Myter	rubric is penciled in by a later hand
Prose 2			
	rubric	2 prose	rubric is penciled in by a later hand
	37	th[e]	torn page
Meter 2			
	rubric	2. Myter.	rubric is penciled in by a later hand
Prose 3			
	50	[]	unrecognized mark; possibly indicating a comma
Meter 3			
	rubric	3. Myter.	rubric is penciled in by a later hand
Prose 4			
	rubric	4. prose.	rubric is penciled in by a later hand
	catchword	What boutes	this catchword anticipates the text on 64-Recto, which continues the first draft inscription; IV Meter 4, at the top of 64-Recto, begins with these words, inscribed in Elizabeth I's hand

Appendix IV
A Third Copy of Book IV, Meter 2

Location Designations	Reference Designations	Notes
52-Recto		
rubric	2. M.	this third-draft inscription of IV Meter 2, is in the italic hand of the amanuensis who also inscribed the fragments of Book I and Book IV; it has been moved from its position at 52-Recto and entered here, in Appendix IV; it has been replaced in the edition by Elizabeth I's inscription, which was moved from 57-Recto

Glossary

Book I

	Location Designations	Words to be Defined	Definitions
Meter 1			
	5	*at Lest*	at least
	6	*mone*	grief; woe
	7	*griny*	green
	11	*powrd*	poured
	15	*wretched*	wretched ones
	15	*wries*	twists or turns [away]
	17	*vading*	fleeting; transitory
	17	*chine*	possibly: shine
	18	*welny*	well nigh
Prose 1			
	2	*in stiles office ment*	in writing [I] mean; or, which means, while writing
	9	*skanted*	lessened; stinted
	12	*hiar*	higher
	14	*wedes*	clothing
	19	*wides*	clothing (alternate spelling)
	37	*Eares*	fruits; crops
	38	*vres*	verse
	50	*sisght*	sight (odd spelling)
	56	*bedsfete*	bed's feet
	59	*pane*	pain

	Location Designations	Words to be Defined	Definitions
Meter 2			
	4	*wons*	once
	5	*Rose*	rosy
	10	*whe*^{n}*s*	whence
	17	*Solne*	swollen
	22	*Sely*	innocent; happy
Prose 2			
	8	*doum*	dumb; speechless
	13	*diseace*	disease
Meter 3			
	4	*Pole*	heavens; L. *polus*
	7	*tracien*	Thracian
	9	*Ligh*	light
Prose 3			
	3	*Curers*	curer's
	5	*Romes*	rooms
	15	*my none*	my own
	42	ravyce	ravish
Meter 4			
	4	*unwonne*	unconquered; "un-won-over"
	10	*hie*	high
	12	*fiers*	fierce
Prose 4			
	6	*sowernis*	sourness
	9	*shop*	chamber
	16	paste of	passed [out] of
	33	ravins	robbery
	40	preiudical	prejudged
	50	forheades markes	foreheads' marks or brands
	57	letted	stopped
	82	wrak	ruin (wrack and ruin)

	Location Designations	Words to be Defined	Definitions
	85	co^{m}mon fall	general indictment
	97	of	off (appears twice in this line)
	97	unwearyed	unforewarned
	119	whilest	whilst
	122	shops	chambers
Meter 5			
	2	*grounsto^{n}e*	groundstone or foundation stone [throne; L. *solium*]
	9	*Nar*	near
	14	*Lefe*	leaf
	19	*Leves*	leaves
	20	*Seφirus*	Zephyrus (the West Wind)
	22	*dokstar*	dog star
	23	*loused*	loosed
	26	*dispice*	despise
	27	*kipe*	keep
	29	*fautles*	faultless or innocent
	37	*othe*	oath
	44	*tost*	tossed
	45	*apeace*	appease
Prose 5			
	20	wantes allso de-servith	also deserves need
	22	shops	chamber's
	44	receites	prescriptions
Meter 6			
	4	*forowes*	furrows
Prose 6			
	16	doutst	doubtest
	48	thy hoste	the Deity, in this instance
	59	lenitives	liniments; balms
	59	fomentations	medicinal compresses; poultices

	Location Designations	Words to be Defined	Definitions
	59	skant	lessen
Meter 7			
	8	*ous*	ooze
	11	*moude*	mud
	30	*snafle*	bridle's bit

Book II

	Location Designations	Words to be Defined	Definitions
Prose 1			
	30	*p*^{re}*nt*	present
Meter 1			
	4	won ma^{n}	defeated man
Prose 2			
	38	amasde	amazed
Meter 2			
	1	*flawes*	flows
	11	*gridy*	greedy
	14	*Chawes*	jaws
Prose 3			
	4	florist	flowed
	5	hard	heard
	28	wayen	infinitive form of the verb *weigh*
	29	trade	trade off
Meter 3			
	1	*poole*	the heavens; L. *polus*
	5	*seΦirus*	Zephyrus (the West Wind)
	8	*stauke*	stalk
	18	*naugh is made*	nothing [that] is made

	Location Designations	Words to be Defined	Definitions
Prose 4			
	16	skantey thy felicitie	your happiness to be little
	22	to	too
	38	leste	least
Meter 4			
	13	*fleing*	fleeing
	19	*plast*	placed
Prose 5			
	16	stones	gem stones
	18	partage	separation; division
	49	leste	least
	72	empty man	empty handed
Meter 5			
	8	*flise*	fleece; silk, in this instance
	9	*venom die*	purple dye
	26	*Sorar*	more sorely; more severely
Prose 6			
	14	bestes	beasts
	14	myse	mice
	29	victorerers	victors'
	40	vitious	vicious
Meter 6			
	7	*domar*	doomer; judge
	7	*dedded*	deceased
	13	*Affraies*	bakes; L. *torret*
Prose 7			
	3	affayres	affairs
	60	*gial*	jail
Meter 7			
	6	*Gridy*	greedy

	Location Designations	Words to be Defined	Definitions
	14	*Lest*	least
	15	*fabritius*	Fabricius
Prose 8			
	17	lest	least
Meter 8			
	6	*Mone*	moon
	9	*kipt*	kept
	12	*hole molde*	whole earth

Book III

	Location Designations	Words to be Defined	Definitions
Prose 1			
	5	to sharp	too sharp; too stringent
	7	cacht	caught
	9	rxd.	received
Meter 1			
	2	*fried*	freed
	2	*Leas*	leaves
	3	*Sithe*	scythe
	8	*hors*	hours
Prose 2			
	48	lest	least
	50	Raygnes	power
Meter 2			
	4	*tijnge*	tying; binding
	7	*Afriche*	African; Punic
	23	*fote*	foot
	24	*Soroing*	sorrowing
	25	*Resontz*	resonates; resounds

	Location Designations	Words to be Defined	Definitions
Prose 3			
	2	playne	plan
	12	amase	amaze
	38	lest	least
Meter 3			
	1	*golfe*	gulf
Prose 4			
	28	foren	foreign
Prose 5			
	5	auto^{r}	author
	9	skanted	lessened
	19	kes	kings
	22	glaives	swords; spears
Prose 6			
	9	skant	lessen
Meter 6			
	5	*Son*^{n}	sun
	6	*mone*	moon
	9	*Limmes*	bodies
	11	*Sede*	seed
	13	*Crake*	boast
Prose 7			
	2	sacientie	satiation
Meter 7			
	1	*deligh*	delight
	2	*stinge*	sting those who enjoy
Prose 8			
	5	lowlynes	lowliness
	16	*soudan*	sudden
	17	Linxes	Lynceus's

	Location Designations	Words to be Defined	Definitions
	22	fyre	fever
	23	Tercian	[of] three [days]
Meter 8			
	3	*griny*	green
	8	*Tyrrhene*	Tyrrhenian
	9	*knoes*	knows
	13	*porpos*	[purple yielding] murex shells
	17	*Cerche*	search
	19	*hest*	behest
	20	*Carke*	toil or work
Prose 9			
	4	se	see
	8	rife	rift
	42	throwe of this	throw this off
	64	Timeo	*Timaeus*
Meter 9			
	8	*mold*	form
	27	*mold*	world
	31	*Last*	goal, in this instance
Prose 10			
	51	reaason	reason
	84	styrre	stir; motion
Meter 10			
	8	*nire*	near
	9	*griny stone*	green stone; emerald
Prose 11			
	37	marish	marshes
	37	stike	stick; adhere
	61	p^{ro}cdith	proceedeth
	76	ruyne	[go to] ruin
	78	m^{r}ke	mark

	Location Designations	Words to be Defined	Definitions
Prose 12			
	1	twise	twice
	47	hard er now	heard err now
	48	Gyantes	giants
	54	yll	ill
	59	Rondell	sphere; L. *orbem*
	59	si^{n}ceritie	the simplicity of the divine; L. *divinae simplicitatis*
	70	prooves	proofs
Meter 12			
	10	*hind*	deer
	10	*Ioin*	join
	14	*ferventar*	more fervent
	31	*Goddes*	goddess
	39	*Tityrus*	Tityus
	42 / 43	*feere / Won*	fairly won
	45	*Tartar*	Tartarus
	57	Chifist	chiefest

Book IV

	Location Designations	Words to be Defined	Definitions
Prose 1			
	9	pas	pass
	15	m^{tr}	master
	25	Charyot	chariot
Meter 1			
	3	*flijing*	flying; ascending
	4	*despice*	despise
	10	*Sorteth*	sorts; assigns

	Location Designations	Words to be Defined	Definitions
	18	*spidy*	speedy
Prose 2			
	20	*optane*	obtain
	94	mightest	mightiest
	95	mightyest	mightiest (alternate spelling)
Meter 2			
	6	*yre*	ire; high emotion
Prose 3			
	1	slowe	pool of mud; L. *in caeno*
	13	rxd	received
	29	plage	plague
	39	shewith	showeth
	45	farvent	fervent
	47	bralles	brawls
	48	chafith	chafes, roars; L. *Fremit*
	49	lyar	lion; L. *leonis*
	56	bestly	beastly
Meter 3			
	3	*Iland*	island
	4	*fear*	fair; L. *pulchra*
	6	*Gestz*	guests
	9	*herber*	herb purveyor
	11	*Marmila*^{n} lio^{n}	lion; L. *Marmaricus leo*
	13	*nu borne*	new born
	14	*houles*	howls
	23	*swin*	swine
Prose 4			
	32	cavill	find fault with unnecessarily; quibble about petty faults
	95	leave	believe
Meter 4			
	5	*bore*	boar

	Location Designations	Words to be Defined	Definitions
	11	*mede*	medication
Prose 5			
	3	exule	an exile
	7	geayle	jail
	13	m^{r}vell	marvel
Meter 5			
	13	*Southest wynde*	actually, *Caurus* is the North-West Wind
	14	*astones*	stuns; astonishes; L. *tundere* (to buffet)
	20	*gase*	gaze
Prose 6			
	5	scacely	scarcely
	6	cut of	cut off
	35	p^{re}ntly	presently
	47	provid.	providence
	52	midst	middle
	78	iombled	jumbled
	113	w[o^{n}] overs	vanquished
	115–116	so much ma^{n}- ner	such a manner
	136	uniniurible	uninjurable
	142	feares	meaning: deters
	165	Actors	perpetrators of acts
Meter 6			
	7	*frosy*	frosty
	15	*fayest*	fairest
Prose 7			
	17	Iarre	jar; collide against
	30	wrestell	wrestling; spite
	40	travells	travail's; labor's

	Location Designations	Words to be Defined	Definitions
Meter 7			
	1	*Twis*	twice
	2	*Φrisians*	Phrygians
	5	*apeced*	appeased
	7	*throte*	throat
	10	*panche*	paunch
	11	*yeles*	yells
	15	*flead*	flayed
	19	*Cheain*	chain
	22	*sered*	seared
	27	*hy heaves*	high heavens
	28	*folme*	foam; froth
	29	*heave*	heaven
	32	*Sample*	example

Book V

	Location Designations	Words to be Defined	Definitions
Prose 1			
	10	bye Crookes	by-ways
	10	Io^{r}ney	journey
	24	rehrest	rehearsed; said
	42	unshu^{n}ning	inevitable
Meter 1			
	5	*Soundred*	sundered
	8	*trunches*	tree trunks
	13	*bit*	bridle
Prose 2			
	13	lymed	limbed; embodied

	Location Designations	Words to be Defined	Definitions
Meter 2			
	4	*pears*	pierce
	12	*Sole*	sun
Prose 3			
	47	mixt	mixed among; intermixed; L. *intermixta*
	49	why science wantes falshed	why science lacks falsehood
	58	*or . . . or*	either . . . or
	85	Prince	L. *principi*
Meter 3			
	8	*overwhelmes*	overwhelming
	12	*gridely*	greedily
	13	*had*	probably meaning: the known things
	27	*kipes*	keeps
Prose 4			
	13	let	stopped
	16	ad	add
	23	sownd	sound
	41	looke	look [at]
	42	Car men	chariot drivers
	68	circuite	circularity
Meter 4			
	3	*lest*	least
	6	*Sea*	flat, as in a level sea; L. *aequore*
	13	*fourmes*	images; L. *imagines*
	15	*Whenche*	whence; L. *Unde*
	23	*truethe*	truth; L. *veris*
Prose 5			
	5	shewith	showeth

	Location Designations	Words to be Defined	Definitions
Meter 5			
	7	*reiois*	rejoice
	8	*grinny*	green
Prose 6			
	15	Arist.	Aristotle
	55	pure	simple
	131	wryes	turns
	134	p^{re}ventes	anticipates

Appendix I
First Variant of the Computation of Days

	Location Designations	Words to be Defined	Definitions
--	5	rwd	rode

Appendix II
Fragmentary Second Draft of Book I

	Location Designations	Words to be Defined	Definitions
Prose 1			
	13	tres.	letters
Meter 2			
	8	vew	view
	12	woo^{n}n	won

Appendix III
Fragmentary Second Draft of Book IV

	Location Designations	Words to be Defined	Definitions
Prose 1			
	14	m^r	master
Prose 2			
	45	preceder	guiding
Meter 2			
	10	guyves	shackles
Meter 3			
	10	Snowte	snout
	11	*Marmican Lyon*	lion; L. *Marmaricus leo*
Prose 4			
	69	hard	heard
	91	Acto^r	actor; perpetrator

Appendix IV
[Book IV, Meter 2]

	Location Designations	Words to be Defined	Definitions
Meter 2			
	10	*gyves*	shackles
	14	*weares*	wears upon; exhausts